Directory of
SCOTTISH SETTLERS
IN NORTH AMERICA

1625-1825

By
David Dobson

VOLUME IX

Baltimore
GENEALOGICAL PUBLISIHING COMPANY

Copyright © 2024
by David Dobson
All Rights Reserved

Published for Clearfield Company by
Genealogical Publishing Company
Baltimore, Maryland
2024

ISBN: 9780806321363

INTRODUCTION

This is the final part of the *Directory of Scottish Settlers in North America, 1625-1825* series that began in 1984. The series was compiled from a wide range of both manuscript and published sources; however, a few of the books concentrated on specific sources that were not accessible to the average North American researcher. Volume VI of the series, for example, was wholly based on the manuscript Register of Deeds of the Commissariat of Edinburgh between 1750 and 1825. Volume III was based on contemporary Scottish newspapers and journals of the eighteenth and early nineteenth century. Since the publication of Volume VII in 1993, my research and publications have concentrated on emigration to particular regions, such as "Scots in the Carolinas, 1680-1820", or subjects, such as "Ships from Scotland to America" and "Scottish Soldiers in Colonial America". Nonetheless, over the last thirty or so years I have accumulated enough miscellaneous Scottish emigration material sufficient to publish "More Scottish Settlers, 1667-1827" in 2005; "Directory of Scottish Settlers to North America, 1625-1825, Volume VIII" and this, Volume IX, the last one of the series.

Libraries at home and abroad provided some interesting material. Most of the libraries were Scotland, such as the National Library of Scotland or the Library of the University of St Andrews. I also consulted sources in London such as the City of London Record Office and the National Maritime Museum. Published sources such as the *Scots Magazine*, the *Gentleman's Magazine*, and the *Royal Gazette of North America* provided valuable, if obscure, references. The matriculation rolls and the graduation records of the Scottish universities, for instance, identified the sons of colonists who were sent to Scotland for their education. The majority of these students bore Scottish surnames, but there were some with continental European names who may have been attracted by the courses offered, especially the medical ones.

Like the other volumes in this series, Volume IX is a compilation of miscellaneous Scottish references abstracted from a wide range of sources, including one source I should like to acknowledge, the Clan Donald Trust, for drawing my attention.

David Dobson

Dundee, Scotland, 2024

REFERENCES

AB   Argyll & Bute Library

ABR   Ayr Burgess Roll

ACA   Aberdeen City Archives

AJ   Aberdeen Journal, series

APCCol Acts Privy Council, Colonial

AUL   Aberdeen University Library

BM   British Museum

BRO   Bristol Record Office

CLRO City of London Record Office

DAB   Dictionary American Biography

DAC   Dumfries Archive Centre

DCA   Dundee City Archives

EAR   Edinburgh Academy Register

ECA   Edinburgh City Archives

EMG   Edinburgh Medical Graduates

ERA   Edinburgh Register of Apprentices

EUL   Edinburgh University Library

F   Fasti Ecclesiae Scoticanae, [Edinburgh 1915]

GCA   Glasgow City Archives

GEU   Graduates of Edinburgh University

GM   Gentleman's Magazine, series

GUL   Glasgow University Archives

HCA Highland Archive Centre

HMC Historical Manuscript Commission

HS History Scotland, series

HWS History of the Writers to the Signet

JCTP Journal of the Committee for Trade and the Plantations

KCA King's College, Aberdeen

MCA Marischal College, Aberdeen

MFA Making for America, [Edinburgh, 2009]

MHS Maryland Historical Society

MI Monumental Inscription

NARA National Archives Records Administration

NLS National Library of Scotland

NMM National Maritime Museum

NRAS National Register of Archives, Scotland

NRS National Records of Scotland, Edinburgh

NWI New World Immigrants, [Baltimore, 1979]

OA Orkney Adveriser, series

PAO Public Archives of Ontario

PANB Public Archives of New Brunswick

PCC Prerogative Court of Canterbury

PHS Pennsylvania Historical Society

RAK Royal Archives, Copenhagen, Denmark

RCPE Royal College Physicians of Edinburgh

RCS Royal Commonwealth Society, London

RGG Register of Glasgow Graduates

RGNA Royal Gazette, North America, series

RGS Register of the Great Seal of Scotland

SAUL St Andrews University Library

SCHS South Carolina Historical Society

SM Scots Magazine, series

SNQ Scottish Notes and Queries, series

SRA Strathclyde Regional Archives

TNA The National Archives, Kew

UAL University of Aberdeen Library

UNC University of North Carolina

VHS Virginia Historical Society

DIRECTORY OF SCOTTISH SETTLERS IN NORTH AMERICA,

1625-1825, Volume IX

ABBOTT, WILLIAM, in Charleston, South Carolina, a letter re the cultivation of cotton, dated 1800. [NRS.GD51.3.259]

ABELL, WILLIAM. An indenture between William Abell in Prince George County, Maryland, and Richard Henderson, factor for John Glassford in Blandenburgh, said county, whereby the said William is to serve the said Richard as an indentured servant, 9 June 1766. [NRS.GD237.21.51]

ABERCROMBY, J., petitioned the boundary commissioners of South and North Carolinas on 14 June 1737. [RPCCol.vi.245]

ABERNETHY, GEORGE, in Aberdeen and Jamaica, a contract of co-partnership, 1750. [NRS.RD4.177/1]

ADAMS, JOHN, of Virginia, to Edinburgh in 1793, residing in St Patrick's Square, Edinburgh, in 1794, a medical student at Edinburgh University 1794-1795, graduated MD at Edinburgh University in 1796. [EUL][EMG][VHS] [ECA.SL115.1.1]

ADDISON, JOHN, in Montreal, Quebec, a letter, 1833. [NRS.NRAS. Blairs]

ADYE, RADULPH, of St Kitts, graduated MD at Edinburgh University in 1778. [EMG]

AFFLECK, JAMES MCVICAR, in Jamaica, a deed of factory with H. I. Wyllie, 14 January 1803. [NRS.RD4.273.497]

AFFLECK, THOMAS, born Aberdeen in 1740, son of Thomas Affleck a tobacconist, was apprenticed to Alexander Rose a cabinetmaker in Ellon, Aberdeenshire, in 1754, emigrated to Philadelphia, Pennsylvania, in 1763, a Quaker, died 5 March 1795. [MFA.45-61]

AFFLECK, WILLIAM, in Grange, Jamaica, testament, 19 October 1826, Comm. Edinburgh. [NRS]

AGNEW, J., petitioned for a grant of mines in Newfoundland on 13 May 1773, which was granted. [RPCCol.vi.543/555]

AGNEW, JAMES, born in Galloway, a merchant in Portsmouth, Virginia, from 1762 to 1776, returned to Stranraer, Galloway, around 1780. [TNA.AO12.99.204]; a deposition, Stranraer, 31 August 1784. [TNA.AO13.27.176]

AGNEW, JOHN, emigrated to Virginia in 1751, rector of Suffolk on the Nansemond River, Virginia, a Loyalist in 1776. [TNA.AO12.56.403]

AIKENHEAD, WILLIAM, in St Thomas, Jamaica, a bond, 8 November 1750. [NRS.RD4.178/1.582]

AIKMAN, ANDREW, in Kingston, Jamaica, brother of Reverend John Aikman, a letter dated 1793. [NRS.GD1.1429.1.1]

AINSLIE, ROBERT, in Quebec, a deed, 25 December 1784. [NRS.RD4.237.916]; a commission, 20 December 1788. [NRS.RD2.246/2.212]

AINSLIE, THOMAS, in Quebec, a deed of factory in favour of Robert Ainslie, 13 July 1777. [NRS.RD4.221.480]; in Quebec, a deed, 19 February 1784, [NRS.RD4.235.280]; in Quebec; in Quebec, a deed, 2 February 1784, [NRS.RD4.235.326]; a bond, 9 July 1785, [NRS.RD4.239.11]

AIR, JAMES, of South Carolina, a medical student at Edinburgh University in 1774-1775. [EUL]

AIRD, DAVID, of Antigua, a student at King's College, Aberdeen, in 1795, graduated MD from Edinburgh University in 1805. [KCA][EMG]

AIRD, JOHN, 'was a practitioner in medicine for several years in Antigua', graduated MA, MD, from Glasgow University, 1772. [RGG]

AITKEN, CHARLES, born in Scotland, settled in New York City in 1772, a Loyalist in 1776. [TNA.AO13.99.9]

AITKEN, JOHN, a weaver in Fayette, Kentucky, testament, 28 January 1820, Comm. Edinburgh. [NRS]

AITKEN, JOHN, a merchant in St Domingo, testament 25 October 1825, Comm. Edinburgh. [NRS]

AITKEN, ROBERT, born in Dalkeith in 1734, settled in Philadelphia as a bookseller by 1759, founded the Pennsylvania Magazine in 1775, printed the Aitken Bible in 1782, died in Philadelphia, Pennsylvania, in 1802.

AITKEN & Company, in Jamaica, a deed of factory with Paterson and Ainslie, 20 July 1802. [NRS.RD3.295.734]

ALDER, CHARLES, in Jamaica, a deed of attorney, 6 December 1788. [NRS.RD4.244.762]

ALEXANDER, ALEXANDER, from Leith, Scotland, a mariner in Charleston, South Carolina, a Loyalist who was killed on the Delaware River in October 1777. [TNA.AO13.96.6]

ALEXANDER, or RUSSELL or CULLEN, MARY, in St Lucia, testament 6 January 1819, Comm. Edinburgh. [NRS]

ALEXANDER, PATRICK, in Jamaica, his relict Elizabeth, testament, 2 August 1821, Comm. Aberdeen. [NRS]

ALEXANDER, THOMAS, emigrated from Scotland to Boston in 1761, a hosiery merchant there, a Loyalist soldier. [PAO.LC.1166]

ALEXANDER, Sir WILLIAM, of Menstrie, a sasine, 1 October 1625, Nova Scotia. [NRS.RS1.18.177]; the King's Lieutenant of Nova Scotia, resigned the land and barony of Lochend in Cape Breton in favour of Sir Thomas Nicholson of Carnock on 31 December 1636. [NRS.GD17.501-2]

ALEXANDER, WILLIAM, Customs Controller, in Philadelphia, Pennsylvania, in 1723. [RPCCol.vi.632]

ALLAN, CHARLES, born 1710 in Edinburgh, son of Benjamin Allan, a lawyer, and his wife Sarah Campbell, was apprenticed to Colin Campbell, an Edinburgh goldsmith, moved to London in 1730s, from there to Kingston, Jamaica, in early 1740s, died there in 1762. [MFA.97-98]

ALLAN, DAVID, in Jamaica, a probative will, 8 November 1783. [NRS.RD2.235/2.210]

ALLAN, JOHN, an attorney at law in Kingston, Jamaica, sasines in Dunbarton, 25 November 1770 and 13 January 1774. [NRS.RS9.10.315/510]

ALLANBY, WILLIAM, Customs Collector on Prince Edward Island, and wife Anne, letters of attorney, from 1772 until 1777. [NLS. Stewart pp.3894/3943]

ALLARDYCE, ALEXANDER, in Jamaica, a bond dated 18 July 1782. [NRS.RD3.241/2.211]

ALMON, WILLIAM BRUCE, of America, graduated MD from Edinburgh University in 1809. [EMG]

ALSTON, JAMES, paymaster of the French Emigrants in Jamaica, a memorandum dated 1811. [NRS.GD1.394.56]

ALVIS, DAVID, Searcher of Customs at Quebec, letter of attorney in 1777. [NLS. Stewart pp.3962]

ANDERSON, ADAM, son of Adam Anderson MD in Jamaica, a student at King's College, Aberdeen, from 1795 to 1799. [KCA.2.377]

ANDERSON, ALEXANDER, emigrated from Scotland to America in 1774, settled on the Susquehanna River, Charlotte County, New York, a Loyalist in 1776, killed by Indians on his way to Niagara in 1779. [TNA.AO12.31.131]; his widow Mary and their family settled in Canada. [PAO.LC.312]

ANDERSON, ANDREW, a merchant in Virginia, a commission, 13 July 1765. [NRS.RD4.198/2.558]

ANDERSON, CHARLES, in Jamaica, testament, 27 October 1815, Comm. Edinburgh. [NRS]

ANDERSON, GEORGE, minister at Pon Pon, South Carolina, a deed subscribed on 16 January 1752. [NRS.RD3.211/2.77]

ANDERSON, Dr J., in St Kitts, a deed dated 16 July 1778. [NRS.RD4.224/1.219]; a deed, 8 October 1789. [NRS.RD3.249.768]; a commission, 20 July 1790. [NRS.RD3.251/2.201]; a commission, 26 June 1791. [NRS.RD3.253.542]; a commission, 16 September 1796. [NRS.RD2.278.744]

ANDERSON, JAMES, of Jamaica, an alumnus in 1731, graduated MD at Marischal College, Aberdeen, on 22 September 1755. [MCA]

ANDERSON, JAMES, a merchant in Boston, Massachusetts, in 1773. [see letter NRS.GD174.1294]

ANDERSON, JAMES, in Jamaica, a deed dated 13 December 1781. [NRS.RD3.245,1274]

ANDERSON, JOHN, of Jamaica, graduated MD from Edinburgh University in 1813. [EMG]

ANDERSON, MURDOCH, a planter in Demerara, testament confirmed 20 December 1803, Comm. Edinburgh. [NRS]

ANDERSON, ROBERT, in Antigua, a deed of factory subscribed on 4 May 1786. [NRS.RD4.247.1094]

ANDERSON, WILLIAM, son of Henry Anderson in Grenada, a student at King's College, Aberdeen, in 1802. [KCA.2.390]

ANDERSON & SUTOR, masons in Grenada and Demerara, from 1791 until 1796. [NRS.CS96.4483]

ANDREW, JOHN, a seaman in Linlithgow, West Lothian, formerly in Boston, New England, a deed in 1698. [NRS.RD3.90.110]

ANDREWS, WILLIAM, an army chaplain, a Loyalist, in Glasgow by 1788. [TNA.AO12.54.240]; a deposition dated 27 July 1784. [TNA.AO13.27.176]

ANGUS, WILLIAM JOHN, son of William Angus at Montego Bay, Jamaica, a student at King's College, Aberdeen, from 1799 to 1803, graduated MA, then at Miranda Hill, Jamaica. [KCA.2.385]

ANNAN, WILLIAM, of Pennsylvania, a medical student at Edinburgh University, 1790-1791, graduated MD at Glasgow University in 1791, died 1797. [EUL][RGG]

ARCHER, GEORGE, from Jamaica, was educated at Edinburgh University, graduated MD at King's College, Aberdeen, on 23 September 1786. [KCA#136]; a student in Edinburgh, versus Helen McLeay, a Process of Declarator of Marriage in 1786. [NRS.CC8.6.759]

ARMSTRONG, ALICE, with two daughters, Loyalists, were driven from their farm near Stoney Point to New York, a petition dated 9 March 1780. [HMC. American. ii.100]

ARMSTRONG, HENRY, born 1613, a passenger aboard the <u>Transport of London</u> bound from London to Virginia on 4 July 1635. [TNA.E157.20]

ARMSTRONG, JOCKY, died in Elizabeth City, Virginia, by 1624. [TNA.CO1.3.]

ARMSTRONG, KATHERINE, born 1615, a passenger aboard the <u>Mathew of London</u> bound from London to St Kitts on 21 May 1635. [TNA.E157.20]

ARMSTRONG, ROBERT, letters from Boston and New Hampshire, re a survey of the Duke of Hamilton's lands there, dated 1729. [NRS.NRAS.0332/1297/1306]

ARMSTRONG, THOMAS, a settler on the north-west branch of the Cape Fear River, North Carolina, petitioned the Synod of Argyle for a Gaelic speaking minister, on 2 September 1748. [NRS.NRAS.1209.553]

ARMSTRONG, WILLIAM, surgeon at the Naval Hospital in St Kitts, graduated MD at King's College, Aberdeen, on 18 October 1798. [KCA]

ARMSTRONG, WILLIAM, a planter and councillor of St Croix, Danish West Indies, around 1803. [NLS.5602/15; 5603]

ARMSTRONG, WILLIAM, in Quebec applied to succeed the late Colonel MacNeal as Consul in New Orleans, Louisiana in 1808. [NRS.GD51.6.1657; 18031.580]

ARNOT, Sir MICHAEL, of Arnot, a sasine, dated 31 July 1630, Nova Scotia. [NRS.RS1.29.61]

ARRAS, DOUGLAS, at Montego Bay, Jamaica, testament confirmed on 16 December 1823, Comm. Edinburgh. [NRS]

ARTHUR, ROBERT, master of the Fortune of Glasgow from Antigua with a cargo of sugar, 1717. [NRS.AC9.595]

ARTHUR, ROBERT, a merchant in Greenock, owner of the snow Christian, master James Montgomerie jr, entered a charter party contract with James Baird jr. and Alexander Walker, merchants in Glasgow, for a trading voyage from Saltcoats to the Rappahannock River, Virginia, in 1758. [NRS.CC5.21.5]

ASHETON, RALPH, of Pennsylvania, a medical student at Edinburgh University in 1758, graduated MD from St Andrews University. [History of Medicine in United States, NY, 1931]

ATHILL, SAMUEL BYAM, of Antigua, graduated MD at Edinburgh University in 1778. [EMG]

AUCHTERLONY, ALEXANDER, purchased land on Dominica in 1765. [NRS.GD126.4]

AULD, ALEXANDER, of Carcoside, late a planter in Demerara, testament, 1 May 1821, Comm. Dumfries. [NRS]

AULD, JOHN, a merchant in Virginia, testament confirmed 28 October 1803, Comm. Edinburgh. [NRS]

AUSTIN, JAMES, of Barbados, graduated MD from Edinburgh University in 1819. [EMG]

AVERY, JAMES F., of Nova Scotia, graduated MD from Edinburgh University in 1821. [EMG]

BAILLIE, ALEXANDER, in Nevis, letters to his cousin Alexander Baillie of Dunain, in 1752. [HCA. Baillie of Dunain pp]

BAILLIE, GEORGE, a trader and planter in Georgia and later Jamaica, a Loyalist, moved to Britain in 1784. [TNA.AO12.74.101]

BAILLIE, HUGH, a Doctor of Laws, applied for a grant of 15,000 acres in Nova Scotia in 1771. [JCTP.78.105]

BAILLIE, J., in Savannah, Georgia, a letter to Thomas Baillie his brother, dated 1734. [NRS.GD170.3558]

BAILLIE, JOHN, born 1767, son of Robert Baillie in Georgia deceased, a student in Scotland. [TNA.AO12.101.94]

BAIN, ALEXANDER, a merchant in Virginia, a sasine, 11 November 1774, Dunbarton. [NRS.RS9.11.109]; Alexander Bain, merchant in Greenock, trading with Sinclair Ferrie in New York, and others in South Carolina, and Newfoundland between 1772 and 1785. [NRS.CS96.76, etc]; a merchant in North America, testament confirmed 19 August 1812, Comm. Edinburgh. [NRS]

BAINBRIDGE, EDMUND, of New York, to Edinburgh in 1793, residing in Drummond Street, Edinburgh, 1794, a medical student at Edinburgh University in 1794-1795. [EUL] [ECA.SL115.1.1]

BAINBRIDGE, RICHARD, of Jamaica, graduated MD from Edinburgh University in 1824. [EMG]

BAIRD, PETER, a mariner in Virginia, testament confirmed 28 March 1812, Comm. Edinburgh. [NRS]

BAIRD, Sir ROBERT, with a financial interest in the Scots Plantation in Carolina, an account dated 1682. [NRS.GD238.box 3, bundle 4]

BAKER, ARCHIBALD, a settler on the north-west branch of the Cape Fear River, North Carolina, petitioned the Synod of Argyle for a Gaelic speaking minister, on 2 September 1748. [NRS.NRAS.1209.553]

BAKER, SIMMONS JONES, of North Carolina, a medical student at Edinburgh University in 1794-1795. [EUL]

BALCANQUEL, R. G., in Jamaica, a deed of attorney dated 15 March 1793. [NRS.RD4.254.934]

BALFOUR, ANDREW, of South Carolina, a medical student at Edinburgh University in 1799. [EUL]

BALFOUR, CHARLES, in Jamaica, a deed of factory in favour of J. Black, dated 27 October 1786. [NRS.RD4.240.845]

BALFOUR, JAMES, from Barbados aboard the sloop True Friendship, master Charles Callahan, bound for Antigua on 4 October 1679. [TNA]

BALFOUR, JAMES, in the county of Charles City, Virginia, a sasine, 17 May 1743, Caithness. [NRS.RS21.2.341]

BALFOUR, JAMES, in St Vincent, a deed, dated 10 February 1776. [NRS.RD3.235.509]

BALFOUR, JOHN, in Tobago, a bond, 20 July 1772, [NRS.RD2.244/1.409]; a deed of attorney in favour of Alexander Hay, dated 18 August 1778. [NRS.RD4.225/1.176]

BALL, INGRAM, in Cape Breton, a deed of factory with Francis Wilson, dated 11 April 1805. [NRS.RD3.315.936]

BALL, JOSEPH, in Jamaica, a deed, dated 5 February 1773. [NRS.RD3.220.767]

BALL, WILLIAM, of Virginia, graduated MD at Edinburgh University in 1773. [EMG]

BALL, WILLIAM J., of America, graduated MD from Edinburgh University in 1808. [EMG]

BALLANTYNE, JAMES and ANN, in Virginia, a deed of attorney dated 28 July 1786. [NRS.RD2.242.2.506]

BANISTER, THEODORIC BLAIR, of Virginia, graduated MD from Edinburgh University in 1804. [EMG]

BANKHEAD, JOHN, of Virginia, a medical student at Edinburgh University in 1783. [EUL]

BANKHEAD, WILLIAM, from Virginia, a medical student at Edinburgh University, from 1762 until 1763, graduated MD from Glasgow University in 1764. [EUL][RGG]

BANKS, ROBERT, was appointed as the Assistant Commissary of the West Indies on 24 December 1807. [NRS.GD51.6.1567.1/2]

BANNERMAN, BENJAMIN, from Scotland to settle in Portsmouth, Virginia, around 1760, a Loyalist, later in Montrose Angus, by 1784. [TNA.AO12.56.367]

BANNERMAN, WILLIAM, born 1617, a passenger aboard the Amity bound from London to St Kitts on 13 October 1635. [TNA.E157.20]

BANNATYNE, JOHN, in Barbados a letter dated 12 June 1710, also, a petition requesting to be made market clerk of Barbados, dated 20 July 1711. [NRS.GD406.1.5635/7585]

BARCLAY, JAMES, in Kingston, Jamaica, a deed of attorney dated 26 November 1751. [NRS.RD3.211/1.521]

BARCLAY, JANET, wife of William Craighead a weaver in Dundee, was found guilty of rioting at Mylnefield, and banished to the American Plantations for life, at Perth in June 1773. [SM.35.332]

BARCLAY, PATRICK, a merchant in Virginia, then in Edinburgh, versus David Young, master of the snow Joseph and Ann, in a case before the High Court of the Admiralty of Scotland in 1745. [NRS.AC8.659]

BARD, SAMUEL, born in 1741, of New York, graduated MD at Edinburgh University in 1765, died in 1821. [EMG][NYAM]

BARHAM, ALEXANDER, born in Scotland, emigrated to America in 1764, a merchant in Philadelphia, Pennsylvania, a Loyalist, in Halifax, Nova Scotia, by 10 May 1786. [PAO.LC.56]

BARNARD, THOMAS, a minister in Salem, America, graduated DD at Edinburgh University on 28 July 1794. [GEU]

BARON, ALEXANDER, of Carolina, graduated MD at Edinburgh University in 1799. [EMG]

BARR, DAVID, born 1795, emigrated to New Brunswick on board the Favourite in 1816. [PANB.RS23]

BARRAND, PHILIP, of Virginia, a medical student at Edinburgh University in 1780. ['Medicine in Virginia in the Eighteenth Century', p87, Richmond, 1931]

BARTON, BENJAMIN SMITH, born in 1766, of Pennsylvania, a medical student at Edinburgh University in 1786, died in 1815. [EUL]

BARTRAM, GEORGE, in Philadelphia, a letter to John Bartram of Carsewell, re Bartram family, dated in 1760. [NRS.GD5.593]

BAYARD, ROBERT, of America, graduated MD from Edinburgh University in 1809. [EMG]

BEARD, NEILL, a settler on the north-west branch of the Cape Fear River, North Carolina, petitioned the Synod of Argyle for a Gaelic speaking minister, on 2 September 1748. [NRS.NRAS.1209.553]

BEECH, JAMES GAMBLE, of Dominica, graduated MD at Edinburgh University in 1801. [EMG]

BEGBIE, JAMES, a shipbuilder in South Carolina before 1776, a Loyalist who settled in Kingston, Jamaica, in 1783. [TNA.AO12.51.184]

BEGG, JOHN, of Jamaica, graduated MD at Edinburgh University in 1793. [EMG]

BELCHES, THOMAS, in Georgia, a deed, dated 30 March 1752. [NRS.RD4.238.1103]

BELL, GEORGE, proposals to establish a colony in Florida, dated around 1712. [NRS.GD95.10, item 38]

BELL, HENRY, a witness to a will in Lancaster County Court, Virginia, on 8 December 1680.

BELL, JOHN, in Jamaica a bond dated 4 August 1786. [NRS.RD2.244/2.530]

BELL, THOMAS, moderator of the Presbytery of South Carolina, re a vacancy in Will Town, South Carolina, letters on 24 September 1750 and 3 December 1750. [NRS.CH1.2.95.400-402]

BELLAMY, JOSEPH, born 20 February 1719 in Cheshire, Connecticut, a minister and author in Bethlehem, Connecticut, from 1740 until his death in 1790. He graduated BA from Yale in 1735, and MD from Marischal College, Aberdeen, on 9 March 1768. [MCA] [SNQ.XII.95/159]

BENNET, GEORGE, in Charleston, [South Carolina?], a probative bill of attorney, dated 15 December 1783. [NRS.RD4.236.795]

BENNET, PARKER, of St Kitts, graduated MD at Edinburgh University in 1745. [EMG]

BERKELEY, CARTER, born in 1768, of Virginia, graduated MD at Edinburgh University in 1793 died 1839. [EMG]

BERNARD, CHARLES, of Jamaica, graduated MD at Edinburgh University in 1800. [EMG]

BERNARD, WILLIAM R., of Jamaica, graduated MD from Edinburgh University in 1817. [EMG]

BERTHELET, BENJAMIN, of Canada, graduated MD from Edinburgh University in 1821. [EMG]

BERTRAM, WILLIAM, of Nisbet, a bond with David Mitchelson, a merchant in New York, dated 1785. [NRS.GD5.416]

BEST, THOMAS, son of Thomas Best a gentleman in Barbados, a student at King's College, Aberdeen, 1814 to 1818, graduated MA, a banker in Aberdeen. [KCA]

BEWS, JOHN, born in the Orkney Islands, Scotland, a Loyalist in South Carolina in 1776. [TNA.AO12.99.278]

BINHAM, GEORGE JAMES, of Jamaica, graduated MD at Edinburgh University in 1792. [EMG]

BISCHOP, J. P., in Essequibo, a probative contract with P. Nisbet, dated 6 February 1802. [NRS.RD3.296.262]

BISSET, GEORGE, probably the son of Alexander Bisset in the Braes of Pitfoddel, Aberdeenshire, baptised in St Paul's Episcopal Chapel, Aberdeen, on 5 December 1743, was ordained by the Bishop of

London in 1767 and installed as Rector of Trinity Church, Newport, Rhode Island, a Loyalist in 1776, died 22 May 1788. [TNA.AO12.75.123]

BLACK, DAVID, emigrated from Scotland to Boston in 1760, a merchant there, a Loyalist, moved to Halifax, Nova Scotia, there on 21 June 1786. [PAO.LC.552]

BLACK, WILLIAM, a mason in Williamsburg, Virginia, letters, from 1774 until 1785. [NLS.Dep.240/19]

BLACK, WILLIAM, 'teacher of an academy in America', graduated MA at Glasgow University in 1800. [RGG]

BLACKBURN, HUGH, in Boston, New England, a deed of factory with William Goddard, dated 8 May 1807. [NRS.RD3.317.299]

BLACKDEN, Mrs ANN, in Halifax, Nova Scotia, a letter dated 1758. [NLS. Yester. 7083.77]

BLACKWOOD, JOHN, son of John Blackwood of Airdsgreen in Lanarkshire, emigrated to Canada in 1780, letters. [NRS.NRAS.0067]

BLAIR, BUCHANAN, born 1794 in Doune, Stirlingshire, emigrated to New Brunswick aboard the *Favourite* in 1816. [PANB.RS23]

BLAIR, DAVID, a merchant in St John, New Brunswick, probate on 10 October 1798, New Brunswick.

BLAIR, JAMES, a merchant in Philadelphia, Philadelphia, was admitted as a burgess and guilds-brother of Ayr on 16 November 1752. [ABR]

BLAIR, JAMES, from Virginia, a medical student at Edinburgh University, from 1760 to 1767. [EUL]

BLAIR, JAMES, in Grenada in 1769. [JCTP.76]

BLAIR, JAMES, Secretary of the Presbyterian Church in Charleston, South Carolina, a letter dated 1810. [NRS.NRAS.0333]

BLAIR, JOHN, from Greenock to St John, New Brunswick, in 1803, settled in Sussex Vale. [PANB.mc1672]

BLAIR, JAMES, a merchant from Glasgow, a planter in St Elizabeth's parish, County Cornwall, Jamaica, a will subscribed to in 1835.

BLAIR, PETER, from Inverness-shire, a merchant in St John, New Brunswick, died on 14 August 1808, administration dated 18 August 1808, New Brunswick.

BLAND, THEODORIC, born in 1740, of Virginia, graduated MD at Edinburgh University in 1763, died in 1790. [EMG][VHS]

BLANE, JOHN, a merchant in Antigua, a deed of factory dated 13 July 1751. [NRS.RD3.211/1.380]

BLANE, THOMAS, in New York, a commission on 17 December 1784. [NRS.RD2.246/2/694]

BLUE, MALCOLM, a settler on the north-west branch of the Cape Fear River, North Carolina, petitioned the Synod of Argyll a Gaelic speaking minister, on 2 September 1748. [NRS.NRAS.1209.553]

BOGLE, JOHN, a merchant in Glasgow, in a charter party, contracted with Anthony Whiteside, a shipowner, to send his vessel the Mary to Virginia, load tobacco on the Rappahannock and return within a specified period. As this did not occur Bogle registered this with Alexander Spotswood, the Lieutenant Governor of Virginia in Williamsburg on 17 August 1716 in an Instrument of Protest. [NRS.AC13.1.60]

BOGLE, ROBERT, in Grenada, a deed, dated 31 March 1772. [NRS.RD2.224/2.650]; a merchant in Grenada, died there on 1 June 1777. [SM.39.459]

BOND, PHINEAS, born in 1717, of Pennsylvania, a medical student at Edinburgh University in 1742, died 1773. [EUL]

BONTEIN, ARCHIBALD, H.M. Engineer General for Jamaica, a commission on 8 October 1750. [NRS.RD2.169.88]; his observations on Kingston Harbour, Jamaica, in May 1754. [JCTP.61/2]

BONTEIN, JAMES, in Jamaica, a deed, dated 16 September 1774. [NRS.RD4.216.299]

BONTEIN, THOMAS, in Jamaica, a deed, dated 20 August 1749. [NRS.RD3.211/2.355]; in Kingston and Port Royal, Jamaica, a deed, dated 16 March 1751. [NRS.RD2.169.499]

BOOTH, FRANCIS, from America, graduated MD from Edinburgh University in 1824. [EMG]

BOOTH, JAMES, in Martinique, French West Indies, later in Aberdeen, inventory on 27 January 1812, Comm. Aberdeen. [NRS]

BORLAND, JOHN, a merchant in Boston, New England, trading with Andrew Russell a Scots merchant in Rotterdam, the Netherlands, papers and letters from 1689 to 1697. [NRS.RH15.106.box 20]

BORELAND, ROBERT, in Jamaica, a deed, dated 9 June 1770. [NRS.RD4.208.1551]

BOSWELL, DAVID, in Jamaica, a deed of attorney, dated 6 July 1773. [NRS.RD4.216.338]

BOTER, JAMES HENRY FITZPATRICK, of Demerara, a student at King's College, Aberdeen, graduated MD from Edinburgh University in 1823. [KCA] [EMG]

BOTT, JOHN BOSWELL, of Virginia, graduated MD at Edinburgh University in 1800. [EMG]

BOURKE, WILLIAM, a native of St Croix, Danish West Indies, to Edinburgh in 1791, residing in Drummond Street, in 1794, graduated MD at Edinburgh University in 1794. [EMG] [ECA.SL115.1.1]

BOUSH, WILLIAM, of Virginia, graduated MD at Edinburgh University in 1778. [EMG]

BOVELL, JOHN WILLIAM, of Barbados, graduated MD at Edinburgh University in 1796. [EMG]

BOWMAN, JOHN, the younger of Skiddoway, presently in Glasgow, mortgaged 500 acres on the island of Skiddoway in the parish of Christ Church, Georgia, in 1775. [NRS.GD77.168]

BOXILL, WILLIAM, of Barbados, a student at King's College, Aberdeen, from 1798 to 1806, later graduated MD at Edinburgh University in 1809. [KCA]

BOWDOIN, JAMES, President of the American Academy of Arts and Science, graduated LL.D. at Edinburgh University on 7 February 1785. [GEU]

BOWEN, WILLIAM, of America, graduated MD from Edinburgh University in 1809. [EMG]

BOWIE, WILLIAM, late of Antigua, now in Ayr, was admitted as a burgess and guilds-brother of Ayr on 24 September 1790 by right of his father John Bowie a merchant burgess and guilds-brother of Ayr. [ABR]

BOYD, JOHN, of New Brunswick, graduated MD at King's College, Aberdeen, on 6 September 1820. [KCA]

BOYD, SPENCER, in Virginia, a deed, dated on 17 February 1782. [NRS.RD2.233/1.108]

BOYS, WILLIAM, of Pennsylvania, a medical student at Edinburgh University from 1794 until 1795. [EUL]

BRAND, JOSEPH, son of John Brand in Virginia, a student at King's College, Aberdeen, 1793. [KCA]

BRANDER, ADAM, in Jamaica, a deed of attorney in favour of Alexander Tulloch, dated 11 October 1783. [NRS.RD2.236/2.612]

BRANT, JOSEPH, the Mohawk chief, letters to, from 1797 until 1798. [NLS.Liston,5584]

BRAUCHILL, JOHN, a mariner aboard the America from the River Clyde to Virginia, was put ashore in Virginia, in a case before the High Court of the Admiralty of Scotland in 1737. [NRS.AC8.541]

BREADIE, HUMPHRY, 'a poor Scotchman aged 103 years' was buried in St Michael's, Barbados, on 26 October 1743. [Parish register]

BREBNER, JOHN, son of Patrick Brebner in Jamaica, a student at King's College, Aberdeen, from 1811 to 1815, graduated MA. [KCA]

BREMNER, GEORGE, emigrated from Scotland to America in 1773, settled in Willisbro, Charlotte County, New York, a Loyalist, moved to St John's, at Montreal, Quebec, on 31 January 1788. [PAO.LC.330]

BREMNER, JOHN, of Jamaica, graduated MD from Edinburgh University in 1818. [EMG]

BREMNER, ROBERT, in Jamaica, later in Huntly, testament, 14 December 1808, Comm. Moray. [NRS]

BRIDGEWATER, EDWARD, of Connecticut, a physician educated at Edinburgh University in 1759. [EUL]

BROCKENBROUGH, JOHN, of Virginia, graduated MD from Edinburgh University in 1795. [EMG][VHS]

BRODBELT, FRANCIS RIGBY, of Jamaica, graduated MD at Edinburgh University in 1794. [EMG]

BRODBELT, JAMES LEE, of Jamaica, graduated MD from Edinburgh University in 1824. [EMG]

BRODBELT, THOMAS, of Jamaica, graduated MD from Edinburgh University in 1824. [EMG]

BROOKE, LAURENCE, born 1758, a medical student at Edinburgh University in 1775-1787, died 1803. [EUL]

BROTHERSON, LUDOVIC, of St Kitts, graduated MD at Edinburgh University in 1776. [EMG]

BROTHERTON, ALEXANDER, a carpenter in Cambridge, Albany County, New York, a Loyalist in 1776, later settled at New Carlisle, Bay of Chaleur, Quebec, by 1786. [TNA.AO13.81.26]

BROWN, ANDREW, a minister in Halifax, Nova Scotia, graduated DD at Edinburgh University on 27 March 1788. [GEU]

BROWN, CHARLES, of Jamaica, graduated MD at Edinburgh University in 1797. [EMG]

BROWN, DAVID, born in Scotland, emigrated to America in 1770, settled in Bridgewater, a Loyalist, moved via New York to Nova Scotia, at Halifax, Nova Scotia, on 20 June 1786. [PAO.LC.548]

BROWN, DAVID, in New Brunswick, a deed of attorney with John Campbell, dated 16 January 1800. [NRS.RD3.286.406]

BROWN, DUNCAN, a settler on the north-west branch of the Cape Fear River, North Carolina, petitioned the Synod of Argyle for a Gaelic speaking minister, on 2 September 1748. [NRS.NRAS.1209.553]

BROWN, FRANCIS FRYE, of Antigua, graduated MD at Edinburgh University in 1795. [EMG]

BROWN, GEORGE CRANSTOUN, of Nova Scotia, graduated MD from Edinburgh University in 1818. [EMG]

BROWN, Dr GUSTAVUS, son of Gustavus Brown and his wife Frances Fowke in Charles County, Maryland, graduated MD at Edinburgh University in 1768, died 1804. [EMG]

BROWN, Dr GUSTAVUS, in Maryland, a deed dated on 9 December 1756. [NRS.RD4.197/2.404]

BROWN, HUGH, a settler on the north-west branch of the Cape Fear River, North Carolina, petitioned the Synod of Argyle for a Gaelic speaking minister, on 2 September 1748. [NRS.NRAS.1209.553]

BROWN, JAMES, a merchant from Glasgow, in Maryland before 1770. [TNA.AO12.9.59]

BROWNE, JAMES, in Newfoundland, his sentence of death for forgery was remitted by Royal Warrant, 13 December 1804. [EUL.Laing.ii.641]

BROWN, JAMES, sr., formerly a merchant in St Augusta, Georgia, died in Paisley, Renfrewshire, in 1810. [GM.80.590]

BROWN, JANET, a vagrant, was found guilty of theft at the St John's fair at Banff, was sentenced to be banished to the American Plantations, with seven years' service there, at Aberdeen in June 1773. [SM.35.333]

BROWN, JOHN, settled in Portsmouth, Virginia, as a shipwright in 1763, a Loyalist, returned to Pressminnan, Stenton, East Lothian, by 1784. [TNA.AO12.100.213]

BROWN, JOHN, emigrated from Scotland to Norfolk, Virginia in 1762, a merchant there and later in New York, a Loyalist, in Halifax, Nova Scotia on 27 December 1784. [PAO.LC.469]

BROWN, JOHN, of Harmony Hall, Tobago, a carpenter, testament confirmed on 31 December 1808, Comm. Aberdeen. [NRS]

BROWN, JOSEPH, son of John Brown in St Kitts, a student at King's College, Aberdeen, from 1795 to 1799, graduated MA. [KCA]

BROWN, R. G., in 'Merryland', a deed, dated 2 June 1774. [NRS.RD2.219.34]; in Maryland, a deed of attorney, dated 30 May 1789. [NRS.RD3.248.851]; a commission, 6 May 1791. [NRS.RD3.253.804]

BROWN, ROBERT, a physician in Richmond, Virginia, a will subscribed in 1785. [NRS.CC5.21.5]

BROWN, ROBERT, in Jamaica, later in Annan, Dumfries-shire, an inventory on 4 July 1820, Comm. Dumfries. [NRS]

BROWN, SAMUEL, born in 1763, of Virginia, to Edinburgh in 1792, residing in the Canongait in 1794, a medical student at Edinburgh University 1792-1793, graduated MD from Marischal College, Aberdeen, in 1794, died in 1830. [EUL][MCA] [ECA.SL115.1.1]

BROWN, THOMAS, in Virginia, a deed of attorney, dated 1787. [NRS.RD2.243.741]

BROWN, WILLIAM, of America, graduated MD at Edinburgh University in 1770. [EMG]

BROWN, WILLIAM, emigrated from Scotland to Norfolk, Virginia, in 1762, a merchant there and later in New York, a Loyalist, in Halifax, Nova Scotia on 27 December 1784. [PAO.LC.468]

BROWN, WILLIAM, born 1726 in Scotland, in 1767 was appointed Customs Controller in America, a Loyalist, settled in Edinburgh by 1788. [TNA.AO12.101.269, etc]

BRUCE, ALEXANDER, from Barbados, graduated MD from Edinburgh University in 1755. [EMG]

BRUCE, ALEXANDER, in Jamaica, died intestate, James Campbell of Snowhill near Kingston, Jamaica, was appointed as his attorney on 4 February 1768. [NRS.GD237.21.51/11]

BRUCE, ANDREW, master of the Betsy from Edinburgh to South Carolina, was captured by a French privateer on the return voyage in April 1761 afterwards he died at sea, letters. [NRS.GD152.35A/8]

BRUCE, ARCHIBALD, born in 1777, of New York, a medical student at Edinburgh University 1799-1800, graduated MD at Edinburgh University in 1801, died 1818. [EMG][EUL]

BRUCE, JAMES, settled in West Florida in 1764, Member of H.M. Council and Customs Collector, also a planter, a Loyalist, moved to Shelburne, Nova Scotia, by 1786. [TNA.AO12.99.62, etc]

BRUCE, JOHN, in Pennsylvania, a deed of attorney dated 12 January 1774. [NRS.RD4.215.734]

BRUCE, NORMAND, in Maryland, a deed of attorney in favour of James Bruce, dated 29 August 1785. [NRS.RD4.239.31]

BRUCE, Sir WILLIAM, of Stonehouse, a sasine, dated 11 August 1629, Nova Scotia. [NRS.RS1.26.308]

BRYAN, JAMES, in Jamaica, a bond with William Fogo, dated 26 August 1771. [NRS.RD2.236/1.571]

BRYANT, WILLIAM, in Jamaica, a deed, dated 17 October 1774. [NRS.RD3. 235.633]

BRYSON, ROBERT, a shipmaster in Leith, master of the Ann of Edinburgh, a charter party for a voyage from Leith to Boston, New England in 1736. [NRS.AC10.246]

BUCHAN, JAMES, in Voe, Walls, Shetland Islands, bound for Georgia or South Carolina, letters, 1774. [NRS.CH2.1071.33]

BUCHAN, ..., from Perth, in Richmond, Virginia, in 1819. [NRS.GD50.186.125.3/3]

BUCHANAN, ALEXANDER, in New York, later in Campbeltown, Argyll, testament confirmed on 27 January 1819, Comm. Argyll. [NRS]

BUCHANAN, ALEXANDER, in Tobago, a probative deed of attorney with J. Buchanan, dated 19 September 1803. [NRS.RD2.289.1173]; sometime in Tobago later in Campbeltown, Argyll, testament, 25 December 1811, Comm. Argyll, [NRS.CC2.3.13/303]

BUCHANAN, ANDREW, born 1732, from Glasgow, a merchant in Maryland before 1775, a Loyalist, died near Baltimore in March 1786. [TNA.AO12.9.1]

BUCHANAN, ARCHIBALD, of Drumhead, sometime a merchant in Williamsburgh, Virginia, later in Norfolk, Virginia, a sasine dated 27 September 1751. [NRS.RS9.8.250]

BUCHANAN, ARCHIBALD, a merchant in Virginia, sasines in Dunbarton, in 1757. [NRS.RS9.9.84/85/86/87/95]

BUCHANAN, DONALD, born 1795 in Kenmore, Perthshire, emigrated to New Brunswick aboard the Favourite in 1816. [PANB.RS23]

BUCHANAN, GEORGE, a surgeon in Baltimore, Maryland, sasines, dated on 1737, and 1741. [NRS.RS9.7.225/323/324]

BUCHANAN, GEORGE, from Glasgow, a merchant in Maryland before 1775, a Loyalist. [TNA.AO12.9.1]

BUCHANAN, GEORGE, born in 1763, of Maryland, graduated MD from Edinburgh University in 1785, died in 1808. [EUL]

BUCHANAN, GILBERT, son of John Buchanan, from Glasgow, a merchant in Maryland before 1775, a Loyalist, later in London. [TNA.AO12.6.181]

BUCHANAN, JAMES, a merchant in Falmouth, Virginia, sasines from 1758 until 1771. [NRS.RS9.9.160/206/40/98/362]

BUCHANAN, JAMES, the British Consul in New York, letters, from 1820 until 1827. [NRS.GD45.59; 313],

BUCHANAN, JANET, in Jamaica, a deed with Walter Monteath, dated 14 May 1808. [NRS.RD3.322.380]

BUCHANAN, JOHN, a partner in the firm of Buchanan, Cochran, and Company of Greenock, Scotland, based in Savannah, Georgia, dead by 1784. [TNA.AO12.109.106]

BUCHANAN, JOHN, in Glasgow, son of the deceased Cunningham Buchanan of Fellowship Hall, Jamaica, in 1821. [NRS.CS228.B15.52]

BUCHANAN, ROBERT, settled in America in 1769, a merchant in Newport, Charles County, Maryland, a Loyalist who returned to Glasgow, by 1784. [TNA.AO12.6.239]

BUCHANAN, ROBERT, of Maryland, a medical student at Edinburgh University in 1790. [EUL]

BUCHANAN, ROBERT, born 1795 in Balquhidder, Perthshire, emigrated to New Brunswick aboard the Favourite in 1816. [PANB.RS23]

BUCHANAN, WALTER, of New York, a medical student at Edinburgh University from 1797 until 1798. [EUL]

BUCHANAN, WILLIAM, formerly in Petersburg, Virginia, settled in Glasgow, by 1786, a deposition. [TNA.AO13.28.415]

BUCKNER, HORACE, of Virginia, a medical student at Edinburgh University from 1776 until 1777, graduated MA, MD, at Glasgow University in 1778. [EUL][RGG]

BUIE, DUNCAN, a settler on the north-west branch of the Cape Fear River, North Carolina, petitioned the Synod of Argyle for a Gaelic speaking minister, on 2 September 1748. [NRS.NRAS.1209.553]

BUIST, GEORGE, minister of the Scots Church in Charleston, South Carolina, graduated DD at Edinburgh University on 27 March 1794. [GEU]

BULFINCH, THOMAS, born in 1728, of Massachusetts, New England, graduated MD at Edinburgh University in 1757, died in 1802. [EMG][MHS]

BURN, ANN, in South Carolina, a probative settlement, dated 15 March 1788. [NRS.RD4.253.747] [spouse of John Burn]

BURN, JOHN, in Charleston, South Carolina, a will dated 22 September 1774. [NRS.RD2.218.68]; a Member of Council for South Carolina before 1772, died in Scotland in December 1774. [TNA.AO12.51.378]

BURN, JOHN, in Dominica, a probative will, dated 12 January 1796. [NRS.RD3.292.419]

BURN, MARGARET, in Maryland, a deed of factory dated 9 August 1763. [NRS.RD4.198/1.246]

BURNETT, JOHN, a passenger aboard the Abraham of London bound from London to Virginia on 24 October 1635. [TNA.E157.20]

BURNET, SAMUEL, a passenger aboard the Paule bound from London to Virginia on 6 July 1635. [TNA.E157.20]

BURNETT, THEODOSIUS, from Aberdeen, in Dominica before 1783. [NRS.GD23.3.51]

BURNET, Sir THOMAS, of Leyis, a sasine, dated 14 June 1626, Nova Scotia. [NRS.RS1.19.212]

BURNS, WILLIAM, in North America, a deed with A. Burns, dated 3 November 1806. [NRS.RD3.315.732]

BURTON, DANIEL, of America, graduated MD from Edinburgh University in 1819. [EMG]

BUSH, BENJAMIN, born in 1745, of Pennsylvania, graduated MD from Edinburgh University in 1768, died in 1813. [EMG]

BUTCHER, JAMES, of Barbados, graduated MD from Edinburgh University in 1803. [EMG]

BUXILL, WILLIAM, of Barbados, graduated MD from Edinburgh University in 1809. [EMG]

BUY, ARCHIBALD, [1], a settler on the north-west branch of the Cape Fear River, North Carolina, petitioned the Synod of Argyle for a Gaelic speaking minister, on 2 September 1748. [NRS.NRAS.1209.553]

BUY, ARCHIBALD, [2], a settler on the north-west branch of the Cape Fear River, North Carolina, petitioned the Synod of Argyle for a Gaelic speaking minister, on 2 September 1748. [NRS.NRAS.1209.553]

BUY, DONALD, a settler on the north-west branch of the Cape Fear River, North Carolina, petitioned the Synod of Argyle for a Gaelic speaking minister, on 2 September 1748. [NRS.NRAS.1209.553]

BUY, GILBERT, a settler on the north-west branch of the Cape Fear River, North Carolina, petitioned the Synod of Argyle for a Gaelic speaking minister, on 2 September 1748. [NRS.NRAS.1209.553]

BYAM, RICHARD SCOTT, of Antigua, graduated MD at Edinburgh University in 1775. [EMG]

BYLES, MATTHEW, graduated BA Harvard in 1725, a minister in Boston, New England, graduated DD, at King's College, Aberdeen, on 17 September 1765. [KCA] [SNQ.XII.94]

CAINES, JAMES T., of St Kitts, graduated MD from Edinburgh University in 1808. [EMG]

CAINES, ROBERT, of St Kitts, graduated MD from Edinburgh University in 1816. [EMG]

CALDERHEAD, ALEXANDER, from Glasgow to Virginia in 1775, a Loyalist in 1776. [TNA.AO12.54.147]

CALDERHEAD, WILLIAM, a merchant in Norfolk, Virginia, a Loyalist. [TNA.AO12.54.147]

CALHOUN, ..., a merchant and planter on Nevis and St Kitt around 1670.

CALLENDER, JAMES, born in Scotland, an editor, was drowned in the James River, Virginia, on 7 June 1803. [GM.73.882] ['The Recorder']

CAMERON, ALLAN, in Jamaica, a deed of factory dated 15 January 1758. [NRS.RD2.218.24]

CAMERON, ANGUS, emigrated from Scotland to America in 1773, settled at Johnson's Bush, Tryon County, New York, a Loyalist soldier, moved to Riviere de Raisin, Canada. [PAO.LC.1054]

CAMERON, CHARLES, settled in Maryland as a shipmaster, a Loyalist in 1776, returned to Scotland. [TNA.AO12.102.70]

CAMERON, CHARLES, Governor of the Bahamas, in 1812, [BM.Add.40223, ff.243-244]; letters, 1804/1805/1806/1819, [NRS.GD46.17.27; GD51.1.589/591.1-2; GD202.77;GD202.70.13]

CAMERON, JOHN, of Lochiel with an estate in New Jersey, was attainted for participating in the 1715 Jacobite Rebellion, court records dated 1713 until 1725. [NRS.E.663, box 205]

CAMERON, JOHN, at La Chene, near Montreal, a letter dated 12 October 1805. [NRS.GD202.70.12]

CAMPBELL, ALEXANDER, in Prince George County, Maryland, a deed of attorney dated 18 July 1757. [NRS.RD3.224.2.480]

CAMPBELL, ARCHIBALD, settled in Norfolk, Virginia, as a surgeon and physician from 1744 to 1776, a Loyalist who moved to Bermuda. [TNA.AO12.55.70]; emigrated from Scotland to Virginia in 1744, a physician in Norfolk, a Loyalist, moved to Bermuda, in Halifax, Nova Scotia, on 9 June 1789. [PAO.LC.61]; Letters from 1783 to 1791. [NLS.5033/5034/5035/5036]

CAMPBELL, ARCHIBALD, of Virginia, graduated MD at Edinburgh University in 1770. [EMG][WMC]

CAMPBELL, ARCHIBALD, Governor of Jamaica, organised a ship to transport the 71st Regiment to the Clyde where it will be reduced, a letter dated 13 August 1783. [HMC. American. iv.274]

CAMPBELL, THOMAS, from Boston, New England, to Amsterdam, Holland, a letter dated 1714. [NRS.RH15.14.139.2]

CAMPBELL, CHRISTIAN, born 1752, widow of Reverend John Campbell the Rector of St Andrew's, Jamaica, died on 11 February 1835. [Edinburgh, Greyfriars, gravestone]

CAMPBELL, COLIN, a missionary in Burlington, New Jersey, in August 1766. [SM.28.558]

CAMPBELL, COLIN, son of Robert Campbell of Smiddygreen, in America, a student at King's College, Aberdeen, around 1772. [KCA]

CAMPBELL, COLIN, settled in Virginia as a factor for Glasgow merchants before 1776, later in St Andrew's, New Brunswick, by 1786. [TNA.AO13.22.40]

CAMPBELL, COLIN, in Charleston, South Carolina, a planter, died by 1783. [TNA.AO12.52.192, etc]; probate on 2 January 1783, Prerogative Court of Canterbury. [TNA]

CAMPBELL, COLIN, formerly a merchant in Greenock, later on Holland's Estate, St Elizabeth's, Cornwall, Jamaica, versus Henrietta Campbell, a Process of Divorce in 1790. [NRS.CC8.6.839]

CAMPBELL, COLIN, of Jamaica, graduated MD from Edinburgh University in 1812. [EMG]

CAMPBELL, DANIEL, DONALD GOVAN, JAMES MONTGOMERIE, ARCHIBALD CAMPBELL, THOMAS GILCHRIST, JAMES MCCUNE, and JOHN BUCHANAN, all merchants in Glasgow also JOHN MCGOUN, a merchant in Boston, contracted to send the <u>Two Brothers of Boston,</u> master Thomas Gunie on a trading voyage from Glasgow to America on 23 September 1692. [Mitchell Library. Campbell of Shawfield ms.1/31]

CAMPBELL, DANIEL, in Jamaica, a deed dated 5 June 1776. [NRS.RD2.220.765]

CAMPBELL, DAVID, of America, graduated MD at Edinburgh University in 1777. [EMG][SM.39.336]

CAMPBELL, Sir DONALD, of Lundie, a sasine, dated 20 May 1628, Nova Scotia. [NRS.RS1.23.327]

CAMPBELL, DONALD, from Scalpay, Harris, Inverness-shire, settled on McClendon's Creek, Cumberland County, North Carolina, died in September 1784. [TNA.AO12.37.31]

CAMPBELL, DOUGAL, was appointed Clerk of the Crown and Clerk of the Crown and Common Pleas in South Carolina on 19 June 1754. [JCTP.61/2]

CAMPBELL, DUGALD, of Glencarradale, formerly in St Andrews, Jamaica, a deed dated 7 May 1745. [NRS.RD2.169.250]

CAMPBELL, DUGALD, with one other, emigrated from Campbeltown, Argyll, aboard the <u>Edinburgh of Campbeltown</u>, master John McMichael, in July 1771 bound for Prince Edward Island. [NRS.SC54.2.106]

CAMPBELL, DUGALD, in Jamaica, a deed of factory dated 26 July 1774. [NRS.RD4.217.5]

CAMPBELL, DUNCAN, in Jamaica, deeds dated 20 May 1770. [NRS.RD2.215.143; RD2.216.141]

CAMPBELL, DUNCAN, from Scotland to New York aboard the brig <u>Commerce</u> in 1774, settled at St John's on Lake Champlain, New York, at Montreal on 10 March 1788. [POA.LC.444]; letters dated New York from 1775 to 1776. [NRS.NRAS.0934]

CAMPBELL, DUNCAN, from Greenock to St John, New Brunswick, in 1803, settled in Sussex Vale. [PANB.mc1672]

CAMPBELL, Sir GEORGE, a letter re a proposed settlement in America, dated 1682. [NRS.GD158.846]

CAMPBELL, GEORGE, in Grenada, a commission, on 4 March 1793. [NRS.RD2.258.578]

CAMPBELL, IVER, in Jamaica, a deed, dated 1 July 1788. [NRS.RD4.246.868]

CAMPBELL, JAMES, on board a ship in the St Lawrence River, Canada, a letter in 1761. [NRS.NRAS.0631]

CAMPBELL, JAMES, settled in Norfolk, Virginia, in 1762, later in Grenada, and Bermuda. [TNA.AO12.90.3]

CAMPBELL, JAMES, in Mobile, a letter dated 1764. [NRS.GD248.box 672.bundle 6]

CAMPBELL, JAMES, of Snowhill near Kingston, Jamaica, was appointed as attorney of the deceased Alexander Bruce who died in Jamaica, intestate, on 4 February 1768. [NRS.GD237.21.51/11]

CAMPBELL, JAMES, in Grenada, a deed dated 1775. [NRS.RD2.247/2.338]

CAMPBELL, JAMES, born 1792 in Killin, Perthshire, with his wife Mary born 1788, and their children – James born 1810, Alexander born 1812, and Janet born 1814, emigrated to New Brunswick aboard the Favourite in 1816. [PANB.RS23]

CAMPBELL, JAMES, in America, an indenture dated 17 October 1793. [NRS.RD4.254.813]

CAMPBELL, JAMES, in Grenada and Tobago, letters around 1809; a probative will, subscribed 19 March 1810. [NRS.RD3.334.1193] [NMM.C107.147]

CAMPBELL, JOHN, in Boston, New England, a letter to his cousin Robert Alexander, re Nova Scotia, in 1706. [NRS.NRAS.0332]; a request for a grant towards providing a minister and church in Boston, around 1717. [NRS.GD152.200]

CAMPBELL, JOHN, Earl of Loudoun, was appointed Captain General and Governor of Virginia on 18 February 1756. [JCTP.63]

CAMPBELL, JOHN, in Jamaica, a deed dated July 1769. [NRS.RD4.223/2.303]

CAMPBELL, JOHN, a settler on the north-west branch of the Cape Fear River, North Carolina, petitioned the Synod of Argyle for a Gaelic speaking minister, on 2 September 1748. [NRS.NRAS.1209.553]

CAMPBELL, JOHN, an engineer in West Florida in 1769. [JCTP.76]

CAMPBELL, JOHN, born 1731, from Glendaruel, Argyll, Superintendent of Indian Affairs in Lower Canada, died on 23 June 1795. [GM.65.703]

CAMPBELL, JOHN, sometime in Grenada, later in Perth, son of John Campbell a merchant in Perth, an edict of executry, 13 January 1801. [TNA.CC2.8.105/3]

CAMPBELL, JOHN, from Auchenwillie, Argyll, died at Besancon, Three Rivers, Upper Canada, on 11 October 1819. [GM.89.568]

CAMPBELL, KENNETH, son of Donald Campbell from Scalpay, resident of North Carolina, a Loyalist, settled in Skye by 1788. [TNA.AO12.109.104, etc]

CAMPBELL, LACHLAN, from Scotland to Virginia in 1764, factor for Glasgow merchants, a Loyalist, in Auchenbreck, Scotland, by 1783. [TNA.AO12.106.23]

CAMPBELL, MARGARET, imprisoned in Aberdeen Tolbooth guilty of infanticide, banished to America in 1742. [ACA]

CAMPBELL, LACHLAN, died aboard the De Caleman at sea when bound from Tobago to Ostend on is way home to Craignish, Argyll on 8 September 1782. [NRS.CC2.8.88/6]

CAMPBELL, Lord NEIL, with his man-servant, from New York to London on 10 June 1687. [NRS.GD112.16.7.1/55] instructed James Campbell to sell property in East New Jersey in 1690. [NRS.GD50.186.65]

CAMPBELL, NEIL, of Lottery, St George's, Surrey, Jamaica, late in Dunoon, deeds in 1793, 1795, and 1803, [NRS.CC2.2.951; 7.39.6, 8.107.10, 13.11.15]

CAMPBELL, PATRICK, a settler on the north-west branch of the Cape Fear River, North Carolina, petitioned the Synod of Argyle for

a Gaelic speaking minister, on 2 September 1748.
[NRS.NRAS.1209.553]

CAMPBELL, PATRICK, in Tobago, a deed of factory dated 3 July 1775. [NRS.RD2.217/2.268]

CAMPBELL, PETER, Lieutenant Governor of Tobago, died there on 9 January 1779. [SM.41.167]

CAMPBELL, ROBERT, born 1712, emigrated to Virginia in 1734, a physician in Hanover County, Virginia, a Loyalist, returned to Edinburgh by 1784. [TNA.AO12.109.108]

CAMPBELL, ROBERT, born in Edinburgh, a bookseller and stationer in Philadelphia, died in Frankford on 14 August 1800. [GM.70.1107]

CAMPBELL, SAMUEL, a merchant in Wilmington, North Carolina, partner in Hogg and Campbell, a militia officer, settled in Shelburne, Nova Scotia, by 1784. [TNA.AO12.35.4]

CAMPBELL, SARAH, in Antigua, a letter dated 1816. [NLS.5646.47]

CAMPBELL, THOMAS, bound on an embassy to the Creek Indians in 1764, a letter in 1767. [NLS.ms24536]

CAMPBELL, THOMAS, in Grenada, a deed of attorney, dated 25 March 1790. [NRS.RD2.257.479]

CAMPBELL, Lord WILLIAM, married Miss Izard in Charleston, South Carolina, in 1763. [GM.32.313]; was appointed Captain General and Governor in Chief of Nova Scotia on 12 August 1766. [SM.28.437]; petitioned for a grant of Grand Manon Island in the Bay of Fundy on 23 May 1767. [RPCCl.vi.448]

CAMPBELL, WILLIAM, in New York, a deed of factory in favour of James Hart, dated 18 October 1783. [NRS.RD2.240/2.202]

CAMPBELL, WILLIAM, in Jamaica, an agreement by his heirs, on 24 March 1807. [NRS.RD3.318.549]

CARDEN, JAMES, of St Cruz Island, (St Croix), graduated MD from Edinburgh University in 1812. [EMG]

CAREY, JOSEPH, of Jamaica, graduated MD from Edinburgh University in 1809. [EMG]

CARGILL, JOHN, Judge of Dominica was buried in St Michael's, Barbados, on 8 November 1764. [Parish register]

CARMICHAEL, S., in Jamaica, a deed of attorney with C. Innes, on 18 June 1789. [NRS.RD3.285.183]

CARMICHAEL, STEPHEN F., of St Vincent, graduated MD from Edinburgh University in 1822. [EMG]

CARMICHAEL, WILLIAM, in Maryland, deeds, on 31 May 1785 and 14 January 1786, [NRS.RD4.239.714/716]

CARPENTER, SAMUEL, of America, a student at King's College, Aberdeen, from 1759 to 1763. [KCA]

CARRINGTON, JOHN WILLIAM WORRELL, of Barbados, graduated MD from Edinburgh University in 1825. [EMG]

CARROLL, EDWARD, of Jamaica, graduated MD at King's College, Aberdeen, on 5 December 1820. [KCA]

CARRUTHERS, JOHN J., a Professor of Theology in Brockville, Upper Canada, letters, 1821-1825. [NLS.MS8984/8987]

CARSON, JACOBINA, daughter of John Carson MD in Philadelphia, Pennsylvania, married Robert Forsyth an advocate, in Edinburgh on 12 July 1803. [GM.73.690]

CARSON, JOHN, of Philadelphia, a medical student at Edinburgh University, 1774, graduated MD there in 1776. [EMG][Cullen Papers, Glasgow University]

CARTER, AMBROSE, of Jamaica, graduated MD at Edinburgh University in 1794. [EMG]

CATHCART, CHARLES, to go to America as a volunteer with General Howe, a letter dated 22 September 1776, possibly fought at the Battle of Brandywine and in the attack on Philadelphia in October 1777. [NRS.GD155.814]

CATHCART, GABRIEL, son of Dr William Cathcart in North Carolina, brother of John Cathcart of Genoch, was educated in Glasgow from 1758 until 1764. [NRS.GD180.480]

CATHCART, JOHN, Writer and Searcher at the Port of Quebec, a letter dated 1769. [NLS.Stewart.5025.130]

CATHCART, Dr WILLIAM, in Virginia and North Carolina, letters from 1760 to 1769. [NRS.GD180.625.1-2]; died by 24 June 1773 see letter from Samuel Johnston there. [NRS.GD180.644]

CATHRALL, ISAAC, of Pennsylvania, a medical student at Edinburgh University in 1791. [EUL]

CAW, THOMAS, born in 1748, of South Carolina, graduated MD at Edinburgh University in 1769, died in 1773. [EMG]

CHALMER, ALEXANDER, in St Kitts, was admitted as a burgess and guilds-brother of Ayr, on 20 December 1665. [ABR]

CHALMERS, BRYCE, from Galloway, an innkeeper in Charlotte County, New Brunswick, probate 20 September 1834, New Brunswick. [PANB]

CHALMERS, DAVID, settled in New York as a type-maker with a print firm, letters in 1823. [NRS.NRAS.CC8.6.425][S.744.3]

CHALMERS, HUGH, in New York, a deed of factory with Thomas Manson, 28 August 1802. [NRS.RD3.294.698]

CHALMERS, JAMES, a planter in St Thomas in the Vale, Surrey, Jamaica, son of James Chalmers of Balnellan, Boharm, Banffshire, married Margaret Marr in May 1759, a Process of Divorce dated 10 September 1766. [NRS]

CHAMBERS, JOHN, in Charleston, South Carolina, moved to Aberdeen, Scotland by 1784. [TNA.AO12.51.332, etc]

CHANDLER, ISAAC, of South Carolina, graduated MD at Edinburgh University in 1768, died 1782. [EMG]

CHAPMAN, MATTHEW JAMES, of Barbados, graduated MD from Edinburgh University in 1819. [EMG]

CHAPMAN, Dr NATHANIEL, a physician in Philadelphia, was admitted as a burgess and guilds-brother of Ayr on 4 1802. [ABR]

CHARLES, JAMES, in South Carolina, a deed of attorney, dated 28 May 1793. [NRS.RD4.254.393]

CHAUNCEY, CHARLES, MA, minister in Boston, New England, graduated DD at Edinburgh University on 2 June 1742. [GEU]

CHEEKES, WILLIAM, of Barbados, graduated MD from Edinburgh University in 1803. [EMG]

CHEVAS, ALEXANDER, emigrated from Scotland to America in 1762, settled at Long Cane, Ninety Six District, South Carolina, as a planter, returned home by 1784. [TNA.AO12.101.87, etc]

CHEYNE, THOMAS, emigrated from Scotland to Virginia, died there in 1775, father of Chichester Cheyne a Loyalist. [TNA.AO13.97.237]

CHISHOLM, JAMES, in New York, a letter, 1783. [NRS.NRAS.0771]

CHISHOLM, Dr WILLIAM, a surgeon in Port Royal, Jamaica, a deed dated 18 February 1752. [NRS.RD2.171/1.182]

CHISHOLM, WILLIAM, settled in Pittenweem near Norfolk, Virginia, as a merchant skipper, around 1754, a Loyalist, settled in Pittenweem, Fife, by 1788. [TNA.AO12.74.95]

CHISHOLM, WILLIAM, emigrated from Scotland to America in 1773, settled in Johnson's Bush, Tryon County, New York, a Loyalist soldier, moved to Riviere de Raisin by 1783. [PAO.LC.1061]

CHISHOLM, WILLIAM, of Charleston, South Carolina, a medical student at Edinburgh University in 1791-1792, graduated MD at Glasgow University in 1793. [EUL][RGG]

CHRISTIE, EDWARD, in Jamaica, a deed, 17 April 1789. [NRS.RD4.245.993]

CHRISTIE, NATHAN, in Montreal, Quebec, two letters dated 1776. [NRS.NRAS.0631]

CHRISTIE, RICHARD, born 1617, a passenger aboard the William and John bound via London to St Kitts on 2 September 1635. [TNA.E157.20]

CHRISTIE, ROBERT, Lord Provost of Glasgow from 1756 to 1757, died in Maryland on 17 January 1780. [SM.42.333]

CHRISTIE, ROBERT, a trader in Maryland from 1764 until 1774, a Loyalist in 1776, to London by 1784. [TNA.AO12.8.73]

CHRISTIE, ROBERT, from Glass, Aberdeenshire, a wharfinger in St Catherine's, Middlesex, Jamaica, versus his spouse Margaret Napier, a Process of Divorce, in 1782. [NRS.CC8.6.666]

CLACHAR, JOHN S., of Jamaica, graduated MD from Edinburgh University in 1814. [EMG]

CLAP, THOMAS, born on 26 June 1703 in Scituate, Massachusetts, pastor of the Presbyterian Church in Windham from 1726 to 1740, President of Yale College in Connecticut from 1740 to 1765, graduated DD at Glasgow University in 1748, died 29 August 1747. [RGG]

CLARK, ALEXANDER, a settler on the north-west branch of the Cape Fear River, North Carolina, petitioned the Synod of Argyle for a Gaelic speaking minister, on 2 September 1748. [NRS.NRAS.1209.553]

CLARK, ANDREW, in Jamaica, a deed of attorney in favour of W. Richmond, 25 August 1770. [NRS.RD4.208.945]

CLARK, ARCHIBALD, a settler on the north-west branch of the Cape Fear River, North Carolina, petitioned the Synod of Argyle for a Gaelic speaking minister, on 2 September 1748. [NRS.NRAS.1209.553]

CLERK, COLIN, born 1750, a merchant in Wilmington, North Carolina, a Loyalist, in London by 1784. [TNA.AO12.34.20]

CLARK, GILBERT, a settler on the north-west branch of the Cape Fear River, North Carolina, petitioned the Synod of Argyle for a Gaelic speaking minister, on 2 September 1748. [NRS.NRAS.1209.553]

CLARK, JAMES, letters re his training as a merchant, including a trading voyage to New England, between 1716 and 1719. He shipped goods on the Mayflower of Boston in 1716. [NRS.GD18.5288]

CLARK, JAMES, emigrated from Scotland to America in 1772, settled at Otter Creek, Charlotte County, Vermont, a Loyalist in 1776, moved to New Johnstown, Canada, by 1787. [TNA.AO12.31 13] [PAO.LC.281]

CLARK, JOHN, a settler on the north-west branch of the Cape Fear River, North Carolina, petitioned the Synod of Argyle for a Gaelic speaking minister, on 2 September 1748. [NRS.NRAS.1209.553]

CLARK, OSWALD, in Tobago, a probative bond with Alexander Gordon, 1 July 1797. [NRS.RD3.292.330]

CLARK, THOMAS, in Jamaica, a deed of factory, dated 25 May 1778. [NRS.RD2.226/1.610]

CLARKE, JOHN, graduated MA at Glasgow University in 1764. Possibly the John Clarke, MA, minister in Boston, New England, who graduated DD at Edinburgh University on 12 September 1795. [RGG][GEU]

CLARK, THOMAS, was sent by Glasgow merchants to sell their goods in Boston and return via Virginia with tobacco around 1690. [NRS.GD3.17.6]

CLARK, THOMAS MILBOURNE, of Jamaica, a student at King's College, Aberdeen, around 1816. [KCA]

CLAXTON, FRANCIS, of the West Indies, graduated MD at Edinburgh University in 1777. [EMG][SM.39.336]

CLAY, SAMUEL, of Virginia, a medical student at Edinburgh University in 1799-. [EUL]

CLAYTON, THOMAS, of Virginia, graduated MD at Edinburgh University in 1758. [EMG]

CLAYTON, THOMAS, from Potterhill, Paisley, died in Poplar Grove, Wilmington, North Carolina, on 1 October 1793. [GM.63.1214]

CLELAND, JAMES, in Jamaica, a will, 29 October 1790. [NRS.RD4.249.727]

CLEMENTS, EWEN, from Virginia, a medical student at Edinburgh University, from 1756 to 1757. [EUL]

CLERK, GEORGE, in America, a deed, 30 April 1781. [NRS.RD4.235.721]

CLARKSON, MARGARET, in Barbados, a deed, 1787. [NRS.RD3.244.893]

CLELAND, WILLIAM, in London bound for Barbados, letters dated 1705. [GD124.12.259]

CLIFTON, BENJAMIN, of St Kitts, a medical student at Edinburgh University in 1764, graduated MD there in 1766. [EUL][EMG]

CLOUDSDALL, Mrs, widow of Thomas Cloudsdall a storekeeper in Philadelphia and a Loyalist, to settle in Dunbartonshire in 1788. [TNA.AO12.30.270]

CLUB, JAMES, born in Scotland, a mariner in Philadelphia, a Loyalist settled in Annapolis, Nova Scotia, by 1786. [TNA.AO13.24.92]

CLYDE, PETER, in Miramachi, New Brunswick, a letter in 1830. [NRS.GD1.620/84]

COBHAM, FRANCIS, in Barbados, graduated MD from Edinburgh University in 1819. [EMG]

CLIFTON, FRANCIS, of St Kitts, a student from 1771 to 1775, graduated MA at King's College, Aberdeen, on 30 March 1775. [KCA]

CLIFTON, HORATIO M., of St Kitts, graduated MD from Edinburgh University in 1810. [EMG]

CLITHERALL, JAMES, in South Carolina, a student in Edinburgh from 1760 to 1761. [UNC]

COCHRANE, ALEXANDER, in Newport, Rhode Island, a letter dated 24 February 1777. [HMC.Laing.ii.496]

COCHRANE, ARCHIBALD, executor Of S. Parry, in Antigua in 1726. [RPCCol.vi.163]

COCHRANE, DAVID, in Virginia, a deed of factory in favour of Alexander Donald, 1 January 1776. [NRS.RD3.242.127]

COCHRANE, Sir JOHN, of Ochiltree, a letter to Joseph Morton the Governor at Ashley River, Carolina, in 1682. [NRS.GD58.847]

COCHRAN, RICHARD, settled in Princeton, Judge of the Court of Common Pleas of New Jersey, in Glasgow by 1783. [TNA.AO12.13.136][NLS.MSS 2590-2596]

COCHRANE, ROBERT, a furniture painter in Edinburgh, aboard the Magdalene, master James Menzies, bound from Leith to Carolina, a petition, 1746. [NRS.AC10.323]

COCHRANE, Sir THOMAS, Governor of Newfoundland, letters, from 1824 until 1835. [NLS.MSS.2268-2276; journal, 1824-1836.]

COCHRAN, WILLIAM, son of Captain Cochran in Greenock, died in Quebec in 1803. [GM.73.1254]

COCK, WILLIAM H., in the West Indies, graduated MD from Edinburgh University in 1822. [EMG]

COCKBURN, ADAM, Customs Officer at Roanoke, North Carolina, in 1723. [RPCCol.vi.632]

COCKBURN, THOMAS, in Jamaica, graduated MD at Glasgow University in 1747. [RGG]

COCKBURN, THOMAS, in Jamaica, a bond, dated 14 November 1793. [NRS.RD3.263,917]

COCKBURN, Sir WILLIAM, of Langtoun, a sasine, dated 22 April 1629, Nova Scotia. [NRS.RS1.25.366]

COLEMAN, BENJAMIN, born in Boston on 19 October 1673, a non-conformist minister in Boston from 1699 to 1747, graduated DD at Glasgow University in 1731, died on 29 August 1747. [RGG]

COLINS, THOMAS, in St Croix, a contract of marriage with C. Aitken, dated 5 December 1784. [NRS.RD4.337.221]

COLLYMORE, SAMUEL, in Barbados, graduated MD from Edinburgh University in 1810. [EMG]

COLQUHOUN, JAMES, in America, graduated MD from Edinburgh University in 1813. [EMG]

COLQUHOUN, Sir JOHN, of Luss, a sasine, dated 26 October 1625, Nova Scotia. [NRS.RS1.18.201]

COLQUHOUN, PATRICK, agent for the Virgin Islands, a memorial re Tortula, dated 1803. [RCS]

COLQUHOUN, ROBERT, via the River Clyde to St Kitts in 1728, a slave master, plantation manager, and planter in St Kitts. [HS.9.3]

COLQUHOUN, SAMUEL, from Virginia, a medical student at Edinburgh University, from 1759 until 1760. [EUL]

COLQUHOUN, WALTER, from Glasgow, married Elizabeth McAlister, daughter of Alexander McAlister of Dominica, there on 22 June 1776, [SM.38.454]; in Antigua, a deed, 9 January1789. [NRS.RD3.248.701]

COLQUHOUN, WILLIAM, a merchant on Nevis, was elected to the Island Assembly in 1677. [HS.9.3]

COLVIL, Captain JOHN, with six others, emigrated from Campbeltown, Argyll, aboard the Edinburgh of Campbeltown, master John McMichael, in July 1771 bound for Prince Edward Island. [NRS.SC54.2.106]

CONNEL, DAVID, in Jamaica, a deed of attorney, dated 15 July 1788. [NRS.RD4.244.793]

CONNELL, JAMES, a merchant in Port Royal, Jamaica, was admitted as a burgess and guilds-brother of Ayr on 17 June 1710. [ABR]

CONNEL, JAMES, in Jamaica, a deed of attorney in favour of Thomas Graham, dated 19 April 1786. [NRS.RD2.241/1.725]

CONNER, EDWARD, a settler on the north-west branch of the Cape Fear River, North Carolina, petitioned the Synod of Argyle for a Gaelic speaking minister, on 2 September 1748. [NRS.NRAS.1209.553]

CONRAD, DANIEL, of Virginia, a medical student at Edinburgh University in 1791-1792. [EUL]

CONVILLE, CHARLES JOHN, later 1st Viscount Toronto, a letter re disturbances in Lower Canada, 1838. [NRS.NRAS.0039]

COOPER, MYLES, in New York, a probative will, dated 7 May 1782. [NRS.RD4.238.540]

COOPER, SAMUEL, MA, in Boston, New England, graduated DD at Edinburgh University on 23 July 1767. [GEU]

COPLAND, CHARLES, son of Patrick Copland, a student at King's College, Aberdeen, 1805 to 1809, Jamaica. [KCA]

COPLAND, GEORGE, son of William Copland in Jamaica, a student at King's College, Aberdeen, from 1803 to 1805. [KCA]

COPLAND, JAMES, son of William Copland in Jamaica, a student at King's College, Aberdeen, from 1816 to 1817. [KCA]

CORBETT, EDWARD, Receiver General of Quit Rents for South Carolina in 1775, a Loyalist, returned home. [TNA.AO13.126.494]

CORMACK, ENEAS, in Montreal, Quebec, a testament, dated 15 January 1814, Comm Caithness. [NRS]

CORRIE, JOSEPH, in St Thomas, Danish West Indies, a deed with William Caddel, dated 11 January 1784. [NRS.RD3.285.248]

COULL, THOMAS, in Antigua, graduated MD at Edinburgh University in 1797. [EMG]

COULTER, MICHAEL, in Virginia, a deed of attorney in favour of James Ewing, dated 9 May 1774. [NRS.RD3.238/1.391]

COULTER, WILLIAM, in Virginia, a commission, dated 14 September 1791. [NRS.RD4.251.300]

COURT, ANTHONY FRANCIS, in Trinidad, graduated MD at King's College, Aberdeen, on 28 July 1821. [KCA]

COUTTS, WILLIAM, youngest son of James Coutts, a merchant in Aberdeen who died in 1729 and his wife Marjory Gray, their son Patrick went to Virginia about 1747 and settled at Richmond Falls and died there in 1776, their youngest son William was bred a preacher and went to Virginia over 30 years before 1797. [ACA.APB.3]

COWAN, ROBERT, settled as a tobacco planter in Bedford County, Virginia, in 1750s, a Loyalist, moved to England by 1778. [TNA.AO13.28.130]

COWARD, GEORGE SCOTT, in Jamaica, graduated MD from Edinburgh University in 1822. [EMG]

COWIE, ANDREW, in Pensacola, West Florida, an account, dated 1 April 1780. [HMC. American. ii.127]

COX, JOHN, in Jamaica, graduated MD from Edinburgh University in 1822. [EMG]

COXE, JOHN REDMAN, from Pennsylvania, a medical student at Edinburgh University in 1784-1795. [EUL]

CRAIG, DAVID, in the Bahamas, a deed of factory with Patrick Craig, dated 28 August 1801. [NRS.RD3.292.350]

CRAIG, GEORGE, and his son Archibald Cumming Craig of Pennsylvania, correspondence and papers re their executries dated between 1782 and 1820. [NRS.GD1.495.35]

CRAIG, Mr., emigrated from Campbeltown, Argyll, aboard the <u>Edinburgh of Campbeltown</u>, master John McMichael, in July 1771 bound for Prince Edward Island. [NRS.SC54.2.106]

CRAMOND, JOHN, a merchant in Norfolk, Virginia, before 1776, a Loyalist who moved to Jamaica. [TNA.AO12.56.389]

CRANE, CHARLES, of Jamaica, Fellow of the Royal College of Surgeons, graduated MD at King's College, Aberdeen, on 1 November 1810. [KCA]

CRAWFORD, GEORGE, born 1809, son of Louis Crawford in Upper Canada, educated at Edinburgh Academy, 1824-1825. [EAR]

CRAUFORD, HUGH SPROULE, of Cowdonhill, spouse of Charlotte Felicity Conner, daughter of Captain William Conner of Craney Island, Norfolk County, Virginia, a sasine 1773. [NRS.RS.Dunbarton.10.463]

CRAWFORD, PATRICK, a seaman, petitioned Sir Robert Baird a partner in the Carolina Society for participating in a voyage to Carolina and returning with a map and description of the country in 1691. [NRS.GD238.box 3, bundle 4]

CRAWFORD, RICHARD, in Jamaica, a deed, 1787. [NRS.RD2.243.329]

CRAWFORD, ROBERT, in St Kitts, a deed of attorney in favour of Archibald Crawford, dated 21 January 1784. [NRS.RD3.243.146]; a deed of attorney, dated 13 October 1785. [NRS.RD3.249.388]

CREIGHTON, WILLIAM, emigrated to America in 1763, a planter in Charleston, South Carolina, a Loyalist, was banished to England in 1778. [TNA.AO12.51.72, etc]

CRIGHTON, ALEXANDER, settled in Georgia before 1776, a Loyalist who moved to England by 1784. [TNA.AO12.112.4]

CRICHTON, Mrs HELEN, in Pictou, Nova Scotia, a letter to her uncle Aaron Lithgow a merchant in Glasgow, 1837. [NLS.ms2543.37]

CRICHTON, JAMES, born 1773 in Newtyle, Angus, late of Antigua, died on 23 April 1819. [Greyfriars, Edinburgh, gravestone]

CRICHTON, WILLIAM, in Charleston, South Carolina, a deed of factory with John Brown, 9 November 1781. [NRS.RD4.230.876]

CROASDAILE, EDWARD, in Jamaica, graduated MD at Edinburgh University in 1799. [EMG]

CROCKATT, CHARLES, a merchant in London, husband of Anna Mulman, a deed, 28 August 1752. [NRS.RD4.178/2.252]

CROCKATT, JAMES, a merchant in Charleston, South Carolina, and in London, husband of Esther Gaillard, a deed, 28 August 1752. [NRS.RD4.178/2.252]

CROCKATT, Dr JAMES, in South Carolina, inherited property in Coupar Angus in Perthshire, papers from 1765 until 1767. [NRS.NRAS.0387]

CROMAS, JAMES, died in North America before 1769. [ACA, APB.3]

CROOKE, CLEMENT, in St Kitts, graduated MD at Edinburgh University in 1753. [EMG]

CROOKS, RICHARD, in Jamaica, graduated MD at Edinburgh University in 1793. [EMG]

CROOKE, ROBERT, servant of Captain Samuel Welch of New York, was admitted as a burgess and freeman of Ayr on 9 February 1708. [ABR]

CROSS, ROBERT, President of the corporation in Philadelphia for the relief of poor Protestant ministers, an address to the General Assembly of the Church of Scotland, 10 February 1763. [NRS.CH1.2.107/301]

CRUDEN, ALEXANDER, a Scottish Episcopalian, ordained as an Anglican priest and appointed minister at South Farnham, Virginia, in 1750, a Loyalist, returned to Aberdeen by 1788. [TNA.AO12.54.11]

CRUDEN, JOHN, born 1754 in Scotland, son of William Cruden, settled in Wilmington, North Carolina, as a merchant, a Loyalist, died in 1787; J. Cruden, a letter to Major C. Nesbit 'to prevent sale of negroes carried from the Southern Provinces, dated Tortula on 25 March 1783. [HMC. American. iii. 401/415]

CRUICKSHANK, ALEXANDER, born in Scotland, a merchant in Albany, New York, before 1771, moved to Canada, died August 1784. [TNA.AO12.26.270] [PAO.LC.779]

CRUICKSHANKS, JAMES, in St Vincent, a deed of attorney, 7 February 1778. [NRS.RD4.243.779]; a bond with Isabel Ogilvy, 16 August 1793. [NRS.RD4.270.1097]

CRUICKSHANK, PATRICK, late of St Vincent, married Jane Lewis, in Edinburgh on 5 May 1780. [SM.42.279]

CRUIKSHANK, ROBERT, born April 1743 in Arbroath, Angus, son of Reverend George Cruikshank, served his apprenticeship as a silversmith in London, a plate-worker there from 1766 to 1773, emigrated to Montreal, Quebec, in 1773, died in 1809. [MFA.101]

CULLING, JOHN H., in Barbados, graduated MD from Edinburgh University in 1809. [EMG]

CUMINE, Reverend ALEXANDER, a schoolmaster in Beaufort, Port Royal, South Carolina, from 1764 to 1777, a Loyalist who settled in Kingston, Jamaica, as a schoolmaster. [TNA.AO12.49.422, etc]

CUMINGS, ARCHIBALD, Customs Officer in Newfoundland in 1723. [RPCCol.vi.633]

CUMING, HELEN, daughter of the deceased Sir Alexander Cuming of Culter, and spouse of Robert Cuming a merchant in Concord, Massachusetts, legal papers, dated from 1725 to 1730. [NRS.GD105.338-348]

CUMING, JOHN, born 1727 from Massachusetts, a medical student at Edinburgh University around 1750, died 1788. [Sibley's Harvard Graduates, Boston, 1873]

CUMMING, JOHN, probably from Moray, bound via Greenock for New York in 1774, a letter. [NRS.GD248.226.2.17]

CUMMING, JOHN, from Maryland or Pennsylvania, a medical student at Edinburgh University 1791-1792, graduated MD from Glasgow University in 1793. [EUL][RGG]

CUMING, LAUCHLANE, in Demerara, a deed with McHenry Parker and Company, 31 January 1810. [NRS.RD3.333.1341]

CUMING, THOMAS, in Demerara, a deed of factory with George Robertson, dated 19 July 1800. [NRS.RD3.287.129]; a deed with Sir George Grant, dated 16 December 1800. [NRS.RD3.288.1]

CUNNINGHAM, ALEXANDER, manager in Virginia and Maryland of Cunninghame, Findlay and Company and of Cunninghame, Browne and Company, from 1768 until his death in 1772, [TNA.AO12.56.285]

CUNNINGHAM, ALEXANDER, a Loyalist in Savannah, Georgia, via St Augustine, Florida, to Dominica in 1785. [TNA.AO13.137.95]

CUNNINGHAM, ANDREW, in Antigua on 9 October 1788. [NRS.GD21.633]

CUNNINGHAM, DANIEL, in Ludlow, formerly in Cayon, St Kitts, a bond, dated 4 April 1751. [NRS.RD2.169.456]. [NRS.RS1.22.15]

CUNNINGHAM, R., was granted lands in St Kitts on 12 June 1728. [RPCCol.vi.200]

CUNNINGHAM, Sir WILLIAM, of Cunninghamhead, a sasine dated 28 July 1627, Nova Scotia. [NRS.RS1]

CUNNINGHAM, WILLIAM, born 1614, a passenger aboard the Speedwell of London bound from London to Virginia on 28 May 1635. [TNA.E157.20]

CUNNINGHAM, WILLIAM, died 8 December 1768 on St Jan, Danish West Indies, probate, 1758-1775, fos.64-67. [RAK]

CUNNINGHAME, WILLIAM, emigrated to Virginia in 1748, a merchant there, returned to Glasgow in 1768. [TNA.AO12.56.285]

CUNNINGHAM, ..., in East Florida, a deed, 31 March 1788. [NRS.RD2.244/2.149]

CURRIE, DAVID, of Drylaw, died on St Thomas in the West Indies on 28 February 1782. [SM.44.221]

CURRIE, Dr JAMES, in Richmond, Virginia, married Mrs Ingles of Princess Anne County, Virginia, in Norfolk, Virginia, on 12 November 1789. [GM.60.178]

CURRIE, WALTER, in Providence, Rhode Island, acquired property in Linlithgow, West Lothian, in 1739. [NRS.GD119.140]

CURRIE, WILLIAM, emigrated to South Carolina in 1772, a Loyalist, moved to Edinburgh by 1784. [TNA.AO12.51.65]

CURTIN, SAMUEL, in Jamaica, graduated MD at Edinburgh University in 1778. [EMG]

CUSTIS, THOMAS, born in Virginia, to Edinburgh in 1792 to study medicine, residing in St James Square, Edinburgh, in 1794. [ECA.SL115.1.1]

CUTHBERT, GEORGE, in Jamaica, a bond, 1785. [NRS.RD3.246.1172]; in Jamaica, a deed of attorney in favour of Lewis Cuthbert, 10 January 1785. [NRS.RD4.239.451]; a deed of factory, 3 December 1788. [NRS.RD4.245.210]; a deed of factory with William P. Litt, 28 January 1808. [NRS.RD3.322.320]

CUTHBERT, JOSEPH, in Savannah, a deed of attorney in favour of L. Cuthbert, 23 July 1783. [NRS.RD4.238.237]

CUTHBERT, LEWIS, in Jamaica, a deed of factory, 2 July 1789. [NRS.RD4.246.441]; a deed of factory, 21 November 1789. [NRS.RD4.247.153]; probative documents, 27 May 1795, 19 November 1793, and 25 July 1800. [NRS.RD3.298.136-140]

DABNEY, JAMES, of Virginia, graduated MD from Edinburgh University in 1804. [EMG]

DALE, THOMAS SIMONS, (1749-1816), in South Carolina, graduated MD at Edinburgh University in 1775. [EMG]

DALLAS, ROBERT, in St Mary's, Jamaica, a letter to his father re his brother John Dallas who was bound for Dominica as an indentured servant, 1 July 1771. [NRS.GD314.19]

DALRYMPLE, Captain HUGH, Commander of <u>HMS Canada</u> died at sea on 28 December 1780. [SM.42.55]

DALRYMPLE, HUGH, in Jamaica, a deed of attorney, dated 27 May 1790. [NRS.RD2.250.597]

DALYMPLE, JAMES, son of James Dalrymple of Clayholes, an apprentice of John Weir a barber and periwig-maker in Edinburgh, was illegally taken aboard the ………of Queensferry, master James Jamieson, bound for the West Indies, a petition before the High Court of the Admiralty of Scotland in 1710. [NRS.AC10.98]

DALZELL, AUGUSTUS EDWARD, in Bermuda, graduated MD from Edinburgh University in 1812. [EMG]

DANA, JAMES, (1739-1823), MA, in Wallingford, New England, a medical student at Edinburgh University in 1764, graduated DD at Edinburgh University on 29 April 1768. [GEU][EUL]

DANCER, THOMAS, a medical practitioner and author in Spanish Town, Jamaica, graduated MD at Marischal College, Aberdeen, in 1773. [MCA]

DANFORTH, THOMAS, from Massachusetts, a medical student at Edinburgh University in 1796. [EUL]

DANIEL, JOHN MONCURE of Virginia, a medical student at Edinburgh University in 1790, graduated MD at Glasgow University in 1791, possibly a surgeon of the US Army, grandfather of John Moncure Daniel editor of the *Richmond Examiner* of Richmond, Virginia. [EUL][RGG][VHS]

DANIEL, JOSEPH, in Nevis, graduated MD from Edinburgh University in 1809. [EMG]

DANIEL, MEADE HOME, in Montserrat, graduated MD at Edinburgh University in 1799. [EMG]

DARROCH, DUNCAN, and family, emigrated aboard the <u>Edinburgh of Campbeltown,</u> master John McMichael, from Campbeltown, Argyll, on 1 July 1771 bound for North Carolina. [NRS.SC54.2.166]

DAVIDGE, JOHN BEALE, (1768-1829), in Maryland, a medical student at Edinburgh University 1792-1793, graduated MD at Glasgow University in 1793. [EUL][RGG]

DAVIDSON, ARTHUR, in Quebec, a letter of attorney, dated 1777. [NLS.Stewart.3962]

DAVIDSON, JOHN, son of John Davidson in Kingston, Jamaica, a student at King's College, Aberdeen, from 1798 to 1800. [KCA]

DAVIDSON, ROBERT, a planter in Virginia, a bond dated 1670. [NRS.RD2.623]

DAVY, JAMES LEWIS, in Jamaica, graduated MD from Edinburgh University in 1823. [EMG]

DAWSON, WILLIAM, a settler on the north-west branch of the Cape Fear River, North Carolina, petitioned the Synod of Argyle for a Gaelic speaking minister, on 2 September 1748. [NRS.NRAS.1209.553]

DAWSON, WILLIAM, in Jamaica, graduated MD from Edinburgh University in 1813. [EMG]

DEAN, HUGH, emigrated from Scotland to America in 1770, a trader on the Eastern Shore of Maryland by 1775, a Loyalist, in Halifax, Nova Scotia, by 20 July 1786. [PAO.LC.102]

DEANS, WILLIAM, son of John Deans in Jamaica, a student at King's College, Aberdeen, from 1824 to 1825. [KCA]

DEAS, DAVID, in Charleston, America, a deed of factory, 12 March 1765. [NRS.RD3.224/1.630]

DEAS, JAMES, born in Alloa, Clackmannanshire, emigrated to New York, a hairdresser there by 1761, a Loyalist in 1776, returned to Alloa in 1786. [TNA.AO12.24.397]

DEAS, JOHN, a merchant in Charleston, South Carolina, in 1776. [TNA.AO12.73.129]

DE KAY, JAMES E., in America, graduated MD from Edinburgh University in 1819. [EMG]

DE LAP, SAMUEL, in Jamaica, a commission, 6 August 1793. [NRS.RD2.259.796]

DE LEON, HANANEL, in Jamaica, graduated MD from Edinburgh University in 1819. [EMG]

DENHAM, THOMAS, emigrated from Scotland to America in 1774, a shipowner in Charleston, South Carolina, settled in Shelburne, Nova Scotia, by 1786. [TNA.AO13.25.138]

DENNISTOUN, RICHARD, a merchant in Glasgow in 1786, formerly in Skidaway Island, Georgia. [TNA.AO13.370]

DEWAR, ANDREW, in Dominica, a petition 10 July 1770. [JCTP.77]

DEWAR, STEPHEN, from Barbados aboard the barque Resolution, master Thomas Gilbert, bound for Antigua on 15 November 1679. [TNA]

DICK, JOHN, in Jamaica, a will, 10 May 1793. [NRS.RD4.253.1025]

DICK, Miss MARY, in South Carolina, a commission with Patrick Duncan, dated 19 October 1810. [NRS.RD4.291.385]

DICK, WALTER, a native of Glasgow, emigrated to America in 1772, a journeyman gunsmith and cutler in Charleston, South Carolina, in 1774, a Loyalist banished in 1778 from S.C., moved to England. [TNA.AO12.50.185, etc]

DICKSON, LIONEL, from Virginia, a medical student at Edinburgh University, from 1762 until 1764. [EUL]

DICKSON, ROBERT, a fur trader in Upper Canada, a memorandum dated 1813. [NRS.NRAS.0069]

DICKSON, WILLIAM, in Jamaica, a deed of factory, 15 January 1765. [NRS.D4.197/2.377]

DICKSON, WILLIAM, in Niagara, a letter, dated 1810. [NLS.Liston.5616/19]

DIGGES, JOSEPH, born in 1747, of Maryland, a medical student at Edinburgh University in from 1765 to1766, graduated MD from Glasgow University in 1767, died in 1783. [EUL]

DINGWALL, RODERICK, in Jamaica, a letter to Kenneth Dingwall in Dingwall, dated 1807. [HCA.Dingwall pp]

DIXON, WILLIAM MAJOR, of Virginia, a medical student at Edinburgh University in 1783, graduated MD at Glasgow University in 1784. [EUL][RGG]

DOBEL, BENJAMIN, of Pennsylvania, a medical student at Edinburgh University from 1793 until 1794. [EUL]

DOBIE, RICHARD, born 1730 in Liberton, Edinburgh, a merchant in Montreal, Quebec, died there on 23 March 1805. [GM.75.773]

DOIG, JAMES, in Antigua, a probative mandate, 25 November 1791. [NRS.RD4.250.1234]

DONALD, JAMES, a merchant in St Augustine, East Florida, trading with timber from Mississippi, papers, from 1776 to 1778. [NRS.NRAS.0159]

DONALD, THOMAS, in Bermuda, a partnership agreement, dated 17 November 1784. [NRS.RD4.243.1316]

DONALDSON, HENRY, born 1610, a passenger aboard the Plain Jane bound from London to Virginia on 15 May 1635. [TNA.E157.20]

DONALDSON, JAMES WEEMYS, late of Antigua, a merchant in St John County, New Brunswick, administration 20 August 1794. [PANB]

DONALDSON, WILLIAM, born in Scotland, emigrated to America in 1763, settled in Portsmouth, Virginia, via New York in 1783 to Shelburne, Nova Scotia. [PAO.LC.118/607]

DONALDSON, WILLIAM, a merchant in St John, New Brunswick, probate 31 July 1797. [PANB]

DONALDSON, WILLIAM, an attorney in New Brunswick, a letter to James Drummond Lundin re his land in America on 27 September 1762. Letters from New York between 1771 and 1776. [NRS.GD160.307]; Later re land for sale in Grenada on 4 April 1780. [NRS.GD160.245.1/3-4-7]

DORSEY, DENNIS, of Maryland, graduated MD at Edinburgh University in 1776. [EMG]

DORWARD, ANNA, imprisoned in Aberdeen Tolbooth guilty of infanticide, was banished to America in 1742. [ACA]

DOUGLAS, ALEXANDER, in America, a deed of factory, 20 March 1792. [NRS.RD4.252.86]

DOUGLAS, CAMPBELL, in Jamaica, a deed of attorney, dated 9 June 1775. [NRS.RD4.218.871]

DOUGLAS, HUGH, born 1613, a passenger aboard the Constance bound from London to Virginia on 24 October 1635. [TNA.E157.20]

DOUGLAS, JAMES, in Jamaica, a deed, dated 25 June 1781. [NRS.RD2.231.242]; in Jamaica, a deed of attorney in favour of John Forbes, dated 3 May 1785. [NRS.RD3.244.320]; a deed in 1785. [NRS.RD3.246.892]

DOUGLAS, JOHN, master of the Primrose bound from London to Virginia on 18 July 1634. [TNA.E190.38/7]

DOUGLAS, JOHN, in St John, a deed of factory, dated 3 June 1789. [NRS.RD4.247.155]

DOUGLAS, JOHN, in Grenada, versus Mrs Elizabeth Handyside or Kennedy, on 23 July 1812. [NRS.CS36.5.100]

DOUGLAS, ROBERT, Governor of H.M. forts on St Kitt's, died there on 24 October 1779. [SM.42.54]

DOUGLAS, THOMAS, and Company, merchants in Montrose, Angus, a charter party, dated 15 July 1752, with Thomas Gibson, master of their ship Potomac to sail from Montrose with a cargo of trade goods to Holland there to load more cargo, then sail to the coast of Africa, there to sell or barter the cargo then to purchase slaves or ivory, then sail to the West Indies or American colonies, and return. [Montrose Museum ms]

DOUGLAS, Sir WILLIAM, of Glenbervie, Kincardineshire, a sasine, dated 27 August 1625, Nova Scotia. [NRS.RS1.18.124]

DOUGLAS, WILLIAM, with his wife Mary, from Edinburgh, emigrated via Leith to Maryland in 1771, a Loyalist who died there, his widow returned home. [TNA.AO13.39.374]

DOULL, JAMES, a surgeon in Maryland, deeds, dated 2/3 August 1751. [NRS.RD4.177/2.158/525]

DOWNIE, DAVID, a silversmith from Edinburgh, a political radical who was exiled in 1794, settled in Augusta, Georgia, in 1798, died there on 25 December 1816. [MFA.96]

DOWNMAN, ROBERT, of Virginia, a medical student at Edinburgh University from 1796 until 1797, graduated MD there in 1798. [EUL][EMG]

DRAYTON, CHARLES, of South Carolina, graduated MD at Edinburgh University in 1770. [EMG]

DRAYTON, WILLIAM, of Barbados, graduated MD from Edinburgh University in 1822. [EMG]

DRUMMOND, A., offered to supply settlers for Cape Breton Island in 1764. [RPCCol.vi.364]

DRUMMOND, COLIN, a Councillor of Quebec, died in 1776. [JCTP.83.46/47]

DRUMMOND, DUNCAN, Commissary of Accounts in New York, a letter dated 27 August 1783. [HMC. American. iv 314]

DRUMMOND, GEORGE, a tinker in Pathhead, fund guilty of horse-stealing, was, on his petition, banished to the American Plantations for life, with seven years' service there, at Perth in June 1773. [SM.35.332]

DRUMMOND, JAMES, in Philadelphia, a deed of attorney, dated 30 October 1791. [NRS.RD4.252.413]

DRUMMOND, JAMES, from Greenock to St John, New Brunswick, in 1803, settled in Sussex Vale. [PANB.mc1672]

DRUMMOND, JOHN, Controller at the Port of Quebec, certificates, from 1766 to 1767. [NLS.Stewart.5025.39/83]

DRUMMOND, JOHN, a merchant late of Blandford, Virginia, settled in Glasgow, by 1786, a deposition. [TNA.AO13.28.415]

DRUMMOND, ROBERT, in Jamaica, a deed, dated 22 July 1790. [NRS.RD3.251/1.198]

DRUMMOND, Lord THOMAS, letters and papers from 1768 and 1780 in New York re his land in New Jersey. [NRS.GD160, box 53, bundle 1]

DUANE, JAMES, Judge of the Federal Court of America, graduated LL.D. at Edinburgh University on 27 April 1792. [GEU]

DU BOIS, JAMES, from Wilmington, North Carolina, matriculated at King's College, Aberdeen, in 1787; a medical student at Edinburgh University from 1790 to 1791, graduated MD at Edinburgh University in 1793. [KCA][EMG][EUL]

DUCKETT, RICHARD JAMES, in America, graduated MD at Glasgow University in 1786. [RGG]

DUFF, ALEXANDER, in Sunbury, South Carolina, [TNA.AO13.96.272]

DUFF, DAVID, emigrated to Maryland, a schoolmaster there, letters from 1772 until 1774. [NRS.GD248.box 249, bundle 3]; a letter from him in Dorset County, Maryland, dated 1780. [NRS.GD248.box 228. Bundle 1]

DUFF, JAMES, in Jamaica, a probative bond with Alexander Gordon, dated 1 January 1782. [NRS.RD4.272.599]

DUFF, WILLIAM, son of Mary Duff, died on a plantation near Georgetown, South Carolina, a letter dated 1741. [NRS.GD185.box 6, bundle 28]

DUFFIELD, BENJAMIN, born 1753, from Pennsylvania, a medical student at Edinburgh University in 1775. [EUL]

DUGUID, JOHN, born 1750 in Aberdeen, son of John Duguid, born in 1689, died in 1763, and his second wife Helen Johnston, born 1730, died in 1778, emigrated to Canada, a cooper at Fort St Jean, near Montreal, Quebec, in 1775, moved to New Jersey by 1778, settled in Antigua in 1783, died there in 1785. [Trenton Federalist.xxii.1266/1] [NARA. Washington pp]

DUGUID, WILLIAM, formerly in Baltimore, Maryland, later in Aberdeen, testament, 7 February 1822, Comm. Aberdeen. [NRS]

DUMMETT, EDWARD JAMES, in Barbados, graduated MD at Edinburgh University in 1799. [EMG]

DUNBAR, GAWEN, in York County debts, Virginia, ca.1675. [York County Order Book, 1675-1684]

DUNBAR, GEORGE, in New York, a deed of attorney in favour of A. Campbell, 11 November 1782. [NRS.RD2.235/1.17]

DUNBAR, GEORGE, in Antigua, deeds, 7 April 1773 and 31 July 1773. [NRS.RD2.249.415]

DUNBAR, JOHN, formerly a merchant in Antigua, 1796. [NRS.CS97.111.132]

DUNBAR, SIMON, son of John Dunbar of Burgie, a privateer at Newport, Rhode Island, a letter dated 11 August 1748. [NRS.GD199.99]

DUNBAR, WILLIAM, born 1620, a passenger aboard the William and John bound from London to St Kitts on 2 September 1635. [TNA.E157.20]

DUNCAN, ALEXANDER, in Wilmington, North Carolina, former partner of Michal Ancrum, a merchant in Edinburgh, a letter dated 21 September 1762. [NRS.GD214.720]

DUNCAN, ALEXANDER, son of Alexander Duncan in Tobago, a student at King's College, Aberdeen, in 1790. [KCA]

DUNCAN, ANDREW, son of Robert Duncan, a baker, 1777-1859], died in Indiana. [St Andrews Cathedral gravestone]

DUNCAN, CHARLES, in New York, a deed of factory with K. McKenzie, dated 5 December 1799. [NRS.RD3.285.190]

DUNCAN, GEORGE, a wine merchant in Charleston, South Carolina, in London by 1779. [TNA.AO13.127.42]; a Loyalist who settled in Jamaica, a letter dated 8 April 1783. [HMC. American.iv.19]

DUNCAN, PATRICK, in South Carolina, a deed with George Farquharson, dated 19 October 1810. [NRS.RD4.291.412]; son of John Duncan, in Achagoimlan, Aberdeenshire, [born 1721- died 1784] and his wife Isabel Farquharson, [born 1733- died 1807. [Crathie gravestone, Aberdeenshire]

DUNCAN, ROBERT, son of Robert Duncan in Boston, America, matriculated at Glasgow University in 1764, graduated MA there in 1770. [RGG]

DUNCAN, THOMAS, in Grenada, letters dated between 1804 and 1818. [NRS.GD267.5.12]

DUNCAN, THOMAS, in Demerara, a deed dated 28 June 1806. [NRS.RD3.323.586]

DUNDAS, ALEXANDER, in Quebec, a letter dated 1778. [NRS.GD16.459]

DUNDAS, WILLIAM, from Barbados aboard the Young William, master Thomas Cornish, bound for Virginia on 1 August 1679. [TNA]

DUNLOP, COLIN, a merchant in Virginia and Maryland before 1776, later in Glasgow. [TNA.AO13.102.58]

DUNLOP, JAMES, a merchant in Montreal, Quebec, letters from 1788 until 1811. [SRA.TD641]

DUNLOP, JOHN, from Kilmarnock, Ayrshire, settled in Aranlise Creek, Pasquotank County, North Carolina, a mariner who died at sea in 1778. [TNA.AO12.36.319, etc]

DUNLOP. JOHN, of Brockloch, Ayrshire, in America, letters from 1820 until 1834. [NRS.NRAS.1239]

DUNLOP, WILLIAM, in Carolina, a letter to Sir James Montgomerie of Skelmorlie, Ayrshire, re trade, African servants, and the Spanish attack on the Scots colony at Port Royal, dated 1687. [NRS.GD3.E2.114-120]

DUNLOP, WILLIAM, in St Croix, Danish West Indies, a deed of factory with Robert Craig, dated 2 November 1805. [NRS.RD3.317.530]

DUNN, ANDREW, in Jamaica, graduated MD from Edinburgh University in 1823. [EMG]

DUTHIE, WILLIAM, in Jamaica, a deed, 14 November 1786. [NRS.RD4.248.304]

DYETT, RICHARD, in Montserrat, graduated MD from Edinburgh University in 1808. [EMG]

EDGAR, ALEXANDER, in Jamaica, a deed, 1 August 1791. [NRS.RD4.250.1260]; from Jamaica, died 26 December 1820. [Edinburgh, Greyfriars, gravestone]

EDGAR, JAMES, in Jamaica, a bond, dated 10 December 1787. [NRS.RD4.253.272]

EDGAR, THOMAS, son of Archibald Edgar in Jamaica, deceased, a student at King's College, Aberdeen, 1795. [KCA]

EDWARDS, HUGH, in Jamaica, graduated MD at King's College, Aberdeen, on 26 May 1823. [KCA]

EDWARD, JAMES, from Greenock to St John, New Brunswick, in 1803. [PANB.mc1672]

EDWARDS, JOSEPH, from Massachusetts, a medical student at Edinburgh University 1756-1757. [EUL]

ELCOCK, GRANT, of America, a medical student at the University of Edinburgh, 1763. [EUL]

ELLIOT, ALLEN, in Demerara, a probative will, dated May 1779. [NRS.RD4.235.748]

ELLIOT, ANDREW, born 1730, Customs Collector and Receiver General for the Port of New York from 1764, a Loyalist in 1776, in Edinburgh by 1787. [TNA.AO12.24.163]

ELLIOT, ANDREW, of Boston, New England, graduated DD from Edinburgh University on 23 July 1767. [GEU]

ELIOT, JOHN, a minister in Boston, New England, graduated DD at Edinburgh University on 24 June 1797. [GEU]

ELLIOT, ROBERT, in Demerara, a probative will, dated May 1779. [NRS.RD4.235.748]

ELLIS, JOHN, son of William Ellis in Jamaica, a student at King's College, Aberdeen, in 1801. [KCA]

ELPHINSTONE, WILLIAM, Cupbearer to the King, a sasine, dated 28 January 1630, Nova Scotia. [NRS.RS1.27.269]

ERSKINE, HENRY, Lord Cardross, a charter party with John Henderson, master of the Stephen of London for a voyage from Carolina to Virginia, dated 1687. [NRS.GD103.2.222]

ERSKINE, JOHN JAMES, in Jamaica, graduated MD at Edinburgh University in 1791. [EMG]

ERVING, GEORGE, in Boston, New England, son of an American diplomat, graduated MA at Glasgow University in 1762, 'during the Revolutionary War he went to Halifax and thence to London'. [RGG]

ESTON, JOHN, in Bermuda, graduated MD at Edinburgh University in 1792. [EMG]

EVANS, CADWALLADER, from Pennsylvania, a medical student at Edinburgh University around 1756. [Toner pp, Library of Congress]

EVE, FRANCIS AUGUSTUS, in Bermuda, graduated MD from Edinburgh University in 1825. [EMG]

EVERLEIGH, NICHOLAS, from South Carolina, a medical student at Edinburgh University from 1763 until 1765. [EUL]

EVERLEIGH, SAMUEL, from South Carolina, a medical student at Edinburgh University from 1764 to 1765. [EUL]

EWEN, JOHN, a medical student at Edinburgh University, from 1797 until 1798. [EUL]

EWING, JOHN, in Philadelphia, graduated DD at Edinburgh University on 21 June 1774. [GEU]

EWING, JOHN, emigrated from Scotland to America in 1766, a baker in Portsmouth, Virginia, a Loyalist, settled in Shelburne, Nova Scotia, at Halifax, St John, on 20 January 1786. [PAO.LC.23]

EWING, WILLIAM, in Carolina, graduated MD from Edinburgh University in 1816. [EMG]

EWING, WILLIAM, from Glasgow, a merchant in St John, New Brunswick, administration, dated 4 November 1831. [PANB]

FAIRBAIRN. JOHN, in Ramsay, Bathurst, Upper Canada, a letter dated 1834. [NRS.NRAS.2177]

FAIRBAIRN, THOMAS, in Antigua, a deed of factory, dated 5 December 1789. [NRS.RD3.259.635]

FAIRBAIRN, THOMAS, in St Vincent, a deed with James Farquharson, dated 18 March 1800. [NRS.RD4.267.440]

FAIRBANKS, GEORGE EDWARD, in Nova Scotia, graduated MD from Edinburgh University in 1821. [EMG]

FAIRHOLM, THOMAS, in Tobago, a deed of attorney in favour of George Fairholm, dated 5 July 1783. [NRS.RD2.236/1.66]

FAIRLIE, JAMES, a merchant in Warwick, Virginia, before 1776, later in Pensacola, West Florida, afterwards in Kingston, Jamaica, by 1789. [TNA.AO13.34.478]; a letter book from 1783 until 1805. [NRS.NRAS.0905]

FALCONER, JOHN, in Jamaica, graduated MD from Edinburgh University in 1823. [EMG]

FARGUES, THOMAS, in Canada, graduated MD from Edinburgh University in 1811. [EMG]

FARNELL, ROBERT, at the College Land, Virginia, in 1624. [TNA.CO1.3.2]

FARNELL, THOMAS, in Barbados in 1656. [CLRO]

FARRAR, JAMES, a merchant in Halifax, Nova Scotia, letters, from 1813 to 1814. [NLS.Wilson.mss.6730, 6737]

FARQUHAR, WILLIAM, settled in America before 1733, a physician in New Jersey and in New York, a Loyalist in 1776, died in Britain by 1783. [TNA.AO12.99.321]

FARQUHARSON, CHARLES, of Jamaica, graduated MD from Edinburgh University in 1807. [EMG]

FARQUHARSON, GEORGE, in Inveraven, Banffshire, was found guilty of stealing a horse and a big coat and sentenced to banishment to the American Plantations for life, with seven years' service there at Aberdeen in June 1773. [SM.35.333]

FARQUHARSON, JOHN, a physician in Charleston, South Carolina, graduated MD at Marischal College, Aberdeen, in 1769. [MCA]; a Loyalist, moved to London by 1780. [TNA.AO12.47.415, etc]

FARQUHARSON, MARGARET, born 1779, widow of John Callam a wright in Newton, died in Canada in September 1870. [Glenbuchat gravestone, Aberdeenshire]

FARQUHARSON, THOMAS, in Jamaica, a deed, dated 9 July 1774. [NRS.RD2.216.923]

FARRE, JOHN RICHARD, born in Barbados on 31 January 1775, graduated MD at Glasgow University in 1802, later graduated MD at King's College, Aberdeen, in 1806. A medical practitioner in Barbados and in London, he founded the Royal London Ophthalmic Hospital, died 7 May 1862. [RGG]

FAUNTLEROY, DAVID, of Virginia a medical student at Edinburgh University in 1800. ['Medicine in Virginia in the Eighteenth Century', p.87, Richmond, 1931]

FAUNTLEROY, GEORGE, in America, a student at King's College, Aberdeen, from 1760 to 1764. [KCA]

FAUNTLEROY, MOORE, of Virginia, a student at King's College, Aberdeen, from 1760 to 1764. [KCA]

FAUNTLEROY, WILLIAM, in America, a student at King's College, Aberdeen, from 1759 to 1763. [KCA]

FAYSSOUX, PETER, born 1745, from South Carolina, graduated MD at Edinburgh University in 1769, died 1795. [EMG]

FENWICK, GEORGE, a silversmith in Edinburgh, son of George Fenwick a silversmith there, emigrated to Tobago in 1820, died on Castara Plantation there on 4 September 1821. [MFA.101]

FERGUSON, ALEXANDER, emigrated from Scotland to America in 1773, settled at Johnson's Bush, Tryon County, New York, a Loyalist, settled at Riviere de Raisin, Canada, dead by 1787. [PAO.LC.1040]

FERGUSON, ARCHIBALD, a merchant in New England, third son of the late John Ferguson a baillie of Ayr, was admitted as a burgess and guilds-brother of Ayr on 17 September 1692. [ABR]

FERGUSON, JAMES, youngest son of the late Sir James Ferguson of Kilkerran, died on his estate in Tobago on 20 December 1777. [SM.39.53]

FERGUSON, JOHN, in Virginia, a letter dated before 1753. [NRS.NRAS.0934]

FERGUSON, JOHN, from Demerara, was admitted as a burgess and guildsbrother of Ayr on 1 October 1802. [ABR]

FERGUSON, ROBERT, born 1719 in Scotland, a shipmaster based in Newport, Rhode Island, a Loyalist in 1776, settled in Perth, Scotland, by 1783. [NRS.AO12.84.2]

FERRIE, ADAM, an importer in Montreal, Quebec, letters in 1828. [NLS.MS.1846.41-43]

FIELD, ALEXANDER SCHAW, of Virginia, graduated MD at Edinburgh University in 1789. [EMG]

FIELD, JAMES, from Virginia, a medical student at Edinburgh University, from 1757 until 1761. [EUL]

FIELD, JAMES, in Virginia, a deed of attorney with John Taylor, 25 April 1802. [NRS.RD4.272.164]

FIELD, RICHARD, of Virginia, graduated MD at Edinburgh University in 1790. [EMG]

FIELD, WILLIAM, son of the late Dr James Field a physician in Petersburg, Virginia, was apprenticed to Alexander and Patrick Crichton, coachbuilders in Edinburgh for three years on 2 June 1796. [ERA]

FIFE, DAVID, of Jamaica, married Miss Hunter, daughter of the late David Hunter of Burnside, Angus, in Edinburgh on 27 December 1779. [SM.41.684]

FIFE, LAWRENCE, son of Laurence Fife in Jamaica, a student at King's College, Aberdeen, 1814 to 1817. [KCA]

FIFE, LAWRENCE, son of MacDuff Fife in St Vincent, a student at King's College, Aberdeen, from 1819 to 1820. [KCA]

FINLAY, ISABELLA, MARGARET, and HELEN, in Barbados, a deed of attorney, dated 1 September 1764. [NRS.RD3.224/1.9]

FINLAY, JANET, emigrated from Campbeltown, Argyll, aboard the Edinburgh of Campbeltown, master John McMichael, in July 1771 bound for Prince Edward Island. [NRS.SC54.2.106]

FINLAY, THOMAS, in Barbados, a letter dated 15 July 1729. [NRS.GD247.171.11]

FINLAYSON, DAVID, in Jamaica, a deed of factory with Charles Bremner, dated on 8 August 1808. [NRS.RD3.325.1186]

FINLAYSON, HENRY, a silversmith who settled in Georgia in 1774, a Loyalist, via Charleston, East Florida and Dominica to England, died in London 1785. [TNA.AO12.101.250]

FISHER, ADAM, in New York Province, a bond, dated 27 June 1751. [NRS.RD4.178/1.59]

FISHER, ALEXANDER, emigrated from Scotland to America in 1775, settled in Charlotte County, New York, a Loyalist, moved to the Bay of Quinty, Canada, in 1787, at Montreal on 5 November 1787. [PAO.LC.273/4]

FISHER, EDWARD, of Virginia, a medical student at Edinburgh University from 1794 until 1795, graduated MD there in 1795. [EUL][EMG]

FISHER, FINLAY, emigrated from Scotland to America in 1775, settled in Charlotte County, New York, a Loyalist, moved to Montreal in 1787, there on 5 November 1787. [PAO.LC.274]

FITT, SAMUEL, of Bermuda, graduated MD at Glasgow University in 1786. [RGG]

FITZGERALD, JOHN, of Virginia, graduated MD at Edinburgh University in 1800. [EMG]

FLEMING, THOMAS, born 1793, son of John Fleming and his wife Grace Cameron, died in Demerara on 29 April 1829. [Kirkmichael gravestone, Perthshire]

FOGO, JAMES, on Harbour Head Plantation, Jamaica, in 1749. [Jamaica Courant, V.295]

FORBES, ANTONY GEORGE, in St Kitts, graduated MD at Edinburgh University in 1788. [EMG]

FORBES, Sir ARTHUR, of Castle Forbes, a sasine, 18 November 1628, Nova Scotia. [NRS.RS1.25.26]

FORBES, HENRY, died in Bermuda on 26 October 1757. [GM.27.482]

FORBES, JOHN, son of Alexander Forbes a gentleman in Jamaica, a student at King's College, Aberdeen, 1812 to 1815. [KCA]

FORBES, Sir WILLIAM, of Monymusk, a sasine, Nova Scotia, 4 April 1626. [NRS.RS1.19.166]

FORBES, WILLIAM, son of William Forbes born 1773 a farmer in Strathlunack died 1853, died in St Mary's, Jamaica, aged 38 years. [Tullynessle gravestone, Aberdeenshire]

FORRESTER, JAMES, in Baltimore, Maryland, a letter of attorney, dated 17 April 1810. [NRS.SC58.59.1.40]

FORSYTH, ALEXANDER, of Halifax, Nova Scotia, graduated MA at King's College, Aberdeen, on 25 May 1817. [KCA]

FORSYTH, JAMES, a printer in Jamaica, was admitted as a burgess and guilds-brother of Ayr on 4 April 1751. [ABR]

FORSYTH, JOSEPH, in Jamaica, graduated MD from Edinburgh University in 1814. [EMG]

FORSYTH, THOMAS and WILLIAM, in Virginia, a deed of co-partnership with John Rowand, dated 29 August 1775. [NRS.RD4.218.642]

FORSYTH, WILLIAM, an itinerant preacher in Glen Muick, Aberdeenshire, was suggested suitable for the vacancy in Wilton, South Carolina by James Hunter in Huntly, a letter, 5 August 1752. [NRS.CH1.2.95.455]

FORSYTH, WILLIAM, a merchant in Halifax, letters, from 1796 until 1801. [NLS.Liston.ms5590/29-34]

FORSYTH, WILLIAM, son of Joseph Forsyth a merchant in Canada, a student at King's College, Aberdeen, around 1814. [KCA]

FOTHERINGHAM, ALEXANDER, married Judith, daughter of Dr Alexander Garden, in Charleston, South Carolina, on 24 November 1791. [GM.61.1961]

FOULAR, JAMES, in Jamaica, a deed with James Stotherts, dated 21 April 1802. [NRS.RD4.271.1229] 53

FOURNOY, DAVID, of Virginia, a medical student at Edinburgh University in 1799-1800. [EUL]

FOUSHEE, WILLIAM, of Virginia, a medical student at Edinburgh University, from 1771 until 1772. [EUL]

FOWLER, ANDREW, born 1755, of Friendship Estate, Trelawney, Jamaica, died there in June 1792. Memorial erected by brother James Fowler of Grange and Raddery in 1821. [Rosemarkie gravestone, Easter Ross]

FOWLER, JOHN, born in 1754, of Friendship Estate, Trelawney, Jamaica, Commander of the Leeward Troop of Horse, died there in June 1792. Memorial erected by brother James Fowler of Grange and Raddery in 1821. [Rosemarkie gravestone, Easter Ross]

FRANKLAND, THOMAS, in Demerara, a deed of attorney with Francis Gordon, dated 13 June 1810. [NRS.RD2.310.691]

FRANKLIN, BENJAMIN, born 1706 in Boston, Massachusetts, son of Joseph Franklin, graduated LL.D at St Andrews University on 12 December 1759, died 1790. [SAU]

FRASER, ALEXANDER, in Quebec, a probative bill, dated 16 November 1764. [NRS.RD2.213.239]

FRASER, ALEXANDER, in Grenada, a deed, dated 19 July 1786. [NRS.RD2.241/2.546]

FRAZER, ALEXANDER, of Virginia, a medical student at Edinburgh University in 1798. [EUL]

FRASER, CHARLES, from Edinkille, Moray, a yeoman in Woodstock, York County, New Brunswick, probate, 22 February 1794. [PANB]

FRASER, DONALD, settled in Georgia in 1768, Customs Collector of Sunbury, a Loyalist, via Jamaica to London by 1789. [TNA.AO12.109.140, etc]

FRAZER, EDMOND, a bachelor in Barbados, administration, 1649, Prerogative Court of Canterbury. [TNA]

FRASER, ELIZABETH, a Loyalist in Albany, New York, then a refugee in New York, a petition dated New York 24 May 1780, certified by John Green, Norman Tolmie and Donald McLean. [HMC. American ii.126]

FRASER, JAMES, in New York, a deed of factory in favour of Isaac Grant, dated 14 August 1782. [NRS.RD4.237.887]

FRASER, JAMES, was granted land at Nashwaak, New Brunswick, in 1785. [PANB]

FRASER, JAMES, in Halifax, Nova Scotia, two letters dated 1786. [NRS. NRAS. Blairs]

FRAZER, JAMES, a minister from Scotland who settled initially in Virginia and later in Hartford, Orange County, North Carolina, a Loyalist who moved to Annapolis, Nova Scotia, by 1786. [TNA.AO12.92.1a]

FRASER, JAMES, in Barbados, a commission, dated 3 March 1786. [NRS.RD2.248.627]

FRASER, JAMES, a shoemaker in Demerara, a letter to Alexander Fraser in Inverness, dated 1801. [HCA. Alex. Fraser pp]

FRASER, JOHN, died in Halifax, Nova Scotia, on 8 May 1795. [GM.65.614]

FRASER, JOHN, a planter in Dominica, letters from 1800 until 1804. [NRS.AD58.263]

FRASER, KENNETH, a Councillor of the Bahamas in 1728. [RPCCol.vi.202]

FRASER, SIMON, an attorney in Quebec, a deed, dated 4 July 1792. [NRS.RD2.256.1057]

FRASER, SIMON, in St Vincent, youngest son of William Fraser of Colbuckie, died in Bermuda on 12 October 1798. [GM.69.252]

FRASER, SIMON, in Demerara, a commission with James Fraser, dated 2 November 1800. [NRS.RD4.170.217]

FRASER, SIMON, late of the Ordnance Department in Bermuda, died in Edinburgh on 16 February 1819. [GM.88.279]

FRASER, WILLIAM, with his sons William Fraser and Thomas Fraser, emigrated from Scotland to America around 1767, settled at Ballston or Johnstown, Tryon County, New York, Loyalists, sons were soldiers based at Yamaska Block House, later settled at Oswegatchie. [PAO.LC.968]

FRENCH, JAMES, of Virginia, a medical student at Edinburgh University from 1798 until 1799. [EUL]

FRENCH, ROBERT, late on Tortola, Elizabeth Dawson, his relict's testament 19 January 1821, Comm. Lauder. [NRS]

FRITH, JOHN, of Bermuda, graduated MD from Edinburgh University in 1821. [EMG]

FULLER, CHRISTOPHER, of South Carolina, a medical student at Edinburgh University from 1796 until 1797. [EUL]

FURLONG, JOHN, in Montserrat, graduated MD from Edinburgh University in 1822. [EMG]

FYFFE, CHARLES, a physician in Craven County, South Carolina, a marriage contract with Anne Rowe, a spinster in Charleston, S.C., dated 1751. [NRS.RH9.7.300]

FYFFE, JOHN, in Antigua, graduated MD at Edinburgh University in 1786. [EMG]

GAILLARD, ESTHER, spouse of James Crockatt of Charleston, South Carolina, a deed, dated 28 August 1752. [NRS.RD4.178/2.252]

GALBRAITH, Lieutenant GEORGE, in St Mary's, Jamaica, a bond, dated 8 November 1750. [NRS.RD4.178/1.582]

GALBRAITH, J., in America, a deed, dated 17 May 1776. [NRS.RD2.224/1.302]

GALBREATH, THOMAS, in New York, deeds, dated in 1776 and 1784. [NRS.RD2.242/2.4 and 8]

GALL, RODGER, in Honduras, a deed of attorney in favour of John Blackwood, 15 December 1775. [NRS.RD4.228.1092]

GALT, JOHN M., from Virginia, a medical student at Edinburgh University, 1767. ['Medicine in Virginia in the Eighteenth Century, p.86, Richmond, 1931]

GANNT, EDWARD, born 1741, from Maryland, a medical student at Edinburgh University from 1764 to 1766, died 1837. [EUL]

GARDEN, Dr ALEXANDER, a planter on Otranto Plantation, South Carolina, before 1780, moved to London. [TNA.AO12.50.146, etc]

GARDNER, ALEXANDER, a physician and surgeon in Westmoreland, Jamaica, deceased, a draft attorney, in 1788. [NRS.GD59.38.6.184]

GARDINER, GORDON, son of the late Edwin Gardiner in Trinidad, a student at King's College, Aberdeen, from 1817 to 1818. [KCA]

GARDINER, JAMES, in Jamaica, later in Banff, testament 30 OCTOBER 1820 Comm. Aberdeen. [NRS]

GARDINER, JOHN, second son of Dr Gardiner MD in Boston, New England, matriculated at Glasgow University in 1752 and graduated MA there in 1755. [RGG]

GARDINER, WILLIAM, second son of the late Edwin Gardiner in Trinidad, a student at King's College, Aberdeen, in 1818, later assistant surgeon of the 56th Regiment of Foot. [KCA]

GARNER, JONATHAN, in Barbados, graduated MD from Edinburgh University in 1819. [EMG]

GASTON, ALEXANDER, from North Carolina, a medical student at Edinburgh University in 1759, a physician in Newbern, NC, by 1759. [EUL]

GEDDES, CHARLES, in New York, a deed of attorney in favour of Samuel Mitchelson, dated 5 July 1781. [NRS.RD2.232/1.86]

GEDDES, THOMAS, in Halifax, [Nova Scotia?], a deed of attorney in favour of S. Mitchelson, dated 27 April 1784. [NRS.RD2.237/2.34]

GEEKIE, WILLIAM, served in the Royal Navy before 1763, settled as a planter at Goose Creek, South Carolina, a Loyalist, moved to Arbroath, Scotland, by 1784. [TNA.AO12.50.138]

GEMMILL, JOHN, in New Lanark, Upper Canada, dated between 1822 and 1830, to Andrew Gemmill. [SRA.TD293][NRS.NRAS.1043]

GENTLE, WILLIAM, a planter in Clarendon, Jamaica, a draft affidavit around 1807. [NRS.B59.38.6.247]

GIBB, Dr ROBERT, born in Edinburgh, emigrated to George Town, South Carolina, in 1754, a physician in Georgetown and a planter on the Peedee River, died in October 1777. [TNA.AO12.51.99, etc]

GIBBONS, JOHN HANNEM, in Pennsylvania, graduated MD at Edinburgh University in 1786. [EMG]

GIBBONS, JOSIAH, in Georgia, graduated MD at Edinburgh University in 1776. [EMG][SM.38.622]

GIBSON, WALTER, a merchant burgess of Glasgow, a charter party to supply the James of Irvine for a voyage from the River Clyde with passengers bound for Carolina, dated 27 September 1682. [Dumfries House deeds A20/1]

GIBSON, WILLIAM, son of Alexander Gibson master of Perth Academy, in the service of John Ritchie in Virgin Valley, Jamaica, letter from 1797 until 1800. [NRS.B59.37.4.29]

GIBSON, WILLIAM, in America, graduated MD from Edinburgh University in 1809. [EMG]

GILCHRIST, JAMES, in Maryland, deeds, dated in 1773 and 1775. [NRS.RD3.246.371-375]

GILCHRIST, JOHN, of Virginia, a medical student at Edinburgh University from 1796 until 1797. [EUL]

GILCHRIST, THOMAS, in Virginia, a deed of attorney in favour of H. Corrie, dated 4 August 1783. [NRS.RD4.235.686]

GILCHRIST, WILLIAM, bound via Boston, Massachusetts, for Jamaica in 1753, [NRS.NRAS.1031]; in Jamaica, a petition for the monopoly of mill building in the West Indies, in 1772. [JCTP.79.115]

GILLIAM, JAMES SKELTON, of Virginia, graduated MD at Edinburgh University in 1786. [EMG]

GILLON, JOHN, a merchant in Dominica, a letter re the war in America, dated 1776. [NRS.NRAS.0131/7677]; a will dated 18 July 1809. [NRS.GD184.2.7.16.3]

GILMER, GEORGE, born in 1742, of Virginia, a medical student at Edinburgh University, 1760-1765, graduated MD from Glasgow University in 1764. [RGG]['The Bland Papers', Petersburg, 1839]

GILMER, THOMAS WALKER, of Virginia, a medical student at Edinburgh University, in 1790. [EUL]

GILMORE, GEORGE, a minister of the Church of Scotland, in Voluntown, Connecticut, a Loyalist, moved to Noble Town, Albany County, New York, in 1776, moved to Canada in 1782, in Halifax, Nova Scotia, on 14 July 1786. [PAO.LC.571]

GILMOUR, ROBERT, a merchant in Norfolk, Virginia, a Loyalist, in 1776. [TNA.AO12.74.335]

GILMORESTONE, ROBERT, in Baltimore, Maryland, letters re John Moncreiff Wellwood, dating from 1801 to 1803. [NRS.NRAS.0333]

GINN, WILLIAM, of St Vincent, a student of the Arts at King's College, Aberdeen, 1819 to 1823. [KCA]

GIRAUD, LUDOVIC ANDREW, of Dominica, graduated MD from Edinburgh University in 1821. [EMG]

GLASFORD, JOHN, emigrated from Scotland to America, settled on the Susquehana in Tryon County, New York, a Loyalist, moved via Niagara to Osswegatchie. [PAO.LC.1097]

GLASGOW, JAMES, in St Vincent, a lease, dated 30 January 1792. [NRS.RD3.259.647]

GLASGOW, Dr ROBERT, in St Vincent, a probative grant with Eleanor Arison, on 27 March 1777. [NRS.RD2.281.430]; a letter re American privateers dated 1777, [NRS.NRAS.0852]; a bond with John Fullerton, dated 16 May 1795. [NRS.RD3.300.273

GLASS, GEORGE, in Jamaica, a deed of attorney, dated 8 September 1790. [NRS.RD3.253.864]

GLASS, Mrs R., in Jamaica, a deed of attorney in favour of .... Bryant, dated 1 December 1785. [NRS.RD4.239.1064]

GLASS, WILLIAM, in St Croix, a deed of attorney in favour of Alexander Tower, dated 21 December 1784. [NRS.RD3.244.530]

GLASSELL, JOHN, in Spotsylvania County, Virginia, returned to Glasgow in 1775. [TNA.AO13.102.63]

GLASSELLS, JOHN, in Fredericksburg, Virginia, a bond, dated 2 March 1779. [NRS.RD3.238/1.322]

GLEN, GEORGE, born in Scotland, settled in Wolfborough, New Hampshire, in 1774, a Loyalist in 1776, later in Glasgow by 1788. [TNA.AO12.100.98]

GLEN, JAMES, Governor of South Carolina, papers from 1739 until 1762. [NRS.NRAS.0336]

GLENNIE, JAMES, in America, a probative attorney, dated 24 May 1801. [NRS.RD4.272.176]

GLENTWORTH, GEORGE, born in 1735, of Pennsylvania, a medical student at Edinburgh University from 1758 until 1759, graduated MD at St Andrews University, died 1792. [EUL]

GLOVER, JOHN, graduated BA from Harvard University in 1650, and MD from King's College, Aberdeen, in 1654. [SNQ.XII.94]

GODWIN, JOSEPH, of Virginia, graduated MD at Edinburgh University in 1769. [EMG]

GOOD, JAMES S., from Paisley, Renfrewshire, from Greenock via Quebec to Ontario, settled in Newhope as a weaver and a carpenter, a letter to his father, dated 23 November 1812. [GUL.ms.A200]

GORDON, Lord ADAM, in New York, a letter, 1765. [NRS.NRAS.0771]

GORDON, ALEXANDER, the secretary of the Governor of South Carolina, letters between 1741 and 1747. [NRS.GD18.5023]

GORDON, Dr ALEXANDER, in Charleston, South Carolina, correspondence with George Ogilvie of Auchinames, from 1779 until 1801. [NRS.NRAS.O426]

GORDON, CHARLES, son of Dr Charles Gordon in Jamaica, was apprenticed to Thomas Carmichael a merchant in Edinburgh, for 5 years on 2 September 1772. [ERA]

GORDON, CHARLES, settled in Maryland around 1750, a landowner there and in Delaware, a Loyalist in 1776. [TNA.AO12.80.168]

GORDON, CHRISTIAN, a vagrant, was found guilty of theft of a piece of calico and two handkerchiefs at the St John's fair at Banff, was sentenced to be banished to the American Plantations, with four years' service there, in June 1773. [SM.35.333]

GORDON, Sir DONALD, of Lesmoir, a sasine, dated 14 June 1629, Nova Scotia. [NRS.RS1.19.219]

GORDON, GEORGE, from Barbados aboard the Plantation, master Aser Sharpe, bound for Carolina on 9 August 1679. [TNA]

GORDON, J.B., in Grenada, an entail, dated 20 December 1769. [NRS.RD4.208.1380]

GORDON, JAB., in Jamaica, a will, dated 6 May 1780. [NRS.RD2.234.1086]

GORDON, JAMES, in Grenada, from 1728 until 1733. [NRS.GD237.12.50]

GORDON, JOHN, a merchant in Charleston, South Carolina purchased land in East Florida around 1764. [NRS.GD172.2548]

GORDON, JOHN, eldest son of George Gordon MD in St Kitts, matriculated at Glasgow University in 1770, graduated MA, MD, there in 1775. [RGG]

GORDON, JOHN, son of William Gordon MD in Jamaica, a student at King's College, Aberdeen, in 1824. [KCA]

GORDON, MARY, died in St Jan, Danish West Indies, on 4 January 1815, probate, St Jan, 1807-1826, fo.62. [RAK]

GORDON, PETER, in Pennsylvania, 'son of Knockspick', matriculated at King's College, Aberdeen, in 1774. [KCA]

GORDON, THOMAS, a merchant from Aberdeen with trading links with Maryland before 1776, returned to Glasgow in 1782. [TNA.AO13.40.61]

GORDON, WILLIAM, in Jamaica, a deed, 5 July 1776. [NRS.RD3.236.1175]

GORDON, WILLIAM, in Jamaica, graduated MD at King's College, Aberdeen, on 23 November 1822. [KCA]

GORDON, WILLIAM, son of William Gordon MD in Jamaica, a student at King's College, Aberdeen, from 1822 to 1825, afterwards a surgeon in the Honourable East India Company Service, later in Jamaica. [KCA]

GORDON, WILLIAM, in Quebec, a letter dated 1773 to Captain Duncan Urquhart in Forres, Moray. [NRS.NRAS.2441]

GOULDING, SAMUEL, in Barbados, graduated MD at Edinburgh University in 1772. [EMG]

GOVAN, ARCHIBALD, emigrated from Scotland to America, a factor in Hanover Town, King William County, Virginia, from 1758 to 1777, a Loyalist who returned home in 1777. [TNA.AO12.109.152]

GRAHAM, ANDREW, at Hudson's Bay, a deed, 7 August 1774. [NRS.RD2.216.744]; a factor for the Hudson's Bay Company, meteorological registers, 1772-1774 [SAUL.36938]

GRAHAM, CHARLES, late of Jamaica, married Janet Yeaman, daughter of James Yeaman of Auchenleck, in Dundee on 29 May 1782. [SM.44.333]

GRAHAM, DUNCAN, a merchant in Yorkmoor, Virginia, a deed of factory, dated 20 December 1764, [NRS.RD2.197.470]; a deed of factory in favour of John Gray a merchant in Glasgow and William McEwan in Edinburgh, document written by Robert Hart in Hanover, Virginia, and witnessed by Alexander Donald a merchant in Hanover, Virginia, George Smith commander of the Charlotte and mariners William Fary and William Smith of the said ship, 18 May 1770. [NRS.RD3.22C9/2.571]

GRAHAM, EBENEZER, from Delaware, a medical student at Edinburgh University in 1796-1797. [EUL]

GRAHAM, ENNIS, died in St Jan, Danish West Indies, on 5 February 1822, probate, St Jan,1807-1826, fo.121. [RAK]

GRAHAM, HUGH, late in Guadaloupe, French West Indies, a bond, dated 21 January 1765. [NRS.RD4.197/2.5]

GRAHAME, JAMES, brother of Harry Grahame of Breckness, indented with William Foulis to go to Virginia as a servant in 1668. [NRS.GD217.586]

GRAHAM, JOHN, President of the Council of Grenada, a letter in 1769. [JCTP.76]

GRAHAM, JOHN, a planter at Taylor's Caymannas, Jamaica, a sasine in Argyll, 15 April 1776. [NRS.RS9.11.223]

GRAHAM, JOHN, in St Augustine, East Florida, a letter to Sir Guy Carleton, dated 20 October 1782. [HMC.American.iii.181]

GRAHAM, JOHN, a planter in Virginia from 1764 to 1777, a Loyalist, in Kilsyth, Scotland, by 1783. [TNA.AO13.96.347]

GRAHAM, JOHN, late of Jamaica, versus Marion Campbell his spouse, a Process of Separation and Aliment, 1788. [NRS.CC8.6.799]

GRAHAM, JOHN ANDREW, in Rutland County, Vermont, graduated DD at King's College, Aberdeen, on 23 March 1795. [KCA]

GRAHAM, Dr JOHN, in Jamaica, his relict Lilias Hay in Dumfries, testament, 2 March 1819, Comm. Dumfries. [NRS]

GRAHAM, ROBERT, an overseer of the lands on Dominica of Lieutenant General Robert Melville of Strathkinness, Fife, deceased by 1784. [NRS.GD222.2.67]

GRAHAM, THOMAS, in Pensacola, West Florida, an account, dated 1 April 1780. [HMC. American. ii.127]

GRAHAM, Sir WILLIAM, of Braco, a sasine, 26 January 1630, Nova Scotia. [NRS.RS1.27.256]

GRAHAM, WILLIAM, emigrated from Scotland to Virginia in 1763, a lawyer in Middlesex County, Virginia, a Loyalist, via Bermuda to London by 1783. [TNA.AO12.56.49]

GRAHAM, Dr WILLIAM, in Westmorland, Jamaica, a letter dated 1757. [NRS.GD219.289/5]

GRAINGER, HELEN, in St Kitts, a deed, dated 10 February 1781. [NRS.RD4.229.487]

GRANT, ALEXANDER, of Dalvey, born 1704, a physician educated at Aberdeen University, to Jamaica in 1721, a doctor, planter, and merchant, later in London; a letter from Kingston, Jamaica. [NRS.GD199.206].

GRANT, ALEXANDER, son of Alexander Grant in St Croix, Danish West Indies, a student at King's College, Aberdeen, from 1796 to 1800, graduated MA. [KCA]

GRANT, ANDREW, in Georgia, a bond, 28 October 1743. [NRS.RD2.171/1.33]

GRANT, ANDREW, in Grenada, a deed of attorney with Isaac Grant, dated 10 June 1769; a deed of factory with S. McNight, dated 21 March 1800. [NRS.RD4.223.481; RD3.285.668]

GRANT, ARCHANGE, relict of Thomas Dickson in Queenstown, Upper Canada, testament, 28 April 1829, Comm. Dumfries. [NRS]

GRANT, Sir ARCHIBALD, was granted land in East Florida on 18 April 1771. [NRS.GD345.1235]

GRANT, CHARLES, in Winsborough, South Carolina, a letter dated 18 December 1780 re the capture of Charleston, S.C. [NRS.GD248.box 509, bundle 5]

GRANT, CHARLES LONGNESH, son of Donald Grant in Montreal, Quebec, a student at King's College, Aberdeen, in 1800. [KCA]

GRANT, DAVID, in America, a student at Marischal College, Aberdeen, from 1759 to 1763, graduated MD at King's College, Aberdeen, on 16 April 1764. [KCA]

GRANT, DAVID, son of David Grant MD in Jamaica, a student at King's College, Aberdeen, 1792 to 1794, graduated MA. [KCA]

GRANT, DAVID, son of David Alexander Grant MD in Jamaica, a student at King's College, Aberdeen, 1791 to 1793. [KCA]

GRANT, FRANCIS, in Albany, New York, and Fort Edward, New York, letters between 1765 and 1768. [NRS.GD248.box 49, b.1]

GRANT, HARRY, in South Carolina, a deed of attorney in 1799. [NRS.RD2.171/1.33]

GRANT, JAMES, in Portsoy, Banffshire, sometime of Montreal, Quebec, a natural son of Cuthbert Grant in Montreal, ultimus haeres, 10 August 1817. [NRS.PS3.14.153]

GRANT, JOHN, a skipper in Kirkcaldy, master of the Industry of Cockenzie trading with Charleston, South Carolina, and Maryland around 1760. [NRS.CS96.1085]

GRANT, JOHN, a Baron of the Exchequer in Scotland and a sugar planter, died in Grenada in 1776. [SM.39.54]

GRANT, JOHN, in New York, a deed, dated on 30 December 1788. [NRS.RD4.245.38]

GRANT, MICHAEL, assistant surgeon at New York General Hospital during the War of Independence, a memorial dated 17 March 1783. [HMC. American. iii.403]

GRANT, THOMAS, in Virginia, a deed, dated 24 January 1775. [NRS.RD2.207/1.824]

GRANT, WILLIAM, in Quebec, a letter, in 1767. [NRS.NRAS.0771]

GRANT, WILLIAM, son of David Alexander Grant in Montreal, Quebec, a student at King's College, Aberdeen, from 1800 to 1803. [KCA]

GRANT, WILLIAM, son of John Grant in Nova Scotia, a student at King's College, Aberdeen, from 1823 to 1827, graduated MA. [KCA]

GRANT, Dr, died in Antigua in 1771. [NRS.NRAS.771, bundle 305]

GRANT, ..., son of John Grant in Leith, a letter from Baltimore, Maryland, dated 30 May 1803. [NRS.GD248.702.5.56]

GRASS, NEIL, a settler on the north-west branch of the Cape Fear River, North Carolina, petitioned the Synod of Argyle for a Gaelic speaking minister, on 2 September 1748. [NRS.NRAS.1209.553]

GRAY, ARCHIBALD, an alumni, minister of Halifax, Nova Scotia, graduated DD at King's College, Aberdeen, on 15 August 1804. [KCA]

GRAY, JOHN, emigrated from Scotland to America, a merchant in Port Royal, Caroline County, Virginia, from 1748 to 1777, a Loyalist who returned to Glasgow in 1777 aboard the Albion, returned to Port Royal where he died in May 1787. [TNA.AO12.109.150]

GRAY, ROBERT, a Loyalist who settled in Jamaica, a letter dated 8 April 1783. [HMC. American.iv.19]

GRAY, THOMAS JOSEPH, of Jamaica, graduated MD from Edinburgh University in 1802. [EMG]

GRAY, WILLIAM, a settler on the north-west branch of the Cape Fear River, North Carolina, petitioned the Synod of Argyle for a Gaelic speaking minister, on 2 September 1748. [NRS.NRAS.1209.553]

GRAY, WILLIAM, in Boreale, Jamaica, former Provost Marshal General of Jamaica, a sasine in Caithness, 27 March 1776. [NRS.RS21.3.360], also on 13 December 1776. [NRS.RS21.3.436]

GRAY, ..., in Jamaica, a bond, dated 18 May 1776. [NRS.RD4.255.1221]

GREATHEAD, RICHARD WILSON, in St Kitts, graduated MD at Edinburgh University in 1771. [EMG]

GREENHOW, JAMES, of Virginia, a medical student at Edinburgh University 1796, graduated MD there in 1797. [EUL][EMG]

GREGORIE, JAMES, from Scotland to Urbanna, Virginia, as a merchant in 1758, Deputy Naval Officer of the Rappahannock, a Loyalist, in Glasgow by 1778. [TNA.AO12.106.5]

GRIFFIN, CORBIN, of Virginia, graduated MD at Edinburgh University in 1765. [EMG]

GRIFFEN, Lady C., in Virginia, a deed of factory in favour of Colquhoun Grant, dated 20 September 1779. [NRS.RD3.209/1.683]

GRIFFIN, CYRUS, of Virginia, a medical student at Edinburgh University, from 1769 to 1770. [EUL]

GRIFFIN, JOHN TAYLOE, of Virginia, graduated MD at Edinburgh University in 1774. [EMG]

GRIFFIN, SAMUEL STUART, of America, graduated MD from Edinburgh University in 1805. [EMG]

GRIFFITTS, SAMUEL POWELL, born in 1759, a medical student at Edinburgh University in 1784, died in 1826. [EUL]

GRIGG, ANTONY, a surgeon at the Royal Hospital, Barbados, graduated MD at King's College, Aberdeen, on 27 March 1769. [KCA]

GRIMKIE, JOHN, of America, graduated MD from Edinburgh University in 1808. [EMG]

GUTHRIE, WILLIAM, in Jamaica, a deed, dated 12 March 1774. [NRS.RD3.233.387]

HADDOW, ARCHIBALD, in New York, a deed of factory, dated 5 May 1781. [NRS.RD3.4/240.]

HAIG, GEORGE, of South Carolina, a medical student at Edinburgh University from 1762 until 1763, graduated MD at King's College, Aberdeen, on 16 May 1764. [EUL][KCA]

HAIG, MAHAM, second son of George Haig a physician in Charleston, South Carolina, matriculated at Glasgow University in 1803, graduated MD in 1807. [RGG]

HAIG, ROBERT MCKEWN, of South Carolina, graduated MD at Edinburgh University in 1798. [EMG]

HALDANE, GEORGE, Governor of Jamaica, a sasine in Dunbarton in 1758. [NRS.RS99.147]

HALIBURTON, WILLIAM, rector in Montreal, Quebec, graduated DD at Edinburgh University on 29 July 1766. [GEU]

HALL, GEORGE, from South Carolina to Edinburgh in 1791, residing at North Richmond Street, Edinburgh, in 1794, graduated MD at Edinburgh University in 1794. [EMG] [ECA.SL115.1.1]

HALL, HARPER, of Barbados, graduated MD at Edinburgh University in 1782. [EMG]

HALL, ISAAC, of Virginia, graduated MD at Edinburgh University in 1771. [EMG]

HALL, JAMES, in Lanark, Upper Canada, a letter dated 20 March 1823. [NRS.GD45.Section 3.470]

HALSEY, JAMES, from North Carolina to Edinburgh in 1792, residing in Bristo Street, Edinburgh, in 1794, a medical student at Edinburgh University from 1793 to1794. [EUL] [ECA.SL115.1.1]

HAMERSLEY, WILLIAM, in New York, a medical student at Edinburgh University in 1784, graduated MD there in 1787. [EMG][EUL]

HAMILTON, ADAM, from Barbados aboard the ketch William and Susan, master Ralph Parker, bound for New England on 21 March 1679. [TNA]

HAMILTON, ALEXANDER, a merchant in Portobacco, Maryland, a letter from James Lawson in Glasgow, dated 31 January 1764. [MHS.MS1301/1-4]; a factor in Pitcataway, Maryland, letter books from 1765 until 1770. [NRS.NRAS.0396.251]

HAMILTON, ALEXANDER, MD, died in Annapolis, Maryland, in 1756. [GM.26.412]

HAMILTON, ALEXANDER, and JOHN HAMILTON, in Maryland, letters to their brother Gavin Hamilton in Edinburgh, 1750s. [NLS.Halkett.6506]

HAMILTON, ANDREW, an estate owner at Massachusetts Bay, died in 1767. [GM.37.563]

HAMILTON, ARCHIBALD, emigrated from Scotland to America in 1755, a trader in Virginia and North Carolina, a Loyalist. [TNA.AO12.36.242, etc.]

HAMILTON, ARCHIBALD, a merchant in Port au Prince, St Dominica, later in Kingston, Jamaica, testament, 8 February 1803, Comm. Edinburgh. [NRS]

HAMILTON, CHARLES, in Jamaica, a deed of attorney, dated 29 August 1787. [NRS.RD2.245.112]

HAMILTON, Sir FRANCIS, of Kilache, a sasine, dated 18 November 1628, Nova Scotia. [NRS.RS1.25.29]

HAMILTON, GEORGE, in Madison County, Virginia, a letter to Hugh Hamilton of Pilmore, describing a property near Fredericksburg, dated 1803. [NRS.GD1.581.1]

HAMILTON, J., of Bargeny, MP, petitioned for a land grant in East Florida on 13 February 1765. [RPCCol.vi.387]

HAMILTON, JAMES, in Virginia, a deed of attorney, dated 17 June 1787. [NRS.RD3.247.124]

HAMILTON, JOHN, in Nansemond, Virginia, a letter dated 1765. [NRS.NRAS.0620]

HAMILTON, JOHN, emigrated to America in 1768, minister of St Bride's, Norfolk, Virginia, a Loyalist, moved to New York, later to Philadelphia, bound to settle in Shelburne. [PAO.LC.567]

HAMILTON, JOHN, a merchant in Ninety-Six District, South Carolina, before 1776, a Loyalist soldier, in St John, Nova Scotia, in 1784. [TNA.AO12.47.92, etc]

HAMILTON, JOHN, born 1780, eldest son of John Hamilton the Lord Provost of Glasgow, died in Kingston, Jamaica, on 4 December 1801. [GM.72.181]

HAMILTON, JOSEPH, in Canada, graduated MD from Edinburgh University in 1818. [EMG]

HAMILTON, MARY ANN, a widow from Edinburgh, married Edward Marshall in St John, Newfoundland, on 23 February 1815. [GM.85]

HAMILTON, ROBERT, letters from America, dated from 1740 until 1749. [NRS.NRAS.0560]

HAMILTON, WILLIAM, in America, testament, 4 November 1825, Comm. Edinburgh. [NRS]

HAMILTON, ..., emigrated from Scotland to America about 1775, a surgeon in New York, a Loyalist, moved to England in 1779, died upon the Centaur in 1781. [PAO.LC.1128]

HAMPDEN, ROBERT, in Barbados, graduated MD from Edinburgh University in 1808. [EMG]

HANCOCK, JOHN, of Wallyford, East Lothian, Joanna Sonmans eldest daughter of Arent Sonmans in Rotterdam, the Netherlands, and Francisca Hancock, relict of Arent Sonmans in Rotterdam, with titles to land in East New Jersey, dated 1683 from to 1685. [NRS.RH15.131.1-3]

HANDY, WILLIAM, in America, graduated MD at Edinburgh University in 1788. [EMG]

HANNAH, ANDREW, a servant of William Strickland, from Barbados aboard the sloop Katherine, master Andrew Gall, bound for Antigua on 27 November 1679. [TNA]

HANNAH, GEORGE, in Tortula in the Virgin Islands, a will subscribed to in 1798. [NMM.C107.81]

HANNAY, PATRICK, in Virginia, testament, 27 February 1823, Comm. Edinburgh. [NRS]

HANSCOMBE, JAMES, of South Carolina, to Edinburgh in 1789, residing in Drummond Street, Edinburgh, in 1794, a medical student at Edinburgh University from 1797 until 1798, graduated MD there in 1799. [EUL][EMG]

HARDIE, THOMAS, in Virginia, a deed of attorney, dated 29 December 1764. [NRS.RD3.224/1.347]

HARDING, BERNARD, in Jamaica, graduated MD at Edinburgh University in 1796. [EMG]

HARDY, CHARLES, an overseer in St Jan, Danish West Indies, died there on 27 December 1819, probate, St Jan, 1807-1826, fo.92. [RAK]

HARKNESS, JAMES, minister of the Presbyterian Church of St Andrews in Quebec, graduated DD from Glasgow University in 1821. [RGG]

HARMAN, WILLIAM, from Greenock to St John, New Brunswick, in 1803. [PANB.mc1672]

HARMONSON, J.S., in Virginia, a deed dated 28 October 1776. [NRS.RD2.220.1267]

HARDTMAN, BENJAMIN, of St Kitts, graduated MD from Edinburgh University in 1807. [EMG]

HARNBAUM, GEORGE F., jr., born in 1771, of South Carolina, a medical student at Edinburgh University from 1790 to 1791, graduated MD from Marischal College, Aberdeen, in 1791, died 1799. [EUL][MCA]

HARVEY, BAIKIA, in Snowhill, Augusta, Georgia, a letter dated 1776. [NRS.NRAS.1031]

HARVEY, WILLIAM, settled in New York as a shipmaster trading with British ports, a Loyalist in 1776, moved to Shelburne, Nova Scotia, in November 1783. [TNA.AO13.24.254]

HARRIS, FRANCIS, of Virginia, to Edinburgh in 1791, residing in Charles Street, Edinburgh, in 1794, graduated MD at Edinburgh University in 1793. [EMG] [ECA.SL115.1.1]

HARRIS, GEORGE, in America, a student at King's College, Aberdeen, from 1760 to 1764. [KCA]

HARRIS, GEORGE, in Kingston, Jamaica, graduated MD at Marischal College, Aberdeen, in 1768. [MCA]

HARRIS, RUSSEL, MA, in America, a student at King's College, Aberdeen, from 1761 to 1765. [KCA]

HARRIS, TUCKER, in South Carolina, graduated MD at Edinburgh University in 1770. [EMG][SCHS]

HARRISON, EDWARD, a merchant in Quebec, a letter, dated 1765. [NLS.Stewart.5045/3]

HARRISON, RICHARD, counsellor at law in New York, graduated LL.D. at Edinburgh University on 27 April 1792. [GEU]

HART, HENRY, in St Kitts, graduated MD at Edinburgh University in 1773. [EMG]

HART, NOSH, from New Jersey, a medical student at Edinburgh University from 1765 to 1766. [EUL]

HARVEY, ALEXANDER, deceased, of Antigua, his widow died in Aberdeen on 24 March 1777. [SM.39.167]

HARVEY, AUGUSTUS WILLIAM, in Bermuda, graduated MD at Edinburgh University in 1794. [EMG]

HASELL, GEORGE PADDON BOND, of America, graduated MD from Edinburgh University in 1804. [EMG]; in Carolina, a deed with M. Linning, dated 11 April 1810. [NRS.RD3.334.718]

HAVEN, SAMUEL, in Portsmouth, New England, graduated DD at Edinburgh University on 24 December 1769. [GEU]

HAY, DUNCAN, in Metis, a letter reporting on a road from Metis to Lake Metadissiac, date 4 May 1827. [NRS.GD45.Section 3.433]

HAY, JAMES, a merchant in Maryland, was the supercargo aboard the Friend Adventure of Leith, master David Scott, bound for Virginia or Maryland with a cargo to be sold there in January 1708, the ship had returned but no financial settlement had occurred, a petition before the High Court of the Admiralty of Scotland in 1709. [NRS.AC10.88]

HAY, JOHN, in Virginia, a deed of factory in favour of James Baird, 1 March 1775. [NRS.RD2.220.10]

HAY, Mr, Governor of Barbados and brother of the Earl of Kinnoull, died in November 1779. [SM.42.55]

HEDDLE, ELIZABETH, in America, notes to her parents in Kirkwall, Orkney, around 1795. [NRS.GD263.167]

HEDLEY, JOHN, a minister in South Carolina, graduated MA from Glasgow University in 1787. [RGG]

HENDENS, ADAM STRUTHERS, from North Carolina, a medical student at Edinburgh University in 1798-1799. [EUL]

HENDERSON, ALEXANDER, in Jamaica, letters, from 1728 to 1730. [HMC. Westmorland]

HENDERSON, ALEXANDER, a factor in Colchester and in Occoqua, Virginia, a letter book from 1758 until 1765. [NRS.NRAS.0396.244]

HENDERSON, JOHN, born in Scotland, settled in St Paul's parish, Georgia, a Loyalist, moved to London by 1787. [TNA.AO12.42.362]

HENDERSON, LOGAN, in Dominica, a deed, dated 26 April 1773. [NRS.RD3.233.208]

HENDERSON, Reverend MATTHEW, born in Kinross, minister at Chartres and Buffalo, died in Pittsburgh, Pennsylvania, on 4 October 1795. [GM.65.1112]

HENDERSON, RICHARD, factor at Bladensburgh for John Glassford, accepted William Abell of Prince George County, Maryland, as an indentured servant to pay off his debt, in 1766. [NRS.GD237.box 10, bundle 3]

HENDERSON, ROBERT, in Jamaica, later in Elgin, testament 28 May 1824, Comm. Moray. [NRS]

HENDERSON, WILLIAM, son of William Henderson an army officer in Jamaica deceased, a student at King's College, Aberdeen, from 1820 to 1824, a Licentiate of the Royal College of Surgeons in Edinburgh, 1826. [KCA]

HENDRY, ROBERT, in Charleston, South Carolina, graduated MA at Edinburgh University on 15 June 1814. [GEU]

HENDY, JAMES, in Barbados, graduated MD at Edinburgh University in 1774. [EMG]

HENDY, JAMES ALLEYNE, in Barbados, graduated MD from Edinburgh University in 1802. [EMG]

HENRY, J., from Aberdeen, died in Halifax, Nova Scotia, in 1813. [GM.83.670]

HERIOT, Mr, in Tobago, a probative will, dated 28 December 1781. [NRS.RD4.234.869]

HEUGH, JOHN, in 'Merryland', a deed of attorney, dated 6 March 1789. [NRS.RD2.252.1227]

HEWAT, ALEXANDER, of Charleston, South Carolina, graduated DD at Edinburgh University on 12 July 1780. [GEU]; minister of the Scotch Presbyterian Church in Charleston, S.C., from 1763 to 1777, a Loyalist who returned home in 1777. [TNA.AO12.47.428, etc]

HEWSON, THOMAS T., of Pennsylvania, a medical student at Edinburgh University from 1795 to 1796. [EUL]

HIGGINS, DAVID, of Three Rivers, Prince Edward Island, a letter of attorney, dated in 1772. [NLS.Stewart.3894]

HILL, JOHN, born 1783, son of Reverend Hill, died in Jamaica in 1800. [St Andrews Cathedral gravestone]

HILLIARD, Mrs ELIZABETH, wife of Reverend Thomas Hilliard, in Gorham, New England, letters from her sister Barbara and her husband Patrick Fotheringham, a writer in Kirkwall, Orkney, dated 1795 to 1797. [NRS.GD263.79]

HISLOP, DAVID, in Brookline, a letter re Bowdoin College in Maine, dated 1816. [NRS.NRAS.0333]

HOAKESLEY, ROBERT, in New York, a deed of attorney in favour of Thomas Williams, dated 7 December 1781. [NRS.RD2.233/1.295]; a Loyalist in Albany, New York, in 1776, [TNA.AO12.20.417]

HODGE, MICHAEL LOVELL, of Antigua, graduated MD at Edinburgh University in 1795. [EMG]

HODGE, WILLIAM, of St Eustatia, graduated MD from Edinburgh University in 1814. [EMG]

HODGES, JOHN, of Virginia, a medical student at Edinburgh University in 1799, graduated MD in 1801. [EUL][EMG]

HODGES, JOHN, of Jamaica, graduated MD from Edinburgh University in 1814. [EMG]

HOGG, JOHN, in Jamaica, a deed of attorney in favour of Patrick Booth, dated 25 December 1781. [NRS.RD2.231.699]

HOLDER, HENRY E., of Barbados, graduated MD from Edinburgh University in 1816. [EMG]

HOLLINGWORTH, ARTHUR ROLLOCK, of Barbados, graduated MD from Edinburgh University in 1805. [EMG]

HOLMES, ABIEL, of Cambridge, Massachusetts, graduated DD at Edinburgh University on 26 January 1805. [GEU]

HOLMES, ANDREW F., in America, graduated MD from Edinburgh University in 1819. [EMG]

HOME, ALEXANDER G., in Dominica, graduated MD from Edinburgh University in 1823. [EMG]

HOME, CHARLES, a merchant in New York, letters dated between 1730 and 1739. [NRS.GD1.384/3/5]

HOME, PATRICK, in Rappahannock Forge, Virginia, a letter, dated 1795, to George Home of Brankston giving news of the latter's brother, Ninian Home, who was murdered in a slave rising in Grenada and offering to go to the West Indies, [NRS.GD267.1.3]; a letter where he states he intends to sell his forge at Rappahannock, around 1800. [NRS.GD1.384.10]

HOOPE, AD. H., in New York, graduated MD from Edinburgh University in 1810. [EMG]

HOPE, ARCHIBALD, in Kingston, Jamaica, a letter, dated 28 August 1740. [NRS.GD277.272.7]

HOPE, HARRY, in Quebec, a probative will, dated 5 May 1800. [NRS.RD4.267.916]

HOPE, Sir JOHN BRUCE, Governor of Bermuda, was pursued by Samuel Eveleigh, a merchant in Carolina, re a ship's cargo condemned as a smuggler, letters and papers between 1735 and 1741. [NRS.GD242.box 34, bundle 10]

HOPE, Sir THOMAS, of Craighall, a sasine, dated 9 May 1628, Nova Scotia. [NRS.RS1.23.31]

HORLER, EDWARD, a surgeon in Jamaica, graduated MD at King's College, Aberdeen, on 18 July 1781. [KCA]

HORN, JOHN, in Grenada, graduated MD at Edinburgh University in 1799. [EMG]

HOSACK, DAVID, born in 1769, from New York, graduated MD from Edinburgh University in 1791, died 1835. [EUL]

HOUSTON, Sir GEORGE, died in Georgia in 1795. [GM.65.580]

HOUSTON, PATRICK, bound for Georgia, a letter dated 1716; letters from him in Savannah and Fredericia, Georgia, between 1736 and 1748. [NRS.GD18.5360/3-9]

HOWARD, SIMON, a minister in Boston, New England, graduated DD at Edinburgh University on 7 February 1785. [GEU]

HOYES, JOHN, son of John Hoyes in Jamaica, a student at King's College, Aberdeen, from 1819 to 1821. [KCA]

HUGER, FRANCIS KINLOCH, born in 1773, of South Carolina, a medical student at Edinburgh University 1791, died in 1855. [EUL]

HUGGINS, DANIEL W., in St Vincent, graduated MD from Edinburgh University in 1809. [EMG]

HUME, J., storekeeper in South Carolina, a memorial, dated 10 May 1762. [RPCCol.vi.336]

HUME, JAMES, in Savannah, a bond, dated 15 May 1775. [NRS.RD4.247.942]

HUME, JAMES, of the Great Black River, Mosquito Shore, testament, 29 July 1785, Comm. Edinburgh, son of Captain James Hume, a skipper in Leith, [NRS]

HUME, JAMES, Chief Justice of East Florida, from 1780, a Loyalist, later in Edinburgh by 1788. [TNA.AO12.3.58]

HUNT, JOHN L., in St Cruz, (St Croix), graduated MD from Edinburgh University in 1812. [EMG]

HUNTER, CHARLES, a merchant in St Kitts, graduated LL.D. at Edinburgh University on 26 February 1766. [GEU]

HUNTER, FRANCIS, in America, graduated MD from Edinburgh University in 1808. [EMG]

HUNTER, JAMES, in Virginia, a deed of factory in favour of John Hunter, dated 1 January 1773. [NRS.RD3.232.188]; a merchant in Smithfield, Southampton County, Virginia, from 1767 to 1774, moved to Antigua, a Loyalist, in London by 1784. [TNA.AO12.56.198][NRS.GD1.384.21]

HUNTER, JOHN, sr., a merchant in Norfolk and in Gosport, Virginia, before 1776, a Loyalist, died in New York in November 1778. [TNA.AO12.54.331]

HUNTER, PETER, in Montreal, a probative will, dated 19 October 1788. [NRS.RD3.247.1060]

HUNTER, ROBERT, Governor of New York, letters to the Earl of Stair between 1712 and 1715. [NRS.GD135.141.1.26/37/82; 4.22]

HUNTER, ROBERT, a mariner lodging with Hendry Sinclair in Boston, New England, a letter from his mother advising of the death of Patrick

Henderson of Hunterston his father and asking him to return to Scotland, dated 1738. [NRS.GD102.2.54]

HURLOCK, GEORGE, in Kingston, Jamaica, a student at King's College, Aberdeen, in 1788. [KCA]

HUSBANDS, WILLIAM, of Barbados, graduated MD from Edinburgh University in 1805. [EMG]

HUTCHINSON, ROBERT, born in Clackmannan, Scotland, settled in King Street, Charleston, South Carolina, from 1769 to 1781, later in Kincardine, Scotland, by 1784. [TNA.AO13.96.606]

HUTCHISON, DANIEL, a shipmaster in New York, a deed of factory and commission, dated 15 April 1752. [NRS.RD3.211/2.196]

HUTCHISON, GEORGE, in Jamaica, was admitted as a burgess and guilds-brother of Ayr on 30 April 1750. [ABR]

HUTCHISON, Captain WILLIAM, in Queen's County, Maryland, was admitted as a burgess and guilds-brother of Ayr on 30 December 1704. [ABR]

HUTCHISON, WILLIAM, born 1815, son of John Hutchison in Trinidad, was educated at Edinburgh Academy from 1824 to 1825. [EAR]

IMRIE, DAVID, a wright from Methven, Perthshire, emigrated to Richmond, Virginia, in July 1819. [NRS.GD50.186.125.3/3]

IMRIE, JOHN, in Florida, a deed of attorney in favour of J. Simpson, dated 11 January 1782. [NRS.RD4.232.597]; emigrated to Charleston, South Carolina, in 1761, a shipbuilder there and later in St Augustine, East Florida, resided in Dutch Church Street, Charleston, settled in Dundee, Scotland, by 1786. [TNA.AO12.3.252, etc]

INGLIS, CHARLES, Rector of Trinity Church in New York, a warrant re salary, 7 September 1782; a letter re the formation of an Episcopate in Nova Scotia, dated 21 March 1783. [HMC. American.iii.108/409]

INGLIS, JAMES, jr., a merchant in Edinburgh trading with Grenada, Boston, Philadelphia, Wilmington, Charleston, and St Kitts between 1771 and 1780. [NRS.CS96.2004]

INGLIS, JOHN, in Philadelphia, letters re seeds to be sent to the Earl of Loudoun, in 1753. [NRS.NRAS.0631]

INGLIS, KATHERINE, second daughter of the late Alexander Inglis in South Carolina, married Dr James Robertson, a physician in Inverness, in Edinburgh, on 20 October 1794. [GM.64.1148]

INGLIS, THOMAS, a Loyalist who settled in Jamaica, a letter dated 8 April 1783. [HMC. American.iv.19]

INNES, ALEXANDER, Provost Marshal of Jamaica, a sasine in Caithness, 2 September 1746. [NRS.RS21.2.374]

INNES, GEORGE, of St Kitts, a student at King's College, Aberdeen, from 1772 until 1776. [KCA]

INNES, Sir ROBERT, of Innes, Moray, a sasine, dated 20 May 1628, Nova Scotia. [NRS.RS1.23.330]

INNES, ROBERT, in North America, a letter dated 24 August 1772. [NRS.NRAS.1100, bundle51]

IRELAND, DAVID, in Virginia, later in Huntsville, Mississippi, and Jamaica, letters from 1817 until 1832. [NRS.NRAS.1252]

IRVINE, CHARLES, in Tobago, a deed, 29 February 1788. [NRS.RD4.245.147]; a commission, dated 18 September 1793. [NRS.RD2.259.264]

IRVINE, Dr JOHN, born in Scotland, a physician and surgeon in Georgia, a Loyalist, moved to England by 1786. [TNA.AO12.109.178, etc]

IVER, THOMAS, in Jamaica, a deed of factory, dated 1787. [NRS.RD]

JACK, THOMAS, to America around 1764, settled in North Carolina and later in Nansemond County, Virginia, a Loyalist in 1776, in Airdrie near Glasgow by 1784. [TNA.AO12.56.70]; testament, 22 September 1814. [NRS]

JACKSON, CHARLES, a practitioner, sometime in the West Indies, graduated MD from Glasgow University in 1767. [RGG]

JACKSON, WILLIAM, born in 1739, of Massachusetts, a medical student at Edinburgh University in 1785, died 1797. [EUL]

JACKSON, WILLIAM, of St Vincent, graduated MD at Edinburgh University in 1794. [EMG]

JAFFREY, JOHN, in Canada, a deed of factory in favour of Henry Galloway, dated 1 September 1779. [NRS.RD3.240.369]

JAMES, GEORGE, in Jamaica, a deed, dated 23 November 1769. [NRS.RD2.207.472]

JAMES, THOMAS C., born in 1766, of Pennsylvania, a medical student at Edinburgh University in 1792, died in 1835. [EUL]

JAMESON, JOHN, in Jamaica, a deed, 20 September 1798. [NRS.RD2.278.422]

JAMIESON, JOHN, a planter and merchant in Savannah, Georgia, a Loyalist, via Holland to England in 1779. [TNA.AO12.51.266]

JAMIESON, NEIL, born in Scotland, emigrated to America in 1760, a merchant in Norfolk, Virginia, a Loyalist in 1776, at Halifax, Nova Scotia, on 16 May 1786. [TNA.AO12.55.46, etc] [PAO.LC.538]

JAMIESON, SAMUEL HEATH, a merchant in Accomack County, Virginia, a Loyalist in 1776, aboard the Logan bound for Greenock by 1778. [TNA.AO13.31.136]

JARVIS, THOMAS, of Antigua, graduated MD at Edinburgh University in 1744. [EMG]

JAY, JAMES, born in 1732, of New York, graduated MD from Edinburgh University in 1753, died in 1815. [EMG]

JAY, JOHN, late President of the American Congress, graduated LL.D. at Edinburgh University on 27 April 1792. [GEU]

JEFFRIES, JOHN, born in 1745, graduated BA from Harvard in 1763, author, a medical student at Edinburgh University in 1761, graduated MD at Marischal College, Aberdeen, in 1769, died in 1819. [EUL][MCA] [SNQ.XII.95]

JOHNSON, CHRISTOPHER, of St Cruz Island (St Croix), graduated MD from Edinburgh University in 1825. [EMG]

JOHNSON, JAMES, from Glasgow, a merchant in Guilford, Surry County, Virginia, in 1752, a Loyalist. [TNA.AO13.102.91]

JOHNSON, WILLIAM MARTIN, of Georgia, a medical student at Edinburgh University, from 1784 to 1785. [Letters of Benjamin Rush, Princeton, 1951]

JOHNSTONE, ANDREW COCHRAN, Governor of Dominica, a letter dated 20 November 1798. [NRS.GD51.9.151]

JOHNSTON, ANDREW, of Georgia, a medical student at Edinburgh University from 1799 to 1800. [EUL]

JOHNSTON, D., in Jamaica, a deed, dated 7 March 1788. [NRS.RD3.252.115]

JOHNSTON, GABRIEL, Governor of North Carolina, a will and inventory subscribed in Edenton, N.C., on 16 May 1751, reference to his sister Elizabeth Ferrier in Fife. [TNA.Prob.11/1208]

JOHNSTONE, Sir GEORGE, of Carskieben, a sasine, dated 25 May 1626, Nova Scotia. [NRS.RS1.19.177]

JOHNSTONE, GEORGE, in Pensacola, West Florida, letters in 1766. [NRS.NRAS.01631.331]

JOHNSTON, GEORGE, of Pictou, Nova Scotia, a Licentiate of the Royal College of Surgeons in 1804, graduated MD from King's College, Aberdeen, on 17 November 1818. [KCA]

JOHNSTON, JAMES, born in Scotland, and a newspaper printer in Georgia, a Loyalist who moved to St Vincent by 1779. [TNA.AO13.36.69]

JOHNSTON, JAMES, emigrated to America in 1764, a Clerk to the Crown in South Carolina, a Loyalist. [PAO.LC.1173]

JOHNSTON, JAMES, son of Alexander Johnston MD in Jamaica deceased, a student at King's College, Aberdeen, from 1797 to 1801, graduated MA, later a surgeon in the Honourable East India Company Service. [KCA]

JOHNSTON, JOHN, son of Alexander Johnston MD in Jamaica deceased, a student at King's College, Aberdeen, 1791. [KCA]

JOHNSTON, JOSEPH, with others from Shetland via Leith bound for Georgia in 1774. [NRS.CH2.1071.33]

JOHNSTON, LEWIS, senior, settled in Savannah, Georgia, for 29 years, a Member of the House of Assembly, a Member of the Council of Georgia, moved via London to Edinburgh by 1788. [TNA.AO12.4.351, etc]

JOHNSTON, ROBERT, applied for a land grant in East Florida on 20 January 1768. [JCTP.75.60]

JOHNSTON, ROBERT, emigrated to South Carolina in 1772, an attorney at law, a Loyalist, moved to St Augustine, East Florida, by 1784. [TNA.AO13.130.129]

JOHNSTON, ROBERT, son of Alexander Johnston MD in Jamaica, a student at King's College, Aberdeen, from 1799 to 1803, graduated MA, later a surgeon in London. [KCA] on 26 February 1767. [RPCCol.vi.441]

JOHNSTONE, ROBERT, of the Johnstone of Wamphrey family, died in Charleston, South Carolina, on 1 March 1812. [GM.82.488]

JOHNSTONE, Sir SAMUEL, of Elphinstoun, a sasine, 2 December 1628, Nova Scotia. [NRS.RS1.25.61]

JOHNSTON, THOMAS RIDOUT, applied for a land grant in East Florida on 20 January 1768. [JCTP.75.60]

JOLLIE, M., was appointed as a Councillor of East Florida on 15 December 1767. [RPCCol.vi.441]

JONES, JAMES, of Virginia, graduated MD at Edinburgh University in 1796. [EMG]

JONES, JOHN, of New York, studied medicine in Edinburgh before 1750. [DAB]

JONES, JOHN PAUL, master of the brigantine John of Kirkcudbright was accused of a causing the death of Mungo Maxwell, a carpenter on the said ship, when in the West Indies, a petition by Robert Maxwell in Clonyards of Buittle in 1770. [NRS.SC16.12.14]; a Customs entry, signed by John Paul [Jones], of the cargo of the John of Dumfries from the West Indies in 1770. [NRS.RH1/2.697]

JONES, JOHN FORSTER DRAKE, of Barbados, graduated MD from Edinburgh University in 1803. [EMG]

JONES, WALTER, of Virginia, graduated MD at Edinburgh University in 1769. [EMG][VHS][LC]

KEITH, Sir BASIL, Governor of Jamaica, died in Spanish Town, Jamaica, on 15 June 1777. [SM.39.459]

KEITH, HENRY, from Barbados aboard the Young William, master Thomas Cornish, bound for Virginia on 2 August 1679. [TNA]

KEITH, JAMES, emigrated from Scotland to South Carolina in 1751, a planter and shoemaker in Church Street, Charleston, a Loyalist, moved to Kingston, Jamaica, settled in Banff, Scotland, by 1785. [TNA.AO12.48.306, etc]

KEITH, WILLIAM, the Earl Marischal, a sasine, 6 September 1625, Nova Scotia. [NRS.RS1.18.150]

KEITH, WILLIAM, of America, a student at King's College, Aberdeen, 1763 to 1767. [KCA]

KELL, JOHN, third son of John Kell of Rockycreek, Chester County, South Carolina, matriculated at Glasgow University in 1802, graduated MA in 1806. [RGG]

KEMP, JAMES, graduated MA from Marischal College, Aberdeen, in 1786, and DD from Columbia in 1802. [SNQ.XII.95]

KEMP, JOHN, graduated MA from Marischal College, Aberdeen, in 1783, and LLD from King's College, Aberdeen, in 1787, Professor of Mathematics at Columbia from 1786 to 1812. [SNQ.XII.95][KCA]

KENNEDY, ALEXANDER, emigrated from Scotland to America in 1773, settled at Johnson's Bush, Tryon County, New York, a Loyalist, moved to River Raisin. [PAO.LC.1037]

KENNEDY, ARCHIBALD, Customs Collector of New York in 1723, [RPCCol.vi.632], deed re his marriages, [1] to .... Mussam, and [2] Mary Waters or Schuyler, 1792. [NRS.GD25.9.44.4]

KENNEDY, ARCHIBALD, son of Daniel Kennedy in Glasgow, died in Norfolk, Virginia, in 1803. [GM.73.86]

KENNEDY, DONALD, a planter of River St Mary, East Florida, since 1768, a Loyalist, moved to London in 1779. [TNA.AO12.99.216, etc]

KENNEDY, HUGH, son of Daniel Kennedy in Glasgow, died in Philadelphia in 1803. [GM.73.86]

KENNEDY, JAMES, son of Alexander Kennedy a cooper in Virginia, was apprenticed to Phin and Paterson merchants in Edinburgh on 16 May1798. [ERA]

KENNY, ANDREW, of St Cruz, (St Croix), graduated MD from Edinburgh University in 1812. [EMG]

KERR, ALEXANDER, son of Alexander Kerr of Graden, Roxburghshire, a silversmith in Edinburgh and a Jacobite transported to Virginia in 1716, settled in Williamsburg as a jeweller and silversmith, died 20 October 1738. [MFA.95-96]

KER, DAVID CORBIN, of Virginia, graduated MD at Edinburgh University in 1792. [EMG]

KERR, GEORGE, a merchant in Williamsburg, Virginia, was imprisoned in York County because of debt due to William Cunningham, late of Falmouth, Virginia, a tobacco merchant in Glasgow, in 1767. [NRS.GD247.box 59, bundles R; box 140]

KERR, ISABELLA, daughter of Reverend Alexander Kerr in Stobo, Peeblesshire, married judge James Kerr, in Quebec on 17 September 1818. [GM.88.170]

KERR, JAMES, born 1765, a judge, died in Quebec on 5 May 1846. [GM.ns 26.322]

KERR, JAMES S., of Jamaica, graduated MD at Edinburgh University in 1794. [EMG]

KERR, JAMES, a planter in Kingston, Jamaica, testament, 1817. [NRS]

KER, JOHN, a shipmaster in Virginia in 1775, a Loyalist, returned to Ecclefechan, Dumfriesshire, in 1783. [TNA.AO12.54.411]

KERR, MARY, relict of James Fraser in Detroit, inventory, 17 June 1820, Comm. Aberdeen. [NRS]

KERR, MONTGOMERY, and Company in Virginia, a deed dated 14 December 1763. [NRS.RD4.197/2.369]

KERR, ROBERT, in Grenada, husband of Elizabeth McConachie in Girthon, testament, 10 October 1814, Comm. Kirkcudbright. [NRS]

KIDD, ALEXANDER, born in Scotland, settled in Philadelphia around 1766, a merchant and a Loyalist, at Halifax, Nova Scotia, on 14 July 1786. [PAO.LC.572]

KIDD, JAMES, in Jamaica, left a legacy for the poor of Scone, a letter dated 8 August 1820. [NRS.B59.38.5.66]

KIDD, WILLIAM, born 1654 in Dundee, son of John Kidd, a seaman, and his wife Bessie Butchart, a privateer in the West Indies, possibly a militiaman in Barbados in 1679, a shipmaster based in New York around 1690, master of the privateer vessel Adventure Galley operating in the Atlantic and Indian Oceans, found guilty of piracy and executed at Wapping, London, on 23 May 1701. [Dundee Old Parish Register] [TNA.HCA.Examinations. Vol.81, 10.1695]

KIDD, WILLIAM CAMPBELL, MA, born 1796, eldest son of Reverend James Kidd DD, Professor of Oriental Languages in Marischal College, Aberdeen, died in Richmond, Virginia in 1825. [AJ.31.8.1825]

KINCAID, GEORGE, a Loyalist who settled in Jamaica, a letter dated 8 April 1783. [HMC. American.iv.19]

KING, BENJAMIN, of America, a student at King's College, Aberdeen, from 1759 to 1763. [KCA]

KING, BENJAMIN WATTS, a practitioner in the West Indies, graduated MD from Glasgow University in 1799, died there in 1841. [RGG]

KING, Dr GEORGE, brother of William King of Newmiln, died in Kingston, Jamaica, on 10 August 1782. [SM.44.615]

KING, WILLIAM, in Jamaica, a bond, dated 23 October 1789. [NRS.RD4.250.1049]

KING, WILLIAM J., of Barbados, graduated MD from Edinburgh University in 1819. [EMG]

KING, Mrs, from Greenock to St John, New Brunswick, in 1803, settled in Sussex Vale. [PANB.mc1672]

KINLOCH, ALEXANDER, a storekeeper at Red Bank, South Carolina, partner of Alexander Nisbet, partnership agreement dated 4 April 1723. [NRS.GD237.box 10, bundle 1]

KINLOCH, JAMES, a Councillor of South Carolina, died in 1757. [JCTP.65.85]

KINLOCH, JAMES, in Jamaica, deed, dated 26 June 1770. [NRS.RD3.235.238/2422]

KIRK, ADAM, in Grenada, son of John Kirk in Kilmarnock, Ayrshire, a letter dated 1811. [NRS.GD1.632.2]

KIRK, JAMES, a merchant in St John's, New Brunswick, son of James Kirk, [1749-1829] and his wife Elspeth Russell, [1751-1832]. [St Andrews Cathedral gravestone]

KIRK, SARAH, in Grenada, letters from Kilmarnock, Ayrshire, from 1817. [NRSGD1.632.8/12/14]

KIRKWOOD, JOHN and WILLIAM, emigrated to Boston, New England, a memorandum dated 1736. [NRS.GD110.1150]

KISSAM, BENJAMIN, of New York, graduated MD at Edinburgh University in 1783. [EMG]

KISSAM, RICHARD SHARPE, of America, graduated MD at Edinburgh University in 1787. [EMG]

KNOLTON, IGNATIUS DANIEL, of Philadelphia, Pennsylvania, graduated MD at Edinburgh University in 1773. [EMG]

KNOX, ANDREW, of North Carolina, a medical student at Edinburgh University in 1791-1792. [EUL]

KNOX, HUGH, a Presbyterian minister and author in Santa Cruz, Danish West Indies, graduated DD at Marischal College, Aberdeen, on 25 November 1773. [MCA]

KNOX, PETER JOHN, son of Hugh Knox in St Croix, in Danish West Indies, a student at King's College, Aberdeen, 1777 to 1781. [KCA]

KNOX, SAMUEL, graduated 1792, minister of a Presbyterian church in Bladensburg, Maryland, later Principal of Frederick Academy and of Baltimore College. [RGG]

KNOX, WILLIAM, a Loyalist who settled in Jamaica, a letter dated 8 April 1783. [HMC. American.iv.19]

KUHN, ADAM, born in 1741, of Pennsylvania, graduated MD at Edinburgh University in 1767, died in 1817. [EMG]

LACY, LAURENCE, of America, graduated MD from Edinburgh University in 1810. [EMG]

LAIRD, JAMES, of Jamaica, graduated MD from Edinburgh University in 1803. [EMG]

LAIRD, WILLIAM, eldest son of John Laird a merchant in Washington, matriculated at Glasgow University in 1815, graduated BA in 1818, and MA in 1819. [RGG]

LANG, JOHN, was appointed minister of St Peter's, New Kent, Virginia, a letter in 1726. [NRS.GD248, box 564, bundle 74]

LANG, WILLIAM, skipper in Glasgow, master of the Nancy trading with Antigua, Maryland, North Carolina, Virginia, Barbados, Jamaica, the Leeward Islands, St Kitts, Greenland, etc between 1756 and 1760. [NRS.CS96.653]

LANGDON, SAMUEL, graduated BA from Harvard in 1740, and DD from Marischal College, Aberdeen, in 1762. [SNQ.XII.60]

LAPSLEY, JAMES, son of James Lapslie minister at Campsie, matriculated at Glasgow University in 1812, died in Tobago on 23 August 1819. [RGG]

LASHLEY, THOMAS, of Barbados, graduated MD at Edinburgh University in 1766. [EMG]

LATHROP, JOHN, a minister in Boston, New England, graduated DD at Edinburgh University on 7 February 1785. [GEU]

LATIMER, HENRY, (1752-1819), of Delaware, a student of medicine at Edinburgh University in 1773. [EUL]

LATTA, WILLIAM, emigrated from Scotland to America around 1768, settled in Taunton, Massachusetts, a Loyalist, in Halifax, Nova Scotia, on 2 June 1786. [POA.LC.555]

LAURENCE, RICHARD, of New York, a medical student at Edinburgh University in 1785. [EUL]

LAURIE, ROBERT, in St Vincent, a will, 4 March 1780. [NRS.RD4.227.1058]

LAW, GEORGE, a merchant in Barbados, a deed, 9 September 1751. [NRS.RD2.170.187]

LAWLOR, WILLIAM DIGBY, of St Kitts, graduated MD at King's College, Aberdeen, on 2 May 1796. [KCA]

LAWRY, ALEXANDER, a labourer from Dumfries, an indentured servant, bound for 4 years in 1658. [BRO]

LAWSON, GEORGE, in Jamaica, a deed, 14 March 1790. [NRS.RD251/1.561]

LAWSON, GEORGE MCFARQUHAR, of Jamaica, graduated MD at Edinburgh University in 1788. [EMG]

LAWSON, HUGH, a cooper in Newton Ayr, was admitted as a burgess and guilds-brother of Ayr, bound for Barbados aboard the Adventure of Ayr in 1746. [ABR]

LEACOCK, JOHN, of Barbados, graduated MD from Edinburgh University in 1816. [EMG]

LEADER, HENRY, of Barbados, graduated MA, MD, from Glasgow University in 1772. [RGG]

LEARMONTH, ALEXANDER, a tanner and merchant in Charleston, South Carolina, his widow in Edinburgh applied to be put on H.M. charity roll for Scotland in 1800. [NRS.NRAS.0063.P31]

LEARMONTH, JOHN, in Philadelphia, Pennsylvania, a deed of attorney in favour of William Mitchell, 11 September 1784. [NRS.RD4.236.782]

LEE, ARTHUR, born in 1740, of Virginia, a medical student at Edinburgh University in 1764, graduated MD at Edinburgh University in 1764, died 1792. [EUL][EMG][VHS]

LEE, ROBERT C., in Philadelphia, Pennsylvania, a deed, 11 August 1784. [NRS.RD4.236.803]

LEE, Colonel, of Virginia, graduated LL.D. at Edinburgh University on 20 June 1754. [GEU]

LEGGE, THOMAS, at Anglesea, Carlisle Bay, Barbados, a letter dated 20 October 1771. [NRS.GD406.1.7538]

LEHRE, WILLIAM, of South Carolina, a medical student at Edinburgh University 1790-1791, graduated MD from Marischal College, Aberdeen, in 1791. [EUL][MCA]

LEHRE, W., in South Carolina, a deed, 19 August 1791. [NRS.RD.250.557]

LEIPER, JAMES, born in 1735, of Maryland, a medical student at Edinburgh University, did in 1771. [EUL]

LEITH, JOHN, in Jamaica, a deed, dated 6 March 1791. [NRS.RD4.249.1185]

LEMAN, JOHN, of Barbados, graduated MD at Edinburgh University in 1778. [EMG]

LENNAN, JOHN, a settler on the north-west branch of the Cape Fear River, North Carolina, petitioned the Synod of Argyle for a Gaelic speaking minister, on 2 September 1748. [NRS.NRAS.1209.553]

LENNOX and DEAS, in Charleston, South Carolina, a deed of factory, dated 12 March 1765. [NRS.RD2.224/1.627]

LEONARD, GEORGE, son of George Leonard, Salt River, Jamaica, a student at King's College, Aberdeen, from 1772 to 1774. [KCA]

LESLIE, ANDREW, formerly President of H.M. Council of Antigua, died on 26 May 1780. [SM.42.280]

LESLIE, GEORGE, in Schenectady, New York, was appointed Receiver General of Upper Canada, 1807. [NRS.GD51.1.195.63]

LESLIE, JAMES, in Montreal, Quebec, letters, 1832. [NRS.NRAS.1081]

LESLIE, Sir JOHN, of Wards, a sasine, 14 June 1626, Nova Scotia. [NRS.RS1.19.216]

LESLIE, Reverend WILLIAM, first Rector of St John's, Barbados, from 1653 to 1676, grandson of the fifth laird of Kincraigie and great great grandson by his grandmother of John Leslie the eighth baron of Balquhain. [St John's, Barbados, plaque]

LEWIS, JOHN TALIFERRO, of Virginia, a medical student at Edinburgh University, from 1777 to 1779. [EUL]

LEWIS, WILLIAM BIRD, of Virginia, graduated MD at Edinburgh University in 1791. [EMG] 88

LEYBURN, ALEXANDER, emigrated from Scotland to Maryland in 1770, a Loyalist in 1776. [TNA.AO12.100.29]

LEYBURN, PETER, emigrated from Scotland to America in 1770, a merchant in Dorchester County, Maryland, a Loyalist, moved to England by 1780. [TNA.AO12.8.193]

LIDDELL, JAMES, in Bridgetown, Barbados, a letter dated 9 September 1718. [NRS.RH15.70.42]

LINCOLN, BELAM, born in 1733, graduated BA from Harvard in 1754, and graduated MD at King's College, Aberdeen, in 1765, died in 1774. [MCA] [SNQ.XII.94]

LINDE, ABRAHAM ALEXANDER, in Jamaica, a deed with Abraham Robarts, dated 2 February 1810. [NRS.RD3.332.740]

LINDSAY, DAVID, and his wife Susanna, in Northumberland County, Virginia, in 1665. [Northumberland County Order Book, 1652-1665, fo.420]

LINDSAY, JAMES, in Jamaica, a deed of factory with Thomas Farquharson, 2 June 1806. [NRS.RD3.315.571]

LINDSAY, JOHN, from Wormistone, Fife, emigrated to Philadelphia in 1729, was granted 3000 acres at Schenectady, New York in 1733, married Penelope Congreves in 1739, was appointed as Lieutenant Governor of the fort at Oswego in 1748, died in 1751. [NRS. GD203]

LINDSAY, JOHN, in Canongate, Edinburgh, formerly in Virginia, a deed, dated 16 December 1752. [NRS.RD2.172.514]

LINDSAY, JOHN, rector of St Thomas, Jamaica, graduated DD at Edinburgh University on 12 January 1773. [GEU]

LINKLETTER, ALEXANDER, in St Andrews, Charlotte County, New Brunswick, admin.10 August 1789. [PANB]

LITTLE, JOHN, of Bahia, Brazil, graduated MD at King's College, Aberdeen, on 18 December 1824. [KCA]

LITTLE, STEPHEN, a physician in Portsmouth, New Hampshire, a Loyalist in 1776, in Dundee, Scotland, by 1788. [TNA.AO.12.104.78]

LITTLE, WILLIAM, son of James Little in Philadelphia, Pennsylvania, a student at King's College, Aberdeen, 1794. [KCA]

LITTLEJOHN, DAVID, Commander of the Robin Hood at Castle Bay, Barbados, a deed of factory, dated 28 June 1749. [NRS.RD4.177/1.397]

LIVINGSTON, Sir DAVID, of Donypace, a sasine, 22 August 1625, Nova Scotia. [NRS.RS1.1.201]

LIVINGSTON, JOHN, a soldier of the King's Army, who was captured at the Siege of Worcester in 1651, escaped having been banished to Barbados, was summoned in 1656. [Middlesex County Records, 17.1.1656]

LIVINGSTON, Sir JOHN, of Kinnaird, a sasine, 23 July 1627, Nova Scotia. [NRS.RS1.22.3]

LIVINGSTONE, ROBERT, of Livingstone Manor, Albany, New York, was admitted as a burgess and guilds-brother of Ayr on 26 June 1705. [ABR]

LOCH, PHILIP, Surveyor of Customs at Montreal, Quebec, letters and papers, 1774-1797. [NLS.Stewart.3297, etc]

LOCK, WILLIAM, in Jamaica, a deed, 12 May 1766. [NRS.RD4.227.1197]

LOGAN, GEORGE, a merchant in Virginia, and Robert Logan a saddler in Glasgow, a deed, 7 August 1750. [NRS.RD3.211/1.295]; George Logan, a merchant of Kemp's Landing, Princess Anne County, Virginia, from around 1746, a Loyalist in 1776, died 15 June 1781. [TNA.AO12.54.100, etc]

LOGAN, GEORGE, of South Carolina, graduated MD at Edinburgh University in 1773. [EMG]

LOGAN, GEORGE, born 9 September 1753 in Philadelphia, Pennsylvania, graduated MD at Edinburgh University in 1779. [EMG]; settled in Pennsylvania, a politician, died 9 April 1821.

LOGAN, JOHN MURDOCH, eldest son of Walter Logan a magistrate of Boston, New England, matriculated at Glasgow University in 1774, graduated MA in 1779, later graduated MD at Edinburgh University in 1784. [RGG][EMG]

LOGAN, WALTER, from 1766 until 1776 was Customs Controller of Perth Amboy, New Jersey, a Loyalist who returned home, in Edinburgh in 1782, and in Glasgow in 1788. [TNA.AO12.104.12]

LOGAN, WILLIAM, of Philadelphia, Pennsylvania, graduated MD at Edinburgh University in 1770. [EMG]

LORIMER, CHARLES, of the presbytery of South Carolina, re a vacancy in Will Town, S.C., letters 24 September 1750 and 3 December 1750. [NRS.CH1.2.95.400-402]

LORIMER, W., in Albany, New York, a letter, 20 May 1758. [NRS.GD348.177.1.46]

LOUDON, JAMES, in Jamaica, a will, 7 March 1792. [NRS.RD4.252.1397]

LOVELL, JOHN, in Boston, New England, a deed, 6 June 1752. [NRS.RD4.178/1; son of Ebenezer Lovell in Boston, New England, deeds, 1752, [NRS.RD4.178/1.566]

LOVELL, ROBERT, of Barbados, graduated MD at Edinburgh University in 1779. [EMG]

LOW, JAMES, of New York, graduated MD from Edinburgh University in 1807. [EMG]

LOWE, JAMES, in Trinidad, a deed with Joseph Lowe, 11 July 1807. [NRS.RD4.284.503]

LOWELL, JOHN, born in 1734, of Massachusetts, a medical student at Edinburgh University around 1754, died in 1776. [EUL]

LOWTHER, WILLIAM, settled in North Carolina around 1755, a merchant in Edenton, a Loyalist, in Dornock, Scotland, by 1788. [TNA.AO12.30.378, etc]

LUCAS, JOHN RAINES, of America, graduated MD from Edinburgh University in 1805. [EMG]

LUDFORD, JONATHAN ANDERSON, of Jamaica, graduated MD at Edinburgh University in 1791. [EMG]

LUDLOW, EDMUND, of New York, a medical student at Edinburgh University from 1794 to 1795. [EUL]

LUNAN, JOHN, in Spanish Town, Jamaica, a letter dated 1819. [ULL.AL.253]

LUNDIE, ARCHIBALD, a merchant in St Augustine, East Florida, trading with timber from Mississippi, papers, from 1776 to 1778. [NRS.NRAS.0159]

LUNDIE, WALTER, MD, born 20 March 1750, son of Reverend James Lundie, settled in Jamaica. [F.111.193]

LUNDIN, JAMES, of Drummond, Earl of Perth, purchased land in East New Jersey on 25 September 1682. [NRS.GD160.245.1]

LYMBURNER, MATTHEW, emigrated from Scotland to Penobscot in 1767, a farmer and miller there, a Loyalist, from Penobscot to Nova Scotia in 1783, in St John on 22 March 1787. [PAO.LC.]; in Charlotte County, New Brunswick, administration 16 May 1788, bondsmen included Robert Pagan and Captain David Mowat. [PANB]

LYMBURNER, Messrs. in Quebec, a deed of attorney with William Parker, 2 November 1805. [NRS.RD2.299.547]

LYNCH, DOMINIC, of Barbados, graduated MD at Edinburgh University in 1796. [EMG]

LYNCH, JOSEPH, and others, on the Wando River, South Carolina, a letter to Robert Sandilands, a minister in Edinburgh, complaining that they were without a minister dated 1704. [NRS.CH1/2.24/1.fos.110-112]

LYNCH, SAMUEL, of Antigua, graduated MD from Glasgow University in 1785. [RGG]

LYON, CHARLES, settled in Princess Anne County, Virginia, a Loyalist in 1776, moved to Halifax, Nova Scotia, by 1786. [TNA.AO12.102.68]

LYON, GILBERT, of Jamaica, graduated MD from Edinburgh University in 1823. [EMG]

LYON, JAMES, of Pennsylvania, a medical student at Edinburgh University, from 1784 to 1785, graduated MD there in 1785. [EMG][RCPE]

LYON, JOHN, in Northampton County, Virginia in September 1667. [Northampton County Order Book, 1666-1674, fo.40]

MCALESTER, ALEXANDER, a settler on the north-west branch of the Cape Fear River, North Carolina, petitioned the Synod of Argyle for a Gaelic speaking minister, on 2 September 1748. [NRS.NRAS.1209.553]

MACALISTER, ALISTER, in Dominica, father of Elizabeth MacAlister, who was married there on 22 June 1776 to Walter Colquhoun from Glasgow. [SM.38.454]

MACALISTER of Loup, ANGUS, a Deed of Factory, dated 7 January 1765. [NRS.RD2.197.348]

MACALISTER, JAMES, in Dominica, a deed with Graham Leny, on 9 April 1807. [NRS.RD4.281.770]

MCALESTER, JOHN, a settler on the north-west branch of the Cape Fear River, North Carolina, petitioned the Synod of Argyle for a Gaelic speaking minister, on 2 September 1748. [NRS.NRAS.1209.553]

MCALPINE, WILLIAM, born in Greenock, Renfrewshire, settled in Boston as a bookseller and stationer in 1754, a Loyalist in 1776, returned to Greenock, died there 13 July 1788. [TNA.AO12.823.290.92]

MCATHUR, DONALD, late in Demerara, son of John McArthur at Ardgavan, died at sea in July 1800 on his passage mome, an edict of executry dated 13 January 1801. [TNA.CC2.8.1]

MCAULAY, Reverend ANGUS, a Church of Scotland minister in Charleston, South Carolina, by 1773, a Loyalist, moved to England by 1777. [TNA.AO12.30.207, etc]

MCBEAN, WILLIAM, in Jamaica, a probative settlement with Jean McBean, dated 18 July 1789. [NRS.RD]

MCBRAIRE, JOHN, of Nova Scotia, graduated MD from Edinburgh University in 1824. [EMG]

MCBRIDE, HUGH, in Maryland, a deed of attorney in favour of Elizabeth McBride, dated 25 August 1782. [NRS.RD2.232/2.642]

MCCALL, ALEXANDER, a partner of George Kippen and Company, merchants in Glasgow, resident in Virginia before 1771, returned to Glasgow by 1789. [TNA.AO12.109.186]

MACCALL, ALEXANDER, in Jamaica, a probative bill, dated 4 July 1782. [NRS.RD2.235/1.39]

MCCALL, ARCHIBALD, emigrated to Virginia in 1752, a merchant on the Rappahannock River, a Loyalist, in London by 1778. [TNA.AO12.106.7]

MCCALLUM, NEILL, with three others, emigrated from Campbeltown, Argyll, aboard the Edinburgh of Campbeltown, master John McMichael, in July 1771 bound for Prince Edward Island. [NRS.SC54.2.106]

MCCAW, JAMES, a surgeon and physician in Norfolk, Virginia, a Loyalist, in Newton Stewart, Galloway, by 1777. [TNA.AO12.56.343]

MACKIE, WILLIAM, in Jamaica, later in Forres, testament,23 June 1826, Comm. Moray. [NRS]

MCCLELLAN, JOHN, from Galloway, an indentured servant bound via Bristol for Barbados in 1655. [BRO]

MCCLELLAN, JOHN, of Pennsylvania, was admitted as a burgess and guilds-brother of Ayr on 4 June 1784. [ABR]

MCCLELLAN, WILLIAM, son of .... McClellan and his wife Margaret Wallace, from Scotland to Virginia in 1759, a merchant moved to Tarborough, North Carolina, a Loyalist, moved to New York city in 1777. [TNA.AO12.35.118, etc]

MCCLOUD, DANIEL, born 1709, died 13 June 1759. [St Andrew's gravestone, Barbados]

MCCLURG, JAMES, born in 1743, of Virginia, graduated MD at Edinburgh University in 1770, died in 1823. [EMG]

MCCOLMAN, DUNCAN, son of Dr McColman in Islay, Argyll, died in Jamaica in March 1795. [GM.65.791]

MCCOLME, JOHN, in Halifax, Nova Scotia, a letter 1762. [NRS.NRAS.0631]

MCCONNELL, JOHN D., in Gaspe, New Brunswick, a letter re the invention of John McKay, a blacksmith in Halifax, Nova Scotia, dated 26 October 1826. [NRS.GD45.Section 3.449]

MCCORMICK, WILLIAM, possibly from Edinburgh, settled in America in 1761, a merchant in Pasquotank, North Carolina, a Loyalist who moved to London in 1778. [TNA.AO12.34.82, etc]

MCCORQUADALE, ALEXANDER, a surgeon in Hanover, Jamaica, a will dated 10 February 1743. [NRS.CC2.13.10.5]

MCCORQUADALE, ARCHIBALD, from Kilbride, Argyll, married Laura Jones from Llanbeblig, Caernarvon, Wales, in St John's, Newfoundland, on 7 November 1813. [GM.83.20]

MCCOULL, DUNCAN, a settler on the north-west branch of the Cape Fear River, North Carolina, petitioned the Synod of Argyle for a Gaelic speaking minister, on 2 September 1748. [NRS.NRAS.1209.553]

MCCOWAN, JAMES, a smith from Perthshire, settled in Richmond, Virginia in 1817, letters, from 1818 to 1819. [NRS.GD50.186.125.3/3]

MACCOWDIN, WILLIAM, born 1616, a passenger aboard the Peter Bonaventure from London bound for Barbados and St Kitts in Spring 1635. [TNA.E157.20]

MACOY, JOHN, a debtor in York County, Virginia, ca. 1677. [York County Order Book 6, p146]

MCCRAE, JOHN, from Greenock to St John, New Brunswick, in 1803. [PANB.mc1672]

MCCRAINE, HUGH, a settler on the north-west branch of the Cape Fear River, North Carolina, petitioned the Synod of Argyle for a Gaelic speaking minister, on 2 September 1748. [NRS.NRAS.1209.553]

MCCRANIE, DONALD, a settler on the north-west branch of the Cape Fear River, North Carolina, petitioned the Synod of Argyle for a Gaelic speaking minister, on 2 September 1748. [NRS.NRAS.1209.553]

MCCRANIE, MURDOCH, a settler on the north-west branch of the Cape Fear River, North Carolina, petitioned the Synod of Argyle for a Gaelic speaking minister, on 2 September 1748. [NRS.NRAS.1209.553]

MCCRAW, JAMES DREW, of Virginia, graduated MD at Edinburgh University in 1792. [EMG]

MACCREE, GEORGE, in New York, a probative bill, dated 25 October 1779. [NRS.RD2.235/1.851]

MCCRUMMEN, DONALD, from Scotland to Anson County, North Carolina, before 1776, a Loyalist, later in Shelburne, Nova Scotia, by 1783. [TNA.AO12.35.28, etc]

MACCULLOCH, DONALD, settled in Charlotte County, New Brunswick, in 1804. [PANB.MC1672]

MCCULLOCH, HENRY, was appointed Secretary of North Carolina on 18 June 1754. [JCTP.61/2]

MCCULLOCH, ROBERT, a memorial dated New York on 8 March 1783 re a consignment of pavo sent to New York by settlers on the River St John's in East Florida. [HMC.American.iii.390]

MCCULLOCH, THOMAS, a merchant in Gosport, Virginia, before 1776, moved to London by 1789. [see TNA.AO1255.106, etc], died in Westfield, Bothwell, Lanarkshire, on 4 November 1794. [GM.64.1150]

MACULLUM, D, a farmer near Henryville, a letter dated 20 October 1820. [NRS.NRAS.1190]

MCDERMEIT, ROBERT, of Jamaica, was admitted as a burgess and guilds-brother of Ayr on 7 February 1784. [ABR]

MACDONALD, ALEXANDER, in Quebec, a deed, 16 January 1784. [NRS.RD4.255.992]

MACDONALD, ALEXANDER, settled in Charlotte County, New Brunswick, in 1804. [PANB.MC1672]

MACDONALD, ALEXANDER, son of Reverend John MacDonald in Albany, New York, a student at King's College, Aberdeen, from 1795 to 1799, graduated MA. [KCA]

MACDONALD, ALLAN or ALEXANDER, a prisoner in Perth, was found guilty of rioting at Mylnefield, and banished to the American Plantations for life, with seven years' service there, at Perth in June 1773. [SM.35.332]

MCDONALD, ARCHIBALD, a settler on the north-west branch of the Cape Fear River, North Carolina, petitioned the Synod of Argyle for a Gaelic speaking minister, on 2 September 1748. [NRS.NRAS.1209.553]

MCDONALD, DONALD, a merchant from Edinburgh, died at Cross Creek, North Carolina, in January 1773. [SM.35.223]

MACDONALD, DONALD, brother of the late Colonel Alexander MacDonald of Kinlochmoidart, died at Banks, St Anne's, Jamaica, on 19 August 1794. [GM.64.1054]

MACDONALD, DONALD, settled in Charlotte County, New Brunswick, in 1804. [PANB.MC1672]

MCDONALD, EDWARD, and THOMAS, fishermen at Caberous Bay, Cape Breton Island, in 1768. [RPCCol.vi.467]

MACDONALD, I. M., in Grenada, a deed, dated 5 November 1770. [NRS.RD3.238/1.139]

MCDONALD, JAMES, on Prince Edward Island, a letter dated 1776. [NRS.NRAS.Blairs Letters]

MACDONALD, JOHN, emigrated from Scotland to America around 1766, settled as a schoolmaster at Nine Partners, New York, a Loyalist, moved to Burton township, New Brunswick, in 1783, at St John's, N.B., on 26 January 1787. [PAO.LC.681]

MCDONALD, JOHN, son of Alexander McDonald an army officer in New Brunswick, a student at King's College, Aberdeen, 1791 to 1792. [KCA]

MCDONALD, JOHN, at Three Rivers, Quebec, a letter, 1810. [NRS NRAS Blairs]

MACDONALD, JOHN, in Antinogish, Nova Scotia, letters 1826 and 1828 to John MacDonald of Borrodale. [NRS.NRAS.Borrodale]

MCDONALD, SOIRLE, emigrated from Scotland to America in 1771, settled as a planter in Cumberland County and Anson County, North Carolina, a Loyalist who moved to Shelburne, Nova Scotia, by 1783. [TNA.AO12.35.41, etc] [PAO.LC.492]

MCDONALD, WILLIAM, of Clarendon, Jamaica, later in Finlarig, testament, 21 November 1807. [NRS.Comm.Moray]

MCDONALD, WILLIAM, from Sutherland, a merchant in St John, New Brunswick, probate 19 February 1815, New Brunswick. [PANB]

MCDONALD, Mrs, born 1725, from America, widow of Lieutenant Colonel D. MacDonald of the 84th [Royal Highland Emigrants] Regiment, died in Edinburgh in 1815. [GM.85.92]

MCDONNELL, ALEXANDER, in Quebec, a letter dated 1778. [NRS NRAS Blairs]

MCDONELL, ALEXANDER, emigrated from Scotland to America in 1772, settled in Tryon County, New York, a Loyalist soldier, moved to Lot 15, 1st Concession, 1st Township, Canada. [PAO.LC.999]

MACDONELL, ALEXANDER, of Glengarry, Ontario, a letter dated 1812. [NRS.NRAS. Preshome]

MCDONELL, ALLAN, emigrated to America in 1773, settled at Johnstown, Tryon County, New York, a Loyalist in 1776, moved to Quebec in 1778, there in1786. [TNA.AO12.27.396][PAO.LC.998]

MCDONELL, ARCHIBALD, in St Kitts, a letter dated 1809. [NRS.GD128.9.2.103]

MACDONELL, HELEN, born 1760, daughter of Allan MacDonell of Lundie, and widow of James McKenzie a settler on the Mohawk and Glengarry, died at Three Rivers, Canada, on 10 November 1839. [GM.ns13.333]

MCDONELL, HUGH, emigrated from Scotland to America in 1773, settled on Johnson's Patent, Tryon County, New York, a Loyalist who moved to Sorel in 1780 and later settled at Riviere du Raisin, Quebec. [PAO.LC.1036]

MCDONELL, JOHN, emigrated to America in 1773, settled in Johnson's Bush, Tryon County, New York, a Loyalist in 1776, there on moved to New Johnstown, Quebec, by 1786. [TNA.AO12.29.214]

MCDONELL, JOHN, emigrated to America in 1773, settled on the Kingsborough Patent, Tryon County, New York, a Loyalist in 1776, moved to the River Raison, Quebec, by 1788. [TNA.AO12.31.179]

MCDONELL, RODERICK, letters re the voyage to Berbice and the Scottish plantations there, from 1807 until 1809. [NRS.GD128.9.2/106]

MCDOUGALL, GEORGE GORDON, only son of William McDougall MD in St Croix, Danish West Indies, matriculated at Glasgow University in 1813. [RGG]

MCDOUGALD, DONALD, a tailor, and wife Ann McGilvray, returned to Glasgow from North Carolina by 1786, he died 15 December 1787. [TNA.AO12.34.181, etc]

MACDOUGALL, DUNCAN, a farmer near Belwood, Montreal, a letter dated 28 January 1789. [NRS.NRAS.1190] 98

MACDOUGALL, MARY, emigrated via Oban to Quebec, settled at Henryville, Canada, a letter dated 25 August 1820. [NRS.NRAS.1190]

MCDOUGALL, PETER, emigrated from Campbeltown, Argyll, aboard the Edinburgh of Campbeltown, master John McMichael, in July 1771 bound for Prince Edward Island. [NRS.SC54.2.106]

MCDOUGAL, PETER, emigrated from Scotland to America after 1763, settled at White Creek, Charlotte County, New York, moved to Canada in 1778. [PAO.LC.942]

MCDOUGALL, WILLIAM, a planter in East Florida and South Carolina, letters dated from 1766 until 1771, died around 12 July 1774. [NRS.NRAS.0181][NRS.GD477.399]

MCDOUGALL, WILLIAM, of Santa Cruz, (St Croix), Danish West Indies, graduated MD at Edinburgh University in 1791. [EMG]

MCDOWELL, EPHRAIM, born in 1771, of Kentucky, to Edinburgh in1793, residing in Potter Row, Edinburgh, in 1794, a medical student at Edinburgh University 1793-1794, died in 1830. [EUL] [ECA.SL115.1.1]

MCDOWELL, JOHN, settled in Virginia about 1750 as a merchant and factor, moved to London by 1780. [TNA.AO12.100.35]

MCDUFFIE, DUNCAN, a settler on the north-west branch of the Cape Fear River, North Carolina, petitioned the Synod of Argyle for a Gaelic speaking minister, on 2 September 1748. [NRS.NRAS.1209.553]

MCEACHINE, HECTOR, emigrated from Campbeltown, Argyll, aboard the Edinburgh of Campbeltown, master John McMichael, in July 1771 bound for Prince Edward Island. [NRS.SC54.2.106]

MACEACHARN, Dr ANGUS, on Prince Edward Island, a letter dated 1807. [NRS.NRAS.Preshome]

MCEWAN, DUNCAN, born 1818, son of Hugh McEwan, a mason in Dunkeld, and his wife Christian McCullam, died in Detroit, Michigan, on 27 July 1859. [Little Dunkeld gravestone, Perthshire]

MCEWAN, Dr WILLIAM, in Jamaica, a deed, 2 February 1785. [NRS.RD2.238.251]; youngest son of William McEwan deceased, a Writer to the Signet, died in Jamaica in 1782. [SM.44.446]

MCFARLANE, ALEXANDER, in Jamaica, a deed, 17 October 1746. [NRS.RD4.219.140]; was admitted as a burgess and guilds-brother of Ayr on 4 April 1751. [ABR]

MCFARLANE, ANDREW, late merchant in New York, son of Walter McFarlane of Stickentibert, Arrochar, deeds, 23 November 1751, 27 February 1752. [NRS.RD2.171/1.233/259]; husband of Elizabeth Cumming, a sasine in Dunbarton, 3 September 1755. [NRS.RS9.9.3]

MCFARLAN, DANIEL, a settler on the north-west branch of the Cape Fear River, North Carolina, petitioned the Synod of Argyle for a Gaelic speaking minister, on 2 September 1748. [NRS.NRAS.1209.553]

MCFARLANE, DUNCAN, in Jamaica, a deed of attorney, dated 25 May 1765. [NRS.RD4.198/1.163]

MACFARLANE, GEORGE, of Santa Cruz Island, (St Croix), Danish West Indies, graduated MD from Edinburgh University in 1803. [EMG]

MCFARLANE, JAMES, via Greenock to St John, New Brunswick, in 1803, settled in Sussex Vale. [PANB.mc1672]

MCFARLANE, JOHN, born in Scotland, a farmer in St Patrick, Charlotte County, New Brunswick, administration, 21 July 1828, St John, New Brunswick. [PANB]

MACFEDERAN, JOHN, formerly a merchant in North Carolina, edict of executry, 19 August 1823. [NRS.CC2.8.128]

MCGEACHY, JAMES, in North Carolina, a deed, 24 July 1784. [NRS.RD2.238.857]

MCGEACHY, NEIL, late of Wilmington, North Carolina, and his wife Margaret Mackay, were executors of Daniel Hendry a skipper in Campbeltown, Argyll, in February 1785. [NRS.CC2.8.88/2; CC2.3.12/51-57]

MCGIBBON, JAMES, son of James McGibbon in Jamaica, a student at King's College, Aberdeen, 1794. [KCA]

MCGIBBON, JOHN, in Quebec, a letter to his father in Paisley, Renfrewshire, dated 1818. [SRA.TD479]

MCGILL, Sir JAMES, of Cranston Riddell, a sasine, 6 December 1627, Nova Scotia. [NRS.RS1.22.278]

MCGILL, DUNCAN, a settler on the north-west branch of the Cape Fear River, North Carolina, petitioned the Synod of Argyle for a Gaelic speaking minister, on 2 September 1748. [NRS.NRAS.1209.553]

MCGILL, JAMES, in Canada, a letter, 22 May 1755. [De Peyster pp, DAC]

MCGILLIVRAY, ALEXANDER, in Little Tallassie, a letter to John Stuart, dated 25 September 1777, and a letter to Lieutenant Colonel Thomas Brown dated 10 April 1783. [HMC.American.1.135; iv.23]

MCGILLIVARY, ARCHIBALD, late in South Carolina, a contract of wadset re the lands of Daviot, Inverness-shire, with Aneas Mackintosh of Mackintosh, dated 19 December 1749. [NRS.GD176.964]

MCGILLIVRAY, LACHLAN, in Savanna, Georgia, a probative bond, 9 April 1781. [NRS.RD2.239/1.129]

MCGILLIVRAY, WILLIAM, a planter on Hutchinson's Island, Georgia, a Loyalist, moved via Charleston, South Carolina, to London by 1779. [TNA.AO12.4.17, etc]

MCGILLIVRAY, WILLIAM, from Drumnaglass, Inverness-shire, the Creek Chief, died in Pensacola, Florida, on 17 February 1793. [GM.63.767]

MCGILLIVRAY, WILLIAM, born 1764 at Peine na Ghael, Mull, late from Montreal, died in London on 16 October 1825. [GM.95.380]

MACGLASHAN, CHARLES, of Jamaica, graduated MD from Edinburgh University in 1813. [EMG]

MCGLON, ANDREW, from Scotland to America, a grocer in Philadelphia, a Loyalist in 1776, died at sea before 1784. [TNA.AO13.71A.155]

MCGOWAN, JOHN, a merchant in Stirling, formerly in Boston, New England, deeds in 1698. [NRS.RD4.82.1316; RD3.90.110]

MCGOWN, ALEXANDER, emigrated to Savannah, Georgia in 1766, a merchant there, a Loyalist, moved to San Domingo then to Jamaica in 1778, settled at Montego Bay, Jamaica, by 1783.
[TNA.AO13.91.230, etc]; a Loyalist who settled in Jamaica, a letter dated 8 April 1783. [HMC. American.iv.19]

MCGRAHAM, OWEN, a settler on the north-west branch of the Cape Fear River, North Carolina, petitioned the Synod of Argyle for a Gaelic speaking minister, on 2 September 1748. [NRS.NRAS.1209.553]

MCGREGOR, ALEXANDER, a tailor who emigrated from Scotland to America in 1772, settled in Blackwater, Isle of Wight County, Virginia, a Loyalist. [TNA.AO12.101.37]

MCGREGOR, JAMES, in Northumberland County, Virginia, in July 1650. [Northumberland County Order Book, 1650-1652, fo.16]

MACGREGOR, THOMAS, in Quebec, a letter dated 15 March 1822. [NRS.NRAS.1256]

MACGROAH, WILLIAM, emigrated from Scotland to America in 1773, settled on the Susquehana, Tryon County, New York, a Loyalist who moved to Niagara in 1778, later settled in Montreal. [PAO.LC.1026]

MCGUGAN, JOHN, with one other, emigrated from Campbeltown, Argyll, aboard the Edinburgh of Campbeltown, master John McMichael, in July 1771 bound for Prince Edward Island. [NRS.SC54.2.106]

MCILCHERE, ALEXANDER, and family, emigrated aboard the Edinburgh of Campbeltown, master John McMichael, from Campbeltown on 1 July 1771 bound for North Carolina. [NRS.SC54.2.166]

MCILROY, JOHN, born 1713, a husbandman from Inch, Galloway, an indentured servant bound via London to Jamaica for 4 years, from 1731. [CLRO]

MCILVAINE, WILLIAM, of Pennsylvania, graduated MD at Edinburgh University in 1771. [EMG]

MCINTOSH, CHARLES, of Jamaica, a student at King's College, Aberdeen, around 1814. [KCA]

MACKINTOSH, DONALD, in Berbice, a letter to Colonel Baillie in Inverness, dated 1796. [HCA. Bailie of Dunain pp]

MCINTOSH, DUNCAN, was granted 100 acres in St Andrew's parish, also in St George's, Dominica in 1765. [NRS.GD126.4]

MCINTOSH, JAMES, a minister in Dominica, married Ann Simpson, daughter of James Simpson at the Miln of Brodie, Moray, on 13 March 1769, parents of David McIntosh born 16 April 1769, a Process of Marriage and Legitimacy, in 1773. [NRS.CC8.6.531]

MCINTOSH, JAMES, landed in New York on 26 July 1775, a school master in West Chester by August 1775, a letter. [NRS.GD248.508.4]

MCKINTOSH, Dr JAMES, in Jamaica, father of Eliza Anglin who married Alexander Duff on 22 August 1776, a Process of Adherence dated 5 September 1781. [NRS.CC8.6.639]

MCINTOSH, LACHLANE, of Jamaica, a student at King's College, Aberdeen, around 1819. [KCA]

MACINTYRE, DUNCAN, a Chelsea Pensioner residing in Killici, found guilty of stealing a horse, was, on his own petition, banished to the

American Plantations for life in June 1773 at Inveraray, Argyll. [SM.35.334]

MCIVER, ALEXANDER, in Liberty County, Georgia, was served heir to his uncle Dr Alexander Munro, in 1824. [NRS.GD128.52.5]

MCIVER, JOHN, in Virginia, a deed of attorney, dated 19 December 1788. [NRS.RD2.254.922]

MACKAY, AENEAS, son of James Mackay in Ross-shire, died in Havanna, Cuba, in May 1817. [GM.87.629]

MCKAY, ALEXANDER, a sailor, with two others, emigrated from Campbeltown, Argyll, aboard the Edinburgh of Campbeltown, master John McMichael, in July 1771 bound for Prince Edward Island. [NRS.SC54.2.106]

MACKAY, AENEAS, a merchant in Boston, New England, and in Greenock, deeds, dated 16 May 1752, 6 June 1752, and 11 July 1752. [NRS.RD4.178/1.566; RD4.178/1.553; RD4.178/2.284]

MCKAY, ALEXANDER, a settler on the north-west branch of the Cape Fear River, North Carolina, petitioned the Synod of Argyle for a Gaelic speaking minister, on 2 September 1748. [NRS.NRAS.1209.553]

MCKAY, ARCHIBALD, emigrated from Campbeltown, Argyll, aboard the Edinburgh of Campbelltown master John McMichael, in July 1771, bound for Prince Edward Island. [NRS.SC54.2.106]

MCKAY, Sir DONALD, of Strathnaver, a sasine dated 8 November 1628, Nova Scotia. [NRS.RS1.25.8]

MACKAY, DONALD, from Inverness to Demerara in 1801, a merchant and planter in Essequibo, died in England after 1815. [NRS.GD23.6.391]

MACKAY, DONALD, settled in Charlotte County, New Brunswick, in 1804. [PANB.MC1672]

MCKAY, DUNCAN, born in Scotland, a carpenter in Portland, New Brunswick, administration, 11 November 1834, New Brunswick. [PANB]

MACKAY, FRANCIS, in Quebec, a memorial in 1772. [JCTP.79.109]

MCKAY, Dr HUGH, in Jamaica, a probative will, 25 December 1780, [NRS.RD2.233/1.50]; a deed of attorney in favour of William Bryant, 1 December 1785. [NRS.RD4.239.1061]

MCKAY, JAMES, formerly a merchant in Glasgow, died 30 January 1828, admin. 21 July 1828, St John, New Brunswick. [PANB]

MCKAY, JOHN, sr., with one other, emigrated from Campbeltown, Argyll, aboard the Edinburgh of Campbeltown, master John McMichael, in July 1771 bound for Prince Edward Island. [NRS.SC54.2.106]

MCKAY, JOHN, a tailor, with one other, emigrated from Campbeltown, Argyll, aboard the Edinburgh of Campbeltown, master John McMichael, in July 1771 bound for Prince Edward Island. [NRS.SC54.2.106]

MCKAY, MELASHUS, born 1623, a passenger aboard the Speedwell of London bound from London to Virginia on 28 May 1635. [TNA.E157.20]

MCKAY, ['MIKAYE']. MICHAEL, born 1627, a witness in Lower Norfolk County, Virginia, on 31 July 1649. [Lower Norfolk County Order Book, 1646-1651, fo.120]

MCKAY, MORE, an indentured servant, emigrated from Campbeltown, Argyll, aboard the Edinburgh of Campbeltown, master John McMichael, in July 1771 bound for Prince Edward Island. [NRS.SC54.2.106]

MCKAY, NEILL, with two others, emigrated from Campbeltown, Argyll, aboard the Edinburgh of Campbeltown, master John McMichael, in July 1771 bound for Prince Edward Island. [NRS.SC54.2.106]

MACKAY, ROBERT, from Bighouse, Scotland, died in Antigua on 29 September 1816. [GM.86.566]

MACKAY, RUPERT, in Jamaica, a bond, 4 June 1785. [NRS.RD2.238/2.894]

MCKENDRICK, ROBERT, and family, emigrated aboard the Edinburgh of Campbeltown, master John McMichael, from Campbeltown on 1 July 1771 bound for North Carolina. [NRS.SC54.2.166]

MCKENNA, JOHN, settled in New York colony, a Loyalist in 1776, moved to London in 1778. [TNA.AO12.24.243]

MCKENNA, SAMUEL, born in Scotland, settled in Woodbridge, New Jersey, in1774, a Loyalist in 1776, moved to Boulston, South Wales, by 1786. [TNA.AO12.101.143]

MCKENNY, JOHN, emigrated from Scotland to America around 1760, settled at White Creek, Charlotte County, New York, a Loyalist soldier, moNLS.Ch.3814]ved to La Chine, Quebec, by 17 1646. [KCA83. [PAO.LC.933]

MCKENZIE, ALEXANDER, a merchant in Norfolk, Virginia a bond dated 1750. [NRS.RD

MCKENZIE, ANDREW, a mariner in Boston, a deposition concerning the Tea Riot, dated 19 February 1774. [RPCCol.vi.554]

MCKENZIE, ARCHIBALD, with one other, emigrated from Campbeltown, Argyll, aboard the Edinburgh of Campbeltown, master John McMichael, in July 1771 bound for Prince Edward Island. [NRS.SC54.2.106]

MCKENZIE, COLIN, born 19 October 1750, son of William McKenzie minister at Glen Muick, Aberdeenshire, settled in Carriacou near Grenada. [F.6.99]

MCKENZIE, COLIN, in Jamaica, a deed, 29 December 1783. [NRS.RD4.235.344]

MCKENZIE, DONALD, settled in Bladen County, North Carolina, a Loyalist, moved to Edinburgh by 1783. [TNA.AO13.91.265]

MCKENZIE, FRANCIS HUMBERSTONE, born 1754, Chief of the Clan in 1783, Colonel of the 78th Regiment, planter in Berbice, Governor of Barbados from 1801 to 1806, died in 1815.

MCKENZIE, HECTOR, of New York State, son of Kenneth McKenzie of Redcastle, married Diana, second daughter of Dr Davidson from Leeds, in Edinburgh on 29 March 1800. [GM.70.588]

MCKENZIE, Sir JOHN, of Tarbat, a sasine, dated 15 March 1630, Nova Scotia. [NRS.RS1.28.6]

MACKENZIE, JOHN, settled in Charlotte County, New Brunswick, in 1804. [PANB.MC1672]

MACKENZIE, NEIL, settled in Charlotte County, New Brunswick, in 1804. [PANB.MC1672]

MACKENZIE, ROBERT, born 1636 in Scotland, emigrated via London aboard the Conquer bound for Virginia in August 1657. [TNA.CO1.13.29i]

MCKENZIE, ROBERT, a merchant in Charleston, South Carolina, a Loyalist soldier, moved to Edinburgh, Scotland, by 1780. [TNA.AO12.51.273, etc]

MACKENZIE, ROBERT, settled in Charlotte County, New Brunswick, in 1804. [PANB.MC1672]

MCKENZIE, RODERICK, born 20 March 1752, son of William McKenzie minister at Glen Muick, Aberdeenshire, settled in Grenada. [F.6.99]

MCKENZIE, RODERICK, son of Captain Kenneth McKenzie of Redcastle, died in Jamaica in 1801. [GM.71.483]

MCKENZIE, SIMON, in Jamaica, a deed, dated 8 December 1783. [NRS.RD4.237.901]

MACKENZIE, THOMAS, of Jamaica, graduated MD from Edinburgh University in 1814. [EMG]

MACKENZIE, WILLIAM, of Grenada, graduated MD from Edinburgh University in 1809. [EMG]

MACKENZIE, WILLIAM LYON, born 1794 in Dundee, emigrated to Canada in 1825, a political radical, died in Toronto on 28 August 1861. [GM.ns.2/11.567] [TNA.CO1.13.29]

MACKEWE, ROBERT, a Scot, born 1636, emigrated aboard the Conquer to Virginia in 1657. [TNA]

MCKICHAN, DONALD, a settler on the north-west branch of the Cape Fear River, North Carolina, petitioned te Synod of Argyle for a Gaelic speaking minister, on 2 September 1748. [NRS.NRAS.1209.553]

MACKIE, ALEXANDER, found guilty of fraud, falsehood, and forgery, in Glasgow, was, in June 1773, sentenced to banishment to the American colonies for life with seven years of service there. [SM.35.334]

MACKIE, JOHN, from Dalry Ayrshire, a mariner, probate 12 December 1806, New Brunswick. [PANB]

MACKIE, RICHARD, a merchant in Nansemond County, Virginia, a Loyalist in 1776, to settle in Nova Scotia in 1787. [TNA.AO12.56.356]

MACKIE, WILLIAM, in the Isle of Wight County, Virginia, appointed Robert Landers of Robroyston, Lanarkshire, as his attorney in Scotland, subscribed aboard the Grozia lying in the Nansemund River, Nansedmond County, Virginia, on 13 July 1768, witnessed by Andrew Sym and James Williamson. [NRS.RD4.210/2.639]

MCKINLAY, WILLIAM, of St Kitts, graduated MA at King's College, Aberdeen, on 31 March 1772. [KCA]

MCKINNON, CHARLES WILLIAM, applied for a grant of 5000 acres in Georgia on 6 March 1771, [JCTP.78.57]; a planter on Skidaway Island, Georgia, a Loyalist in 1776, died in Charleston in 1776, his widow, Helen McKinnon, moved to Kingston, Jamaica, by 1787. [TNA.AO12.101.341, etc]; a letter from St Augustine, East Florida, in 1776, [NRS.NRAS.01631.76]

MCKINNON, DONALD, born 1653 on Skye, second son of Lachlan Mor McKinnon, settled on Antigua by 1693, a planter, died in 1720. A petition to the Privy Council Colonial on 25 August 1719. [RPCCol.vi.119/132]

MCKINNON, DONALD, born 1745 in North Uist, son of John McKinnon, emigrated to North Carolina in 1771, settled in Jamaica as a merchant. [TNA.AO12.109.204, etc]

MCKOWEN, ARCHIBALD, of Jamaica, graduated MD from Edinburgh University in 1818. [EMG]

MCLACHLAN, DUGALD, sometime in Jamaica, lately in Callart, Argyll, testament, Comm. Argyll, 4 July 1800. [NRS.CC2.3.12/344]

MCLACHLAN, HUGH, a settler on the north-west branch of the Cape Fear River, North Carolina, petitioned the Synod of Argyle for a Gaelic speaking minister, on 2 September 1748. [NRS.NRAS.1209.553]

MCLACHLAN, JAMES, in North Carolina, dead by 1758, brother of Florence McLachlan daughter of Lachlan McLachlan of Strathlachlan, a deed, 1762. [NRS.GD64.1.197]

MACLAE, WALTER EWING, son of Walter Ewing MacLae a merchant in Glasgow, died in Charleston, South Carolina, on 2 September 1797. [GM.67.1069]

MCLAINE, ARCHIBALD, an agreement to settle 100 families in Virginia, dated 1784. [NRS.GD174.175]

MCLAINE, HECTOR, in New York, a letter describing a shipwreck in which he lost all his family, dated 1776. [NRS.GD174.130]

MCLAREN, ALEXANDER, born 1707, a cook and butcher from Muthill, Perthshire, an indentured servant bound via London to Jamaica, 7 August 1731. [CLRO]

MCLAREN, ALEXANDER, born 1783, son of James McLaren [1733-1806], died in Jamaica on 17 January 1808, buried there. [Moulin gravestone, Perthshire]

MCLARTY, ARCHIBALD, a settler on the north-west branch of the Cape Fear River, North Carolina, petitioned the Synod of Argyle for a Gaelic speaking minister, on 2 September 1748. [NRS.NRAS.1209.553]

MCLARTY, JOHN, emigrated from Campbeltown, Argyll, aboard the Edinburgh of Campbeltown, master John McMichael, in July 1771 bound for Prince Edward Island. [NRS.SC54.2.106]

MACLAUCHLAN, JAMES A., the supervisor of 'the great road leading to Canada' a report to Sir Howard Douglas, Lieutenant Governor of New Brunswick, dated 30 December 1826. [NRS.GD45.Section 3.451]

MCLEAN, ARCHIBALD, born in Mull, a surgeon in New York, lately in Jamaica, a will dated in 1772. [NRS.GD174.159-160]

MCLEAN, Captain COLIN, of the 42nd Regiment, deceased, his widow Helen McLean in Fort William, testament 28 November 1801, Comm. Argyll, [NRS.CC2.3.13/23]

MCLEAN, DANIEL, from Scotland to Cumberland County, North Carolina, a Loyalist in 1776, died in Jamaica. [TNA.AO12.100.282]

MCLEAN, JOHN, a merchant in Norfolk, Virginia, who returned to Britain in 1774. [TNA.AO13.31.331]

MCLEAN, JOSEPH, emigrated from Campbeltown, Argyll, aboard the Edinburgh of Campbeltown, master John McMichael, in July 1771 bound for Prince Edward Island. [NRS.SC54.2.106]

MCLEAN, LAUCHLIN, Collector of Customs in Philadelphia, a letter of attorney dated 1773. [NLS.Ch.3906]

MCLEAN, MALCOLM, arrived in Boston, New England, on 30 October 1773, with his wife, also his mother in law and John Livingstone his father in law, settled in New Boston, a letter to John MacLaine, tacksman of Gruline, Mull, dated 20 December 1773. [NRS.GD174.1294]; a letter to John McLean a farmer in the parish of Glenbuy, dated 1773. [NRS.GD174.1294]

MCLEARAN, ..., a settler on the north-west branch of the Cape Fear River, North Carolina, petitioned the Synod of Argyle for a Gaelic speaking minister, on 2 September 1748. [NRS.NRAS.1209.553]

MCLELLAN, JOHN, born in St Ninian's, Stirlingshire, a farmer who emigrated to America in 1775, settled in Cambridge, Albany County, New York, a Loyalist who returned to Scotland by 1782. [TNA.AO13.56.107]

MCLELLAN, JOHN, emigrated from Scotland to America as an apprentice storekeeper in 1768, later a merchant in Hillsborough, North Carolina, a Loyalist, moved via Nova Scotia to London by 1784. [TNA.AO12.101.38, etc]

MCLEOD, DONALD, the elder, settled in Charlotte County, New Brunswick, in 1804. [PANB.MC1672]

MCLEOD, GEORGE, settled in Charlotte County, New Brunswick, in 1804. [PANB.MC1672]

MCLEOD, HUGH, settled in Charlotte County, New Brunswick, in 1804. [PANB.MC1672]

MCLEOD, JANE, a widow, settled in Charlotte County, New Brunswick, in 1804. [PANB.MC1672]

MCLEOD, JOHN, emigrated from Scotland to North Carolina in 1753 with his father Alexander McLeod, a Loyalist, via Charleston and New York to Shelburne, Nova Scotia, at Halifax on 16 February 1786. [PAO.LC.491]

MCLEOD, JOHN, of New York, a student at King's College, Aberdeen, in 1785. [KCA]

MCLEOD, JOHN, brother of Roderick McLeod in Skye, a minister and planter in Cumberland County, North Carolina, died at sea in 1779 or 1780. [TNA.AO13.95.464]

MCLEOD, NEIL, settled in Charlotte County, New Brunswick, in 1804. [PANB.MC1672]

MCLEOD, NORMAN, a merchant in Boston, Massachusetts, invoices from 1761 until 1765. [NRS.NRAS.0623]

MCLEOD, NORMAN, born on Skye, died in Montreal, Quebec, on 27 January 1796. [GM.66.614]

MCLEOD, RODERICK, born in Scotland, a resident of Carolina, Georgia, and East Florida for 12 years as a trader, a Loyalist, moved to Shelburne, Nova Scotia, by 1786. [TNA.AO13.80.319]

MCLEOD, WILLIAM, settled in Charlotte County, New Brunswick, in 1804. [PANB.MC1672]

MCLEONAN, ..., emigrated from Campbeltown, Argyll, aboard the Edinburgh of Campbeltown, master John McMichael, in July 1771 bound for Prince Edward Island. [NRS.SC54.2.106]

MACLOUGHLIN, DAVID, of Canada, graduated MD from Edinburgh University in 1810. [EMG]

MCMASTER, DANIEL, from Galloway, in New Hampshire collecting his brothers' debts, in Halifax, and St John, 26 December 1785. [PAO.LC.15]

MCMASTER, JAMES, born in Galloway, emigrated to Boston in 1765, a merchant there and in Portsmouth, New Hampshire, a Loyalist in 1776. [TNA.AO12.12.23]; settled in Shelburne, Nova Scotia, by 26 December 1785. [PAO.LC.15]

MCMASTER, JOHN, born in Galloway, emigrated to Boston in 1768, a merchant there and in Portsmouth, New Hampshire, a Loyalist in 1776. [TNA.AO12.12.23]; moved to London. [PAO.LC.15]

MCMASTER, PATRICK, born in Galloway, emigrated to Boston in 1767, a merchant there and in Portsmouth, New Hampshire, a Loyalist in 1776. [TNA.AO12.12.23]; a merchant in Halifax by 26 December 1785. [PAO.LC.15]

MACMORAN, HUGH, in Tobago, a deed, dated 22 October 1778. [NRS.RD2.224/2.576]

MCMULLIN, DONALD, emigrated from Scotland to America in 1773, settled on Johnson's Bush, Tryon County, New York, a Loyalist soldier, settled on River Raisin. [PAO.LC.1066]

MCMURCHIE, DONALD, a settler on the north-west branch of the Cape Fear River, North Carolina, petitioned the Synod of Argyle for a Gaelic speaking minister, on 2 September 1748. [NRS.NRAS.1209.553]

MCMURDO, GEORGE, in Enrick, Dumfries-shire, father of George, Thomas, and Charles James, in Virginia, letters, from 1770 to 1797. [NLS.Acc.7199, box 40]; testament, 1801. [NRS.Comm.Kirkcudbright]

MCNAB, DUNCAN, in Northampton County, Virginia in September 1667. [Northampton County Order Book, 1666-1674, fo.40]

MCNAB, JOHN, at Niagara, a letter, dated 1802. [NRS. NRAS. Blairs]

MACNAB, Mr and Mrs, in Jamaica, a deed with Walter Monteath, dated 14 May 1808. [NRS.RD4.322.380]

MCNAUGHTON, RONALD, a settler on the north-west branch of the Cape Fear River, North Carolina, petitioned the Synod of Argyle for a Gaelic speaking minister, on 2 September 1748. [NRS.NRAS.1209.553]

MCNEA, JOHN, in Tobago, a bond, dated 8 August 1769. [NRS.RD2.224/2.646]

MCNEILL, ARCHIBALD, a settler on the north-west branch of the Cape Fear River, North Carolina, petitioned the Synod of Argyle for a Gaelic speaking minister, on 2 September 1748. [NRS.NRAS.1209.553]

MCNEIL, Captain DONALD, from North Uist, settled at Mira River, Cape Breton, a letter to his brother, Captain William McNeil in Newton, North Uist, dated June 1849. [NRS.GD403.27.2]

MCNEILL, DANIEL, in Wilmington, a deed, dated 2 October 1792. [NRS.RD3.258.193]

MCNEILL, DONALD, a settler on the north-west branch of the Cape Fear River, North Carolina, petitioned the Synod of Argyle for a Gaelic speaking minister, on 2 September 1748. [NRS.NRAS.1209.553]

MCNEILL, HECTOR, [1], a settler on the north-west branch of the Cape Fear River, North Carolina, petitioned the Synod of Argyle for a Gaelic speaking minister, on 2 September 1748. [NRS.NRAS.1209.553]

MCNEILL, HECTOR, [2], a settler on the north-west branch of the Cape Fear River, North Carolina, petitioned the Synod of Argyle for a Gaelic speaking minister, on 2 September 1748. [NRS.NRAS.1209.553]

MCNEILL, HECTOR, [3], a settler on the north-west branch of the Cape Fear River, North Carolina, petitioned the Synod of Argyle for a Gaelic speaking minister, on 2 September 1748. [NRS.NRAS.1209.553]

MCNEIL, HECTOR, from Kingerloch, died in Pictou, Nova Scotia, in 1810. [GM.80.395]

MCNEILL, JAMES, born around 1734, emigrated to Virginia in 1762, later a planter in North Carolina and a merchant in Halifax County, North Carolina, a Loyalist who returned to Scotland.
[TNA.AO12.91.32, etc]

MCNEILL, LACHLAN, a settler on the north-west branch of the Cape Fear River, North Carolina, petitioned the Synod of Argyle for a Gaelic speaking minister, on 2 September 1748.
[NRS.NRAS.1209.553]

MCNEILL, MALCOLM, a settler on the north-west branch of the Cape Fear River, North Carolina, petitioned the Synod of Argyle for a Gaelic speaking minister, on 2 September 1748.
[NRS.NRAS.1209.553]

MCNEILL, NEILL, [1], a settler on the north-west branch of the Cape Fear River, North Carolina, petitioned the Synod of Argyle for a Gaelic speaking minister, on 2 September 1748.
[NRS.NRAS.1209.553]

MCNEILL, NEILL, [2], a settler on the north-west branch of the Cape Fear River, North Carolina, petitioned the Synod of Argyle for a Gaelic speaking minister, on 2 September 1748.
[NRS.NRAS.1209.553]

MCNEILL, N., in St Kitts, an agreement with William Reeves, dated 19 February 1799. [NRS.RD4.267.1096]

MCNEILL, TORQUIL, a settler on the north-west branch of the Cape Fear River, North Carolina, petitioned the Synod of Argyle for a Gaelic speaking minister, on 2 September 1748.
[NRS.NRAS.1209.553]

MCNEILL, WILLIAM, a settler on the north-west branch of the Cape Fear River, North Carolina, petitioned the Synod of Argyle for a Gaelic speaking minister, on 2 September 1748.
[NRS.NRAS.1209.553]

MCNEILL, ..., a settler on the north-west branch of the Cape Fear River, North Carolina, petitioned the Synod of Argyle for a Gaelic speaking minister, on 2 September 1748. [NRS.NRAS.1209.553]

MCNEILL, ..., in St Kitts, a deed, dated 6 June 1762. [NRS.RD4.226.817]

MCPHADZEAN, ANGUS, a planter in Westmoreland, Jamaica, son of the late Duncan McPhadzean, from Kilmartin, Argyll, a tidewaiter in Greenock, an Edict of Executry, 9 December 1785. [NRS.CC8.8.88/14][NRS.CC2.3.12/65]

MCPHAILE, DUGALD, a settler on the north-west branch of the Cape Fear River, North Carolina, petitioned the Synod of Argyle for a Gaelic speaking minister, on 2 September 1748. [NRS.NRAS.1209.553]

MCPHAILE, JOHN, [1], a settler on the north-west branch of the Cape Fear River, North Carolina, petitioned the Synod of Argyle for a Gaelic speaking minister, on 2 September 1748. [NRS.NRAS.1209.553]

MCPHAILE, JOHN, [2], a settler on the north-west branch of the Cape Fear River, North Carolina, petitioned the Synod of Argyle for a Gaelic speaking minister, on 2 September 1748. [NRS.NRAS.1209.553]

MACPHERSON, ALEXANDER, of Antigua, graduated MD from Glasgow University in 1785. [RGG]

MACPHERSON, ANDREW, of Balchor, in America, a letter, dated 1782. [NRS.NRAS.0771]

MCPHERSON, CATHERINE, in Quebec, a deed of attorney in favour of Alexander McDonald, dated 1 September 1783. [NRS.RD4.235.19]

MCPHERSON, DONALD, in Jamaica, later in Strathdearn, testament 24 May 1803. [NRS. Comm. Inverness]

MCPHERSON, JAMES, the Secretary of West Florida, a letter dated 1764. [NRS.NRAS.01631]

MCPHERSON, JOHN, a settler on the north-west branch of the Cape Fear River, North Carolina, petitioned the Synod of Argyle for a Gaelic speaking minister, on 2 September 1748. [NRS.NRAS.1209.553]

MCQUEEN, ARCHIBALD, in Miramachi, a letter dated 1820. [NLS.ms791]

MCQUEEN, JAMES, born 1798, a blacksmith from Kilmadock, Perthshire, emigrated to Canada in 1822, settled in Esquesing in 1824, but moved to Pilkington, Upper Canada, in 1846. [Wellington County Museum]

MCRAE, ALEXANDER, son of Alexander McRae in Kingston, Jamaica, a student at King's College, Aberdeen, 1793 to 1797. [KCA]

MCRAE, FARQUHAR, of Inverinate, born 1764, a doctor in China later in Demerara, Lieutenant Colonel of the Demerara Militia, died in 1806. [History of Clan Macrae, 1899, 104]

MCRAE, GEORGE, a merchant in Norfolk, Virginia, a Loyalist in 1776. [TNA.AO13.123.129]

MCRAE, WILLIAM GORDON, son of Adam Gordon in Jamaica, a student at King's College, Aberdeen, 1785 to 1788. [KCA]

MCROBBIE, JOHN, of Jamaica, graduated MD from Edinburgh University in 1824. [EMG]

MCSHENOIG, HECTOR, emigrated from Campbeltown, Argyll, aboard the Edinburgh of Campbeltown, master John McMichael, in July 1771 bound for Prince Edward Island. [NRS.SC54.2.106]

MCTAVISH, D., from Stratherick, a partner of the North West Company of Canada, was drowned in the River Columbia, near Cape Disappointment on 22 May 1815. [GM.85.376]

MCVICAR, JAMES, in Jamaica, a deed of factory, 14 September 1771. [NRS.RD4.210/2.550]; a deed of factory with H. S. Wyllie, 9 July 1800. [NRS.RD4.268.552]

MCVICAR, JOHN, emigrated from Campbeltown, Argyll, aboard the Edinburgh of Campbeltown, master John McMichael, in July 1771 bound for Prince Edward Island. [NRS.SC54.2.106]

MCVICAR, JOHN, a carpenter from Argyll, in Jamaica by 1806. [ABLibrary-Kilberry pp]

MCVIE, ANDREW, from Greenock to St John, New Brunswick, in 1803, settled in Sussex Vale. [PANB.mc1672]

MCWHANN, WILLIAM, settled in Blandford, Virginia, as a merchant in 1763, a partner in John Baird and Company, a Loyalist in 1776, in London by 1779. [TNA.AO12.109.210]

MCWILLIAM, DUNCAN, with three others, emigrated from Campbeltown, Argyll, aboard the Edinburgh of Campbeltown, master John McMichael, in July 1771 bound for Prince Edward Island. [NRS.SC54.2.106]

MABEN, MATTHEW, in Petersburg, Virginia, brother of John Maben in Dumfries, a copy will dated 1818. [NRS.NRAS.0118]

MADDOX, THOMAS H., of America, graduated MD from Edinburgh University in 1816. [EMG]

MAIR, JAMES, of the West Indies, graduated MD at Edinburgh University in 1795. [EMG]

MAITLAND, RICHARD, at Quebec, a letter to his brother Colonel Maitland, 1759. [NRS.NRAS.0631]

MAITLAND, WILLIAM, emigrated to Virginia in 1771, a merchant in Williamsburg, a Loyalist who moved to London by 1777. [TNA.AO13.31.344]

MALCOLM, JOHN, of Portalloch, Argyll, a merchant in Jamaica, died in 1773.

MALCOLM, WILLIAM, a millwright and carpenter in Kingston, Jamaica, later in Dunmore, testament, 29 January 1814, Comm. Stirling. [NRS]

MALLONEY, DANIEL THOMAS, of Barbados, graduated MD from Edinburgh University in 1805. [EMG]

MANSON, WILLIAM, a former shipmaster who settled as a planter in St Paul's parish, Georgia, in 1774, a Loyalist, moved via Charleston, South Carolina, to England in 1781, settled in Kirkwall, Orkney, Scotland, by 1783. [TNA.AO12.100.28, etc]; Papers from 1771 until 1782. [NRS.NRAS.1015]

MARCH, WILLIAM, of Jamaica, graduated MD from Edinburgh University in 1802. [EMG]

MARSHALL, JOHN, a mason in Aberdeen, brother-german of James Marshall deceased innkeeper in Charleston, South Carolina, sons of James Marshall a merchant in Stonehaven, Kincardineshire and his wife Jean Rhind, a deed, 5 May 1767. [ACA.APB.2]

MARSHALL, JOHN, in Halifax, [Nova Scotia?], a deed of attorney in favour of A. Moneypenny, dated 8 July 1782. [NRS.RD4.233.163]

MARSHALL, JOHN, in Jamaica, a deed, dated 1 May 1782. [NRS.RD3.242.875]

MARSHALL, JOHN, a planter in South Carolina, papers from 1796 until 1819. [NRS.NRAS.1232]

MARSHALL, LEWIS, of Virginia, a medical student at Edinburgh University 1794-1795. [EUL]

MARSHALL, SAMUEL, emigrated from Skye to North Carolina before 1756, settled in Wilmington, N.C., moved to London by 1780. [TNA.AO12.3.218, etc]

MARSHALL, THOMAS, of South Carolina, a medical student at Edinburgh University 1790-1791. [EUL]

MARSHALL, WILLIAM, of Virginia, a medical student at Edinburgh University, 1758. [Medicine in Virginia in the Eighteenth Century, p86, Richmond, 1931]

MARTIN, JAMES, born in Dundee, Scotland, emigrated to Charleston, South Carolina, in 1771, settled in Savannah, Georgia, as a baker and merchant, returned to Dundee in 1776. [TNA.AO12.109.206]

MARTIN, JOHN, in Cupar, and his wife Elspeth Pearson, were found guilty of rioting at Mylnefield, and banished to the American Plantations for life, with seven years' service there, at Perth in June 1773. [SM.35.332]

MARTIN, SAMUEL, a farmer in Anson County, North Carolina, a Loyalist soldier, in London in 1783. [TNA.AO12.37.37, etc]

MARTIN, SAMUEL, of New York, graduated MD at Edinburgh University in 1765. [EMG]

MARYE, WILLIAM, of Virginia, a medical student at Edinburgh University, 1758. ['Medicine in Virginia in the Eighteenth Century, p.86, Richmond, 1931]

MATHER, BENJAMIN, son of Reverend Cotton Mather DD in Boston, New England, graduated MA from Glasgow University in 1731. [RGG]

MATHER, ..., a minister in North America, possibly Samuel son of Cotton Mather, BA Harvard in 1723, graduated DD at Marischal College, Aberdeen, on 17 March 1762. [MCA]

MATHESON, JOHN, settled in Charlotte County, New Brunswick, in 1804. [PANB.MC1672]

MAXWELL, DANIEL, a merchant in Beaufort County, North Carolina, was murdered on 27 November 1775, brother of Archibald Martin a writer in Edinburgh, [TNA.AO13.95.567]

MAXWELL, ELISHA, a settler on the north-west branch of the Cape Fear River, North Carolina, petitioned the Synod of Argyle for a Gaelic speaking minister, on 2 September 1748. [NRS.NRAS.1209.553]

MAXWELL, JAMES, of South Carolina, a medical student at Edinburgh University in 1786, graduated MA at King's College, Aberdeen, on 30 March 1779, and MD in 1790. [EUL][KCA]

MAXWELL, JOHN, Governor of the Bahamas, a letter from Alexander Gillon, Commodore of the Navy of South Carolina, dated 7 May 1782. [HMC. American. ii.483]

MAXWELL, JOSEPH WILLIAM, of America, graduated MD from Edinburgh University in 1803. [EMG]

MAXWELL, MARIE, born 1614, a passenger aboard the Amity bound from London to St Kitts on 13 October 1635. [TNA.E157.20]

MAXWELL, PATRICK, in Grenada, a deed, 6 July 1789. [NRS.RD4.246.229]

MAYCOCK, JAMES D., of Barbados, graduated MD from Edinburgh University in 1811. [EMG]

MAYHEW, JONATHAN, a minister in Boston, Massachusetts, graduated DD at King's College, Aberdeen, on 25 December 1749. [KCA]

MEADE, RICHARD EVERARD, of Virginia, graduated MD at Edinburgh University in 1800. [EMG]

MELVILLE, ADAM, from Edinburgh, now in Jamaica, a deed, 10 July 1764. [NRS.RD2.198.705]

MELVILLE, ALEXANDER, of St Vincent, graduated MD at King's College, Aberdeen, on 26 December 1795, graduated MD from Edinburgh University in 1801. [KCA][GEU]

MELVILLE, ALEXANDER, of the West Indies, graduated MD at Edinburgh University in 1801. [EMG]

MELVILLE, JOHN, of St Vincent, graduated MD from Edinburgh University in 1811. [EMG]

MELVILLE, ROBERT, late Governor General of Jamaica, 1772. [NRS.RS27.200.240]

MENZIES, ARCHIBALD, of Culdair, a Customs Commissioner in Scotland, married Fanny Rutherford, only daughter of John Rutherford, in North Carolina, on 17 October 1776. [GM.46.530]

MENZIES, ARCHIBALD, in Jamaica, a deed of factory with Colin Menzies, dated 10 December 1809. [NRS.RD3.333.971]

MENZIES, JOHN, settled in Georgia, a Loyalist, moved to St John, New Brunswick, died there in 1786. [TNA.AO13.21.300]

MERRILEES, JAMES, in Savannah, Georgia, a deed of attorney, dated 12 March 1792. [NRS.RD2.255.26]

MERIWEATHER, CHARLES, born in 1766, of Virginia, graduated MD at Edinburgh University in 1792, died in 1843. [EMG]

MICHIE. HARRY, a merchant in Charleston, South Carolina, a Loyalist in 1776, moved via the West Indies to England by 1784. [TNA.AO12.50.417, etc]

MICHIE, JAMES, a merchant in Charleston, South Carolina, letters to Sir Alexander of Dean between 1745 and 1747, [NRS.GD237.box 10, bundle 2]; was appointed as a Councillor of South Carolina on 24 June 1755, [JCTP.62,264]; a planter in Camden District, South Carolina, deceased by 1784. [TNA.AO12.28.95, etc]

MIDDLETON, Dr PETER, in New York, re a tack to Archibald Douglas of the mansion house of Barnsdale, in the parish of Newbattle, dated 14 May 1770. [NRS.RD2.212.386]; in New York, a deed of attorney in favour of William Donaldson, dated 6 March 1780. [NRS.RD3,229.370]; in New York, a deed of attorney in favour of P. Rolland, dated 20 June 1775. [NRS.RD2.235/2.730]

MIGNOT, DAVID, of Jamaica, graduated MD from Edinburgh University in 1813. [EMG]

MILL, DAVID, in Tobago, a deed, dated 11 January 1776. [NRS.RD2.232/2.613]

MILLAR, ARCHIBALD, from Greenock to St John, New Brunswick, in 1803. [PANB.mc1672]

MILLER, ARCHIBALD, born in Scotland, settled in the West Indies as a mason from 1769 until1781. [TNA.AO100.348]

MILLER, GEORGE, emigrated from Scotland to Virginia in 1758, moved to North Carolina in 1763, a merchant in Dobbs County, N.C., a Loyalist, moved to Dumfries, Scotland by 1782. [TNA.AO12.36.174, etc]

MILLER, HUGH, in Virginia, a deed, 3 July 1718. [NRS.RD2.224/1.234]

MILLER, JAMES, late merchant in New Providence in the Bahamas, later in Edinburgh, executor for Reeves Fowler late of New Providence, a summons in 1815. [NRS.GD63.478]; also, versus Elizabeth Fowler, wife of Dr Mitchell in Virginia, 27 October 1815.

MILLER, JOHN, of Seamill, husband of Elizabeth Muir, sasines in Bute, 6 May 1653. [NRS.RS9.3.126/127]

MILLAR, MATTHEW, a periwig maker in Barbados, was admitted as a burgess and guilds-brother of Ayr on 7 September 1748. [ABR]

MILLER, SAMUEL, son of Francis Miller a merchant in Barbados, a student at King's College, Aberdeen, from 1798 to 1799, graduated MA, graduated MD from Edinburgh University in 1802. [KCA][EMG]

MILLAR, WILLIAM, of Antigua, graduated MA from Glasgow University in 1767. [RGG]

MILLAR, Dr WILLIAM, in Antigua, was admitted as a burgess and guilds-brother of Ayr on 17 October 1767. [ABR]

MILLER, WILLIAM, emigrated to New England in 1771, Deputy Customs Controller at Newbury Piscataqua, a Loyalist in 1776, returned to Glasgow. [TNA.AO12.81.44]

MILLIGAN, ROBERT LINDSAY, of America, graduated MD from Edinburgh University in 1822. [EMG]

MILNE, GEORGE, graduated MD from Yale in 1785, and MD from Marischal College, Aberdeen, in 1784. [SNQ.XII.95]

MINOR, CHARLES, of Virginia, graduated MD at Edinburgh University in 1793. [EMG][VHS][UVC]

MINTO, Dr WALTER, arrived in Philadelphia, Pennsylvania, on 1 August 1786, a letter. [HMC.Laing.ii.524]

MITCHELL, ALEXANDER G., of Virginia, graduated MD from Edinburgh University in 1811. [EMG]

MITCHELL, HENRY, born in Scotland, a factor in Fredericksburg, Virginia, for twenty years, for McCall, Smillie and Company, merchants in Glasgow, a Loyalist who returned to Glasgow by 1784. [TNA.AO13.31.635]

MITCHELL, JAMES, in Weathersfield, Kentucky, New England, a deed, dated 12 August 1752. [NRS.RD4.178/2.198]

MITCHELL, JAMES, youngest son of Alexander Mitchell, died at Morant Bay, Jamaica in May 1767. [ACA.APB.3]

MITCHELL, JOHN, a merchant in St Augustine, East Florida, trading with timber from Mississippi, papers, from 1776 to 1778. [NRS.NRAS.0159]

MITCHELL, JOHN, of Carolina, graduated MD from Glasgow University in 1787. [RGG]

MITCHELL, JOHN, in Jamaica, a deed, dated 25 January 1791. [NRS.RD2.252.108]

MITCHELL, ROBERT CARY, of Virginia, a medical student at Edinburgh University in 1784. [EUL]

MITCHELL, SAMUEL LATHAM, born in 1764, of New York, graduated MD at Edinburgh University in 1786, died in 1831. [EMG]

MITCHELSON, DAVID, in New York, a deed of factory, dated 18 October 1790. [NRS.RD2.250.950]

MOFFAT Dr THOMAS, born in Scotland, a physician who was educated at Edinburgh University, emigrated to America in 1729, settled in Connecticut as Customs Controller of New London, brother of John Moffat in Boston, [probate 21 November 1777]; a Loyalist in 1776, moved to London, died there on 23 March 1787. [TNA.AO12.82.1] [GM.57.278]

MOIR, HENRY, in Tortula, a probative letter, dated 18 September 1775. [NRS.RD2.236/1.499]

MONCRIEFF, Sir JOHN, of Moncrieff, a sasine, dated 30 June 1626, Nova Scotia. [NRS.RS1.19.259]

MONCREIFF, JOHN, a merchant in Charleston, South Carolina, before 1776, moved to England by 1778. [TNA.AO13.131.452]

MONCREIFF, PHILIP, son of Colonel Moncreiff, a merchant in Virginia before 1776, a loyalist, bound for India in 1778. [TNA.AO13.31.640]

MONCREIFF, ROBERT, in St Vincent, letters to his brother Archibald Wellwood in Baltimore, Maryland, from 1773 until 1799. [NRS.NRAS.0333]

MONTEITH, WILLIAM, in Jamaica, a deed, dated 21 October 1777. [NRS.RD4.237.607]

MONTGOMERY, HUGH, with four others, emigrated from Campbeltown, Argyll, aboard the Edinburgh of Campbeltown, master John McMichael, in July 1771 bound for Prince Edward Island. [NRS.SC54.2.106]

MONTGOMERY, JAMES, Lord Advocate of Scotland, applied for a grant of three small islands off Prince Edward Island, a memorial dated 1772. [JCTP.79.106]

MONTGOMERY, JAMES, a merchant in New York, later in Urr, testament, 19 August 1801, Comm. Dumfries. [NRS]

MONTGOMERIE, JAMES, was appointed Governor of Dominica on 21 December 1808. [NRS.GD142.45]

MONTGOMERY, NEIL, emigrated from Campbeltown, Argyll, aboard the Edinburgh of Campbeltown, master John McMichael, in July 1771 bound for Prince Edward Island. [NRS.SC54.2.106]

MONTGOMERY, Sir ROBERT, of Skelmorlie, a sasine, dated 29 December 1628, Nova Scotia. [NRS.RS1.25.112]

MONTGOMERY, THOMAS, a merchant in Norfolk, Virginia, before 1776, a Loyalist who settled in Coylsfield, Ayr, by 1781. [TNA.AO12.106.47]

MONTGOMERY, KERR, and Company in Virginia, a deed, dated 14 December 1763. [NRS.RD4.197/2.369]

MOODIE, ROBERT, in Jamaica, a deed, dated 17 January 1774. [NRS.RD3.233.38]

MOORE, CHARLES, born in 1724, of Pennsylvania, a medical student in Edinburgh from 1748, graduated MD at Edinburgh University in 1752, died in 1801. [NRS.GD24.1.833][EMG]

MOORE, WILLIAM, of New York, graduated MD at Edinburgh University in 1780. [EMG]

MOORES, DANIEL, born in 1745, of Maryland, graduated MD at Edinburgh University in 1787, died in 1802. [EMG]

MORGAN, GEORGE THOMSON, son of James Morgan a merchant in Jamaica, a student at King's College, Aberdeen, from 1821 to 1825, graduated MA, a Licentiate of the Royal College of Surgeons in Edinburgh, later a surgeon and an author. [KCA]

MORGAN, JOHN, (1735-1789), of Pennsylvania, graduated MD at Edinburgh University in 1763. [EMG][CPP]

MORRIS, BENJAMIN, of Pennsylvania, a medical student at Edinburgh University in 1748. [NRS.GD24.1.833]

MORRIS, JAMES MAURY, of Virginia, graduated MD from Edinburgh University in 1805. [EMG]

MORRIS, JOHN G., born in New York, eldest son of John Morris a merchant, matriculated at Glasgow University in 1819, graduated BA in 1822. [RGG]

MORRIS, WILLIAM, and his wife Elizabeth Cochrane, in Perth, Upper Canada, letters, from 1825 until 1828. [NRS.NRAS.0362].

MORRISON, ALEXANDER, a merchant in Newcastle on the St John's River, East Florida, a Loyalist, returned to Greenock, Scotland, by 1788. [TNA.AO9913.7.88, etc]

MORRISON, ANGUS, settled in Charlotte County, New Brunswick, in 1804. [PANB.MC1672]

MORRISON, HUGH, settled in Charlotte County, New Brunswick, in 1804. [PANB.MC1672]

MORRISON, JAMES, a physician in Jamaica, graduated MD at Marischal College, Aberdeen, in 176-. [MCA]

MORRISON, JOHN, settled in Charlotte County, New Brunswick, in 1804. [PANB.MC1672]

MORRISON, MALCOLM, emigrated to America in 1762, settled in Fredericksburgh, Dutchess County, New York, as a merchant, a Loyalist in 1776, moved in 1783 to Nova Scotia, died by 1786. [TNA.AO12.22.1]

MORRISON, NORMAN, of Connecticut, a medical student at Edinburgh University in 1730. [EUL]

MORRISON, PETER, settled in Charlotte County, New Brunswick, in 1804. [PANB.MC1672]

MORRISON, RODERICK, settled in Charlotte County, New Brunswick, in 1804. [PANB.MC1672]

MORISON, ….., a planter in Tobago, deeds etc, from 1804 until 1830. [NMM.C104.178-180]

MORSE, JEDIDIAH, a minister in Charleston, South Carolina, graduated DD at Edinburgh University on 28 July 1794. [GEU]

MORSON, WALTER S., of Antigua, graduated MD from Edinburgh University in 1821. [EMG]

MORTIMER, WILLIAM, in Antigua, died at sea, testament 12 June 1819, Comm. Moray. [NRS]

MORTON, SAMUEL GEORGE, of America, graduated MD from Edinburgh University in 1823. [EMG]

MOULTRIE, JAMES, of South Carolina, graduated MD at Edinburgh University in 1788. [EMG]

MOULTRIE, JOHN, born in 1729, of South Carolina, graduated MD at Edinburgh University in 1749, died in 1798. [EMG]

MOULTRIE, JOHN, to East Florida in 1767, a planter there, was appointed Lieutenant Governor there in 1771, a Loyalist, to London by 1786. [TNA.AO12.3.393]

MUDIE, ALEXANDER, in Jamaica, a deed of factory with William Mudie, dated 19 July 1810. [NRS.RD3.336.705]

MUIR, GEORGE, emigrated from Scotland to America, a planter in Georgia and in Virginia, in London by 1779. [TNA.AO13.31.650]

MUIR, JOHN, of Antigua, graduated MD from Glasgow University in 1790. [RGG]; MUIR, Dr JOHN, of Antigua, was admitted as a burgess and guilds-brother of Ayr on 2 October 1790. [ABR]

MUIR, JOHN, late of Quebec, residing in Dalserf House, testament, 15 October 1823. [NRS]

MUIR, WILLIAM, in Lynchburg and in Richmond, Virginia, letters to his aunt in Kirkcudbright, Scotland, dated from 1796 until 1815. [NRS.NRAS.0118]

MUIR, WILLIAM, in Grenada, a deed, dated 24 January 1786. [NRS.GD4.239.287]

MUNN, ALEXANDER, emigrated via Greenock aboard the Murdoch, master Archibald Orr, for Virginia in 1769, later settled as a merchant in Wake County, North Carolina, a Loyalist in 1777, moved to London by 1784. [TNA.AO12.35.1, etc]; in Halifax, or St John's, on 17 December 1785. [PAO.LC.67]

MONROE, DANIEL, was proposed for the Council of Jamaica on 20 October 1753. [JCTP.61/2]

MUNROW, DANIEL, a settler on the north-west branch of the Cape Fear River, North Carolina, petitioned the Synod of Argyle for a Gaelic speaking minister, on 2 September 1748. [NRS.NRAS.1209.553]

MUNRO, GEORGE, born in 1760, of Delaware, a student of medicine at Edinburgh University, graduated MD in 1786, died in 1819. [EUL]

MUNRO, H., in Jamaica, a deed of factory, dated 27 September 1788. [NRS.RD4.246.353]

MUNRO, Dr HARRY, a clergyman in Albany and a military chaplain before and after the Revolution, moved to Stirling, Scotland by 1788, [TNA.AO12.24.36]; in New York, a deed of settlement, dated 17 July 1797. [NRS.RD3.289.704]; a will, dated 17 July 1797. [NRS.RD3.289.717]

MUNRO, JAMES, in Grenada, a probative will, dated 7 January 1779. [NRS.RD3.242.460]

MUNRO, JOHN, a settler on the north-west branch of the Cape Fear River, North Carolina, petitioned the Synod of Argyle for a Gaelic speaking minister, on 2 September 1748. [NRS.NRAS.1209.553]

MUNRO, JOHN, in New York, a deed of factory with John McKenzie, 1 August 1801. [NRS.RD3.290.467]

MUNRO, ROBERT H., in Jamaica, a deed, dated 3 September 1793. [NRS.RD3.263.659]

MUNRO, WILLIAM, in Jamaica, later in Forres, testament, 9 November 1809, Comm. Moray. [NRS]

MURDOCH, ANDREW, probably from Moray, in Philadelphia, a letter dated 1785. [NRS.GD248.box 354. Bundle 4]

MURRAY, ALEXANDER, in Middlesex County, Virginia, in 1685. [Middlesex County Order Book, 1680-1694, fos.216-217]

MURRAY, Sir ARCHIBALD, of Blackbarony, a sasine, dated 10 October 1628, Nova Scotia. [NRS.RS1.24.421]

MURRAY, CORDELIA, in Quebec, a letter, in 1784. [NLS.Stewart.50]

MURRAY, GEORGE, in Jamaica, a deed of attorney in favour of Jean Murray, dated 13 August 1782. [NRS.RD3.241/2.281], papers from 1811 until 1815. [NLS.Adv.ms46]

MURRAY, JAMES, in Quebec, letters, dated 1764. [NRS.NRAS.0631]

MURRAY, JAMES, in Jamaica, a bond, dated 15 August 1766. [NRS.RD2.236/2.634]

MURRAY, JAMES, a Member of the Council of North Carolina, was suspended from duty by Governor Dobbs, a memorial, dated 15 March 1758, [JCTP.65]; once President of the Council of North Carolina, a Loyalist, died in Halifax, Nova Scotia, before 1784. [TNA.AO12.99.319, etc]

MURRAY, JAMES, born in 1739, of Maryland, a medical student at Glasgow University in 1765 and at Edinburgh University in 1764, died 1819. [EUL]

MURRAY, JAMES, of Demerara, a student at King's College, Aberdeen, around 1800. [KCA]

MURRAY, J., petitioned for land in East Florida on 2 April 1767. [RPCCol.vi.447]

MURRAY, JOHN, in Kingston, Port Royal Harbour, a letter to Patrick Home, surgeon aboard <u>HMS Squirrel</u> at Charleston, South Carolina, a letter dated 1733. [NRS.GD267.3.21]

MURRAY, Dr JOHN, in Charleston, South Carolina, correspondence with his cousin John Murray of Murraywhat, from 1747 to 1763. [NRS.GD219]

MURRAY, JOHN, of Philiphaugh, in Roxburghshire, born 1715, a planter in Savannah, Georgia, a Loyalist, moved to Nova Scotia in 1787, and to Jamaica by 1789. [TNA.AO12.4.268, etc]

MURRAY, J. O., a Loyalist who settled in Jamaica, a letter dated 8 April 1783. [HMC. American.iv.19]

MURRAY, Sir PATRICK, of Elibank, a sasine, dated 23 October 1630, Nova Scotia. [NRS.RS1.29.162]

MURRAY, PETER, of Jamaica, graduated MD from Edinburgh University in 1802. [EMG]

MURRAY, RICHARD, Collector of Customs at Quebec, certificates and letters, from 1767 until 1771. [NLS.Stewart.5025/83, etc]

MURRAY, SAMSON, and Company in New York, a deed of factory in favour of Anthony Barclay, dated 9 August 1786. [NRS.RD3.245.1215]

MURRAY, THOMAS, of Trinidad, graduated MD from Edinburgh University in 1823. [EMG]

MURRAY, WALTER, Deputy Naval Officer of Jamaica in 1770. [JCTP.77]

MURRAY, WILLIAM, of Dunairne, a sasine, dated 30 December 1630, Nova Scotia. [NRS.RS1.29.369]

MURRAY, WILLIAM, from Edinburgh, formerly a merchant in Virginia, died in London on 2 January 1791. [GM.61.91]

MURRAY, WILLIAM, in Hyde Park estate, St Thomas in the Vale, deceased, brother of James Murray an innkeeper in Perth, a letter dated 15 September 1813. [NRS.B59.38.6.257]

MUSGRAVE, ANTONY, of Antigua, graduated MD from Edinburgh University in 1814. [EMG]

MUSHET, ROBERT, in Jamaica, a deed, dated 15 January 1774. [NRS.RD2.218.1162]; a deed, dated 18 December 1776, [NRS.RD2.221/1.842]

MUTCH, ALEXANDER, born 1756 in Aberdeen, to Prince Edward Island in 1786, died at Mount Herbert in 1828. [Crossroads, Christian Church Cemetery, Prince Edward Island]

MYERS, JOSEPH HART, of America, graduated MD at Edinburgh University in 1779. [EMG]

MYRES, LEVI, born in 1768, of South Carolina, a medical student at Edinburgh University in 1785, graduated MD from Glasgow University in 1797, died 1822. [EUL][RGG]

NAPIER, THOMAS, son of Archibald Napier in Tobago, student from 1807 to 1811, graduated MA at King's College, Aberdeen, on 29 March 1811. [KCA]

NAPIER, VALENTINE, in New Kent County, Virginia, in 1677. [York County Order Book]

NAPIER, WILLIAM, a surgeon in Charleston, South Carolina, a sasine in Dunbarton on 24 June 1748. [NRS.RS10.8.2]

NEILSON, ARCHIBALD, settled in North Carolina in 1770, a public official, returned to Britain in 1777, in Dundee by 1788. [TNA.AO.13.349.]

NEILSON, WILLIAM, from Greenock, Renfrewshire, to St John, New Brunswick, in 1803. [PANB.mc1672]

NESBIT, ALEXANDER, of Tobago, a Licentiate of the Royal College of Surgeons in 1813, graduated MD from King's College, Aberdeen, on 7 January 1820. [KCA]

NESBITT, ..., Attorney General of Nova Scotia in 1754. [JCTP.61/2]

NEUFVILLE, THOMAS, of Jamaica, graduated MD at Edinburgh University in 1776. [EMG]

NEUFVILLE, ZACHARY, of South Carolina, graduated MD at Edinburgh University in 1778. [EMG]

NEWBURGH, Lord EDWARD, a sasine, 28 January 1629, Nova Scotia. [NRS.RS1.25.155]

NEWELL, JAMES, of New Jersey, a medical student at Edinburgh University around 1745. [EUL]

NEWTON, HENRY, Collector of Customs in Nova Scotia, letters of attorney, dated 1768, and 1772. [NLS.Stewart.3823/3889]

NEWTON, JOHN, Surveyor of Customs at Halifax, Nova Scotia, letters of attorney, in 1768, and 1772. [NLS.Stewart.3823; 3831; 3892]

NIBBS, HENRY, of Dominica, graduated MD at Edinburgh University in 1796. [EMG]

NICHOLSON, ALEXANDER, born on Skye, Inverness-shire, died on Prince Edward Island on 26 September 1820. [Polly Cemetery, Belfast, PEI]

NICHOLSON, WILLIAM THOMAS, of Nevis, graduated MD from Edinburgh University in 1822. [EMG]

NICOLL, GEORGE, in Jamaica, a bond with George Marshall, dated 24 July 1783. [NRS.RD2.235/1.275]

NICOLL, Dr JOHN, in New York, was admitted as a burgess and guilds-brother of Ayr on10 April 1724. [ABR]

NICOLL, SAMUEL, of America, graduated MD at Edinburgh University in 1776. [EMG][SM.38.622]

NIHILL, LAURENCE, of Antigua, graduated MD at Edinburgh University in 1780. [EMG]

NISBET, CHARLES, in Pennsylvania, a deed of attorney with Alexander Tweedie, on 10 March 1800. [NRS.RD3.286.415]

NISBET, JOHN, in Jamaica, a deed, dated 6 September 1784. [NRS.RD2.238/1.940]

NISBET, JOSEPH, of the West Indies, graduated MD at Edinburgh University in 1768. [EMG]

NISBET, ROBERT, a merchant in Charleston, South Carolina, trading with the Netherlands, a cash book from 1720 to 1723. [NRS.GD237.box 10, bundle 4/1]

NISBET, WILLIAM, Collector of Customs on Prince Edward Island, letters, 1786. [NLS.MS5034.190-198]

NOBLE, RACHEL, spouse of Major Isaac Noble of Ramapough, Bergen County, New Jersey, a compensation claim, 1780s. [NRS.GD531.36]

NOEL, PERRY ECCLESTON, born in 1768, of Maryland, graduated MD at Edinburgh University in 1794, died in 1813. [EMG]

NORIE, JAMES, in Truro, Nova Scotia, correspondence with George Duncan in Elgin, Moray, from 1833 until 1840. [AUL.3015]

NORRIS, HENRY, of Pennsylvania, graduated MD at King's College, Aberdeen, on 7 December 1786. [KCA]

NORRIS, JAMES, master of the brig Rambler of Leith, with 130 passengers, 14 seamen, and a surgeon, from Thurso in September 1807, and Stromness on 1 October 1807, was totally wrecked near the Bay of Bulls, Newfoundland, on 29 October 1807, only 3 passengers, the 2nd mate, and 3 crewmen survived. [Inverness Journal. 13.11.1807]

NORTON, DAVID, a surgeon in Spanish Town, Jamaica, graduated MD at King's College, Aberdeen, on 1 September 1768. [KCA]

NUGENT, NICOLAS, of Antigua, graduated MD from Edinburgh University in 1804. [EMG]

NUTTALL, GEORGE R., of Jamaica, graduated MD from Edinburgh University in 1809. [EMG]

ODLUM, WILLIAM EYRE, of Antigua, graduated MD at St Andrews University on 4 May 1821. [SAU]

O'DONELL, ELLIOT, of America, graduated MD from Edinburgh University in 1821. [EMG]

OGILVIE, CHARLES, emigrated from Scotland to Charleston, South Carolina, a merchant in Charleston and St Augustine, East Florida, a Loyalist, returned to Auchiries, Aberdeenshire, by 1783. [TNA.AO12.48.63, etc]; a letter re the evacuation of Charleston 10 September 1782; a letter from Jamaica dated 8 April 1783. [HMC.American.iii.113/iv.19]

OGILVY, DAVID, from Brechin, Angus, a stone-mason in St John, New Brunswick, died on 9 January 1828, administration 29 October 1828. [PANB]

OGILVY, Sir GEORGE, of Carnousie, a sasine, 30 June 1626, Nova Scotia. [NRS.RS1.19.262]

OGILVIE, GEORGE, in Jamaica, a will, 1 August 1780. [NRS.RD4.249.42]

OGILVIE, GEORGE, emigrated to South Carolina in1774, a planter there, a Loyalist, via St Eustatia to England in 1779. [TNA.AO12.51.227, etc]

OGILVIE, GEORGE, in South Carolina, letters to Mr Forbes of Pitsligo, Aberdeenshire, from 1778 until 1786. [NRS.NRAS.0426]

OGILVIE, Mrs HANNAH, a widow in Charleston, South Carolina, a Loyalist, via Pensacola, West Florida, and Jamaica to England in 1779, settled in Dundee, Scotland, by 1784. [TNA.AO13.133.223]

OGILVIE, JAMES, from Banff, Scotland, to Virginia in 1771, rector of Westover, Charles City, Virginia, from 1772 to 1776, a Loyalist, moved to Surrey, England, by 1784. [TNA.AO12.56.379]

OGILVIE, JAMES, a clergyman in Virginia, graduated DD at King's College, Aberdeen, on 16 May 1781. [KCA]

OGILVIE, Sir JOHN, of Innerquharitie, Angus, a sasine, dated 23 July 1627, Nova Scotia. [NRS.RS1.22.9]

OGILVIE, JOHN, graduated BA from Yale in 1748, and DD from Marischal College, Aberdeen, in 1769. [SNQ.XII.95]

OGILVIE, PATRICK, emigrated via London aboard the Patience and Judith bound for Boston, New England, 30 June 1716. [NWI.I.463]

OGILVIE, PETER, a blacksmith at Bryer Creek, Georgia, moved to Halifax, Nova Scotia, by 1786. [TNA.AO13.25.342]

OGILVY, WILLIAM, emigrated to South Carolina in 1764, settled in Ninety-Six District, Secretary to the Superintendent of Indian Affairs for the Southern District from 1765 to 1775, moved to England in 1775, settled at Newton Mill, Forfar, Angus, by 1790. [TNA.AO12.47.141, etc]

OLIPHANT, Dr DAVID, in Jamaica, a deed of attorney, 5 May 1772. [NRS.RD3.235.265]; letters, 1789. [TNA.AO13.88.96]

OLIPHANT, DAVID, in Jamaica, a commission with J. Oliphant, 26 October 1809. [NRS.RD3.334.1050]

OLIPHANT, Sir JAMES, of Newtoun, a sasine, 28 August 1629, Nova Scotia. [NRS.RS1.26.341]

OLIPHANT, JEAN, in South Carolina, a deed of attorney, 5 February 1791. [NRS.RD3.252.629]

OLIPHANT, JOHN, bound for Virginia, letters in 1775. [NRS.GD136.410.77-78]

OLIVER, PETER, born in 1749, of Middleborough, Massachusetts, graduated BA from Harvard in 1769, and MD from Marischal College, Aberdeen, in 1790. He was a Loyalist in 1776, who died in Shrewsbury, England, in 1822. [MCA] [SNQ.XII.60/159]

ORR, JOHN DALRYMPLE, born in 1772, a medical student at Edinburgh University from 1790 to 1791, died in 1816. [EUL]

OSBURNE, JOHN HUSBAND, of Connecticut, a student of medicine at Edinburgh University in 1761. [EUL]

OSBURNE, ROBERT F., of Antigua, graduated MD from Edinburgh University in 1819. [EMG]

OSWALD, RICHARD, was granted 20,000 acres in Nova Scotia in June 1764; a planter near St Augustine, East Florida, deceased, probate 1780. [RPCCol.vi.368] [TNA.AO.12.3.84, etc]

PAGAN, ROBERT, emigrated from Scotland to Casco Bay, New England, in 1769, factor at Falmouth for Joseph Tucker and Company of Greenock, later Robert Pagan and Company, a Loyalist, moved to Barbados, later at New York and Penobscot, settled at St Andrews, Nova Scotia, in 1783, at St John on 9 March 1787. [PAO.LC.208]

PAGAN, WILLIAM and THOMAS, merchants in New Brunswick, a letter, 1796. [NLS.Stewart.5039.15]

PAIN, JOHN, of North Carolina, a medical student at Edinburgh University in 1791-1792. [EUL]

PAINE, WILLIAM or JOHN, born 1750, of Worcester, Massachusetts, graduated BA from Harvard in 1768, and graduated MD at Marischal College, Aberdeen, on 1 November 1775, army surgeon in 1775, physician to the British Forces on the North America station in 1784. He died in Worcester on 19 April 1833. [MCA] [SNQ.XII.95/159]

PALMER, ROBERT, born in Scotland, Surveyor General of Nova Scotia and Customs Collector of Bath, North Carolina, from 1753 until 1771, returned home. [TNA.AO12.36.41, etc]

PANTON, GEORGE, graduated MA from Marischal College, Aberdeen, in 1763, and MA from Columbia in 1774. [SNQ.XII.95]; Reverend George Panton, born in Scotland, emigrated to America in 1770, a minister in Trenton, New Jersey, a Loyalist soldier, in Halifax, St John, by 17 December 1785. [PAO.LC.12]; settled at Port Roseway, Shelburne, Nova Scotia, a certificate, 2 August 1787. [EUL.Laing II.526]; a memorial, 3 May 1793. [EUL.Laing ii.559]

PARKE, THOMAS, (1749-1835), of Pennsylvania, a medical student at Edinburgh University in 1771. [Pennsylvania Historical Society, Pemberton Papers]

PARKER, JAMES, emigrated to America in 1773, a farmer in Tryon County, New York, a Loyalist in 1776, moved to Niagara by 1783. [TNA.AO12.28.69][PAO.LC.838]

PARKE, WILLIAM, in Mecklenburg, County, Virginia, a factor for Dinwiddie and Company in Glasgow in 1776. [TNA.AO13.102.78]

PARKMAN, GEORGE, of Boston, USA, graduated MD at King's College, Aberdeen, on 5 July 1813. [KCA]

PARNHAM, JOHN, born in 1740, of Maryland, a medical student at Edinburgh University from 1769, graduated MD at Edinburgh University in 1772, died in 1800. [EMG]

PATTERSON, ARCHIBALD, a settler on the north-west branch of the Cape Fear River, North Carolina, petitioned the Synod of Argyle for a Gaelic speaking minister, on 2 September 1748. [NRS.NRAS.1209.553]

PATERSON, CHARLES, son of George Paterson a medical practitioner in Grenada, a student at King's College, Aberdeen, from 1821 to 1824. [KCA]

PATTERSON, DUNCAN, a settler on the north-west branch of the Cape Fear River, North Carolina, petitioned the Synod of Argyle for a Gaelic speaking minister, on 2 September 1748. [NRS.NRAS.1209.553]

PATERSON, GEORGE, son of George Paterson in Grenada, a student at King's College, Aberdeen, 1815 to 1816. [KCA]

PATERSON, JAMES, a surgeon in Dundee, formerly in Jamaica, a deed, 6 December 1752. [NRS.RD3.211/2.595]

PATERSON, JAMES, son of George Paterson a medical practitioner in Grenada, a student at King's College, Aberdeen, from 1820 to 1823. [KCA]

PATTERSON, JOHN, [1], a settler on the north-west branch of the Cape Fear River, North Carolina, petitioned the Synod of Argyle for a Gaelic speaking minister, on 2 September 1748. [NRS.NRAS.1209.553]

PATTERSON, JOHN, [2], a settler on the north-west branch of the Cape Fear River, North Carolina, petitioned the Synod of Argyle for a Gaelic speaking minister, on 2 September 1748. [NRS.NRAS.1209.553]

PATERSON, JOHN, and his wife Jean, emigrated from Scotland to Philadelphia in 1771, a shopkeeper and a Loyalist in 1776, he died in New York. [TNA.AO12.40.40]

PATERSON, JOHN, son of John Paterson MD in Jamaica deceased, a student at King's College, Aberdeen, 1792 to 1796. [KCA]

PATERSON, JOHN LIGHTBODY, of Nassau, New Providence, a Member of the Royal College of Surgeons in 1813, graduated MD at King's College, Aberdeen, on 13 October 1820. [KCA]

PATERSON, THOMAS, sometime a ropemaker in Leith, afterwards in Baltimore, Maryland, a sasine, 28 March 1780. [NRS.RS27.250.260]

PATTERSON, WALTER, Governor of Prince Edward Island, papers, 1771, 1780. [NLS.Stewart.3885, 3982]

PATERSON, Mrs, in Charleston, South Carolina, a deed, 16 April 1782. [NRS.RD2.234.450]

PATON, SARAH, in New York, a deed, 2 October 1783. [NRS.RD3.242.1069]

PATRICK, WILLIAM, in New York, a a letter dated 1784. [NRS.NRAS.0852]

PATTY, JOHN, late in Lucea, Jamaica, then in Park of Troqueer, testament 1 July 1816 Comm. Dumfries. [NRS]

PATULLO, Captain ROBERT, born in Scotland, a mariner. Probate 23 April 1807, New Brunswick. [PANB]

PAYNE, JAMES THEOBALD, of Nevis, graduated MD at Edinburgh University in 1775. [EMG]

PAYTON, VALENTINE, from Virginia, graduated MD from Edinburgh University in 1754. [EMG]

PEAKIE, JOHN, of Virginia, a medical student at Edinburgh University in 1788. [RCPE, Cullen ms]

PENICUIK, Captain R., journal of voyage from Madeira to Darien, Panama, in 1698. [BM.Add.mss.40796, ff1-16]

PENMAN, EDWARD, in South Carolina, letters from 1797 until 1802. [NRS.NRAS.0426]

PENMAN, JAMES, in East Florida, a deed of factory in favour of Andrew Gardner, 22 May 1772. [NRS.RD4.224/2.250]; Governor Patrick Tonyn of East Florida, claimed that James Penman was aiding the rebels, a letter dated St Augustine on 27 May 1780. [HMC. American. ii.127]; a letter from Charleston dated 20 December 1771. [NRS.GD477.399]

PENMAN, EDIE, and Company, in Carolina, a deed of factory in favour of Robert Walker, 27 January 1786. [NRS.RD3.245.725]

PEREIRA, JOACHIM B., of Brazil, graduated MD from Edinburgh University in 1815. [EMG]

PERONNEAU, ROBERT, of South Carolina, graduated MD at Edinburgh University in 1775. [EMG]

PERRAULT, CHARLES NORBERT, of Canada, graduated MD at King's College, Aberdeen, on 18 July 1817. [KCA]

PERRY, WILLIAM, son of William Perry a notary in Trinidad, a student at King's College, Aberdeen, in 1823. [KCA]

PETRIE, WILLIAM, of Halifax, Nova Scotia, a Licentiate of the Royal College of Surgeons in 1812, graduated MD from King's College, Aberdeen, on 2 August 1820. [KCA]

PETTIGREW, JOHN, from Glasgow, a merchant in Sunbury, Georgia, in partnership with Simon Paterson, died in Savannah in November 1775. [TNA.AO12.101.190, etc]

PEYTON, FRANCIS, of Virginia, a medical student at Edinburgh University 1793-1794, graduated MD there in 1796. [EUL][EMG]

PEYTON, GEORGE, of Virginia, a medical student at Edinburgh University, from 1763 to 1767. [EUL]

PEYTON, VALENTINE, of Virginia, graduated MD at Edinburgh University in 1754. [EMG]

PHILIP, JOHN BAPTIST, of Trinidad, graduated MD from Edinburgh University in 1815. [EMG]

PHILLIPS, SAMUEL, searcher and writer of Customs in Quebec, letter of attorney, 1774. [NLS, Stewart pp.3916] 1

PHILLIPS, JAMES, a settler on the north-west branch of the Cape Fear River, North Carolina, petitioned the Synod of Argyle for a Gaelic speaking minister, on 2 September 1748. [NRS.NRAS.1209.553]

PHILLIPS, STEPHEN, a settler on the north-west branch of the Cape Fear River, North Carolina, petitioned the Synod of Argyle for a Gaelic speaking minister, on 2 September 1748. [NRS.NRAS.1209.553]

PHIMMER, SWABY, of Jamaica, graduated MD from Edinburgh University in 1821. [EMG]

PHINNIE, RICHARD, born 1605, emigrated via London bound for St Kitts on 13 October 1635. [TNA.E157.20]

PHINNIE, ROBERT, a sailor, emigrated via Bristol aboard the Little John bound to serve William Lindsay, a mariner in Barbados for four years, on 8 March 1635. [BRO]

PIERCE, THOMAS POLLARD, of Barbados, graduated MD at Edinburgh University in 1792. [EMG]

PITT, Mr and Mrs, in Virginia, a deed in favour of Patrick Colquhoun, 26 October 1785. [NRS.RD3.245.92]

POINSETT, J. R., of South Carolina, a medical student at Edinburgh University from 1797 to 1798. [EUL]

POLLOCK, ALLAN, in Virginia, correspondence from 1800 until 1807. [NRS.NRAS.0905]

POLLOCK, HUGH, a saddler in Charleston before 1776, a Loyalist who moved via St Eustatia and St Kitts to Kingston, Jamaica, in 1778 where he died in 1782. [TNA.AO.12.99.336]

POLLOCK, ROBERT, in Virginia, correspondence from 1800 until 1807. [NRS.NRAS.0905]

POLLOCK, WALTER, of Braemar, St Mary's, Jamaica, the attorney of Laurence Graeme in Pemberton Valley, Jamaica, on 22 December 1803. [NRS.B59.38.6.242]

POLLOCK, WALTER, son of Walter Pollock in Jamaica, a student at King's College, Aberdeen, from 1818 to 1822. [KCA]

POLLOCK, WILLIAM, in Tobago, a deed, 1 November 1775. [NRS.RD3.244.419]

POLSON, HUGH, in Jamaica, a deed, 8 August 1779. [NRS.RD4.237.908]

PORTER, WILLIAM, in Virginia, a deed of attorney, 1787. [NRS.RD4.242.372]

POWRIE, WILLIAM, the King's Commissioner in Barbados, 1640. [SPCol.]

PRESTON, JOHN, in New York, a deed in favour of A. Abercromby, 18 July 1777. [NRS.RD4.223/2.147]

PRINGLE, ROBERT, born in 1755, of South Carolina, a medical student at Edinburgh University from 1776 until 1778, died in 1811. [EUL]

PRINGLE, WALTER, a Customs officer on St Kitts in 1754. [JCTP.61/2.279]; his wife died in St Kitts on 19 August 1766. [SM.28.558]

PRINGLE, ..., was appointed Lieutenant Governor of Grenada in 1767. [RCS]

PROUDFIT, DANIEL, of New York, residing in Richmond Street, 1794, a medical student at Edinburgh University from 1794 until 1795, graduated MD at Edinburgh University in 1795. [EUL][EMG] [ECA.SL115.1.1]

PUE, ARTHUR, of Maryland, a medical student at Edinburgh University from 1796 until 1797. [EUL]

PULLAR, THOMAS, born 1833, died in New Britain, Connecticut, on 3 March 1901. [Little Dunkeld gravestone, Perthshire]

PURDIE, JAMES HYNDMAN, of Virginia, a medical student at Edinburgh University in 1792-1793, graduated MD from Glasgow University in 1793. [EUL][RGG]

PYOTT, THOMAS, born in Angus, Scotland, a flour dealer and bread baker in New Berne, North Carolina, before 1776, a Loyalist who moved to London by 1777. [TNA.AO13.123.48]

QUYNN, WILLIAM, born in 1760, of Maryland, a medical student at Edinburgh University in 1783, died there in 1784. [Maryland Hist. Mag.XXXI.181]

RAE, DAVID, in St Vincent, a bill of exchange, a protest, 30 September 1774. [NRS.RD4.216.332]

RAE, GEORGE, a merchant in Norfolk, Virginia, from 1771, a Loyalist who moved to London by 1776, from there to Dumfries, Scotland, by 1789. [TNA.AO12.99.21]

RAE, ROBERT, emigrated to America in 1763, schoolmaster of the Free School in Dorchester, South Carolina, a Loyalist, moved to Elgin, Morayshire, by 1783. [TNA.AO12.51.133, etc]

RAMSAY, Sir GILBERT, of Balmayne, a sasine, 8 November 1625, Nova Scotia. [NRS.RS1.18.233]

RAMSAY, JAMES, son of George Ramsay a physician in Virginia, a student at King's College, Aberdeen, from 1746 to 1750, graduated MA, an advocate in Aberdeen by 1759. [KCA]

RAMSAY, JAMES, of Virginia, a medical student at Edinburgh University 1783-1788. [EUL]

RAMSAY, JAMES, emigrated to New York in 1794, a merchant in Albany, New York, by 1810, a letter. [NRS.GD23.6.469]

RAMSAY, THOMAS, in Jamaica, a deed of attorney, 21 July 1790. [NRS.RD3.263.473]

RAMSAY, WILLIAM, Moderator of the Synod of New York and Philadelphia, a letter, 27 May 1771. [NRS.CH1.2.113.379]

RANDALL, ANN, born in Scotland, a soldier's widow in New York city, a Loyalist. [TNA.AO13.92.222]

RANDOLPH, BATHURST, of Virginia, a medical student at Edinburgh University 1797-1799, graduated MD at Edinburgh University in 1799. [EUL][EMG]

RANDOLPH, THOMAS MANN, of Virginia, a medical student at Edinburgh University in 1786. [EUL]

RANKIN, JAMES, at Greenock bound for Quebec on 2 August 1804. [NRS.GD202.70.11]

RANKIN, JAMES, in Jamaica, a deed of factory with Walter Finlayson, 9 July 1807. [NRS.RD3.317.1096]

RANKIN, JOHN, at Greenock bound for Quebec on 2 August 1804. [NRS.GD202.70.11]

RANNIE, JAMES, of Demerara, died at St Kitt's on 14 May 1779. [SM.41.455]

RAPIER, CHRISTOPHER, in Grenada, a deed of attorney, 6 September 1790. [NRS.RD2.250.599]

RATTRAY, ALEXANDER, in Trinidad, a deed of factory with Robert Rattray, 26 June 1807. [NRS.RD4.282.512]

RAVENSCROFT, JOHN, of Virginia, graduated MD at Edinburgh University in 1770. [EMG][NLS: Maxwell, MacMurdo and Newhall pp]

REACH, ALEXANDER, emigrated from Scotland to South Carolina, a merchant in George Town, dead by 1779. [TNA.AO13.80.408]

REACH, KENNETH, emigrated via London to South Carolina, in 1779, settled in George Town, a Loyalist, moved to Frenchman's Bay, Nova Scotia, by 1783. [TNA.AO13.80.408]

REDHEAD, JOHN, of Antigua, graduated MD at Edinburgh University in 1789. [EMG]

REDMAN, JOHN, (1722-1808), a medical student at Edinburgh University in 1746. [Redman ms., National Library of Medicine, Bethesda]

REEDER, HENRY, of Maryland, a medical student at Edinburgh University 1765-1766. [EUL]

REES, THOMAS, Rector of Kingston, Jamaica, graduated DD from King's College, Aberdeen, on 8 May 1787. [KCA]

REID, ALEXANDER, from Inverness, Scotland, a clerk for John Glen, an attorney in Savannah, Georgia, a Loyalist who returned to Britain in 1776. [TNA.AO13.36.1173]

REID, JAMES, son of John Reid and his wife Margaret in Lanark, Scotland, a storekeeper in St John, New Brunswick, probate 9 September 1788. [PANB]

REID, MARCUS DILL, youngest son of Robert Reid a surgeon in Antigua, matriculated at Glasgow University in 1802, graduated MD in 1803. [RGG]

REID, ROBERT, in Savannah, Georgia, a will, 10 March 1787. [NRS.RD3.250/1.538]; emigrated to Georgia in 1763, a partner in the merchant firm of Reid, Storr, and Reid, in Savannah, then a planter on Skidaway Island, a Loyalist, from St Augustine via the Bahamas to London by 1786, in Edinburgh by 1788. [TNA.AO12.101.352, etc]

REID, ROBERT, in Miramachi, New Brunswick, a letter, 1785. [GUL:ms1035]

REID, THOMAS, settled in Virginia around 1763, partner of the merchant firm Reid and Barrett, a Loyalist. [TNA.AO12.54.161]

REID, WILLIAM, from Montrose, Angus, then in Grenada, versus Susan Adamson or Reid, in 1817. [NRS.CC8.6.1631]

RENNALLS, JOHN POWELL, of Jamaica, graduated MD at Edinburgh University in 1797. [EMG]

RENNY, JAMES, in Jamaica, a deed of factory in favour of ... Strachan, 19 July 1779, [NRS.RD3.242.387], also deeds, 5 September 1783. [NRS.RD3.242.1202.1266]

RENNIE, ROBERT, in Jamaica, a deed, 1 November 1770. [NRS.RD4.224/2.43]

REVERE, JOHN, of America, graduated MD from Edinburgh University in 1811. [EMG]

RHIND, WILLIAM, born 1713, from Prestonpans, Midlothian, an indentured servant bound via London to Pennsylvania for 4 years in July 1731. [CLRO]

RICHARDSON, G. A., of Demerara, graduated MD at King's College, Aberdeen, on 5 May 1823. [KCA]

RICHARDSON, JOHN, a malt-maker from Stirling and Dunbarton, in New York, heir to the deceased Major James Livingstone, an affidavit dated 1798. [NRS.GD1.660.1]

RICHARDSON, ROBERT, a mariner in Leith, was bound for Guinea and the West Indies, died abroad, his testament dated 8 January 1707. [NRS.CC8.8.83.25]

RICHARDSON, ROBERT, possibly from Perth, died in Nassau, in the Bahamas, father of James Richardson, a letter dated 18 June 1819. [NRS.B59.38.5.63]

RICHMOND, WALTER, in Jamaica, bonds, 10 December 1770. [NRS.RD4.215.563]

RIDDELL, GEORGE, a physician in Yorktown, Virginia, brother of Sir James Riddell, a Loyalist who died on 20 January 1779. [TNA.AO2.71.86][SM.41.167]

RIDDELL, JOHN, a factor in Virginia for Glassford and Henderson of Glasgow, returned to Glasgow in July 1776, a deposition. [TNA.AO12.109.166]; in Prince William County, Virginia, before 1779. [TNA.AO13.102.81]

RIDDLE, JAMES, late of Grenada, now in Ayr, was admitted as a burgess and guilds-brother of Ayr on 27 July 1776. [ABR]

RIDDEL, JAMES, of Pennsylvania, a medical student at Edinburgh University, 1792. [EUL]

RIDDELL, WALTER, of Bermuda, graduated MD at Edinburgh University in 1774. [EMG]

RIDDOCH, COLIN, in Jamaica, a deed of attorney, 15 September 1774. [NRS.RD.4.216.788]

RIDDICK, ALEXANDER, merchant formerly in Virginia, now in Dumfries, 1800. [NRS.CS17.1.19/23]

RITCHIE, ANDREW, emigrated from Scotland to Boston, New England, in 1753, a shopkeeper there, a Loyalist, settled in Annapolis, Nova Scotia, at Halifax, N.S., on 29 April 1789. [PAO.LC.521]

ROBBINS, CHANDLER, MA, of Plymouth, Massachusetts, graduated DD at Edinburgh University on 3 August 1792. [GEU]

ROBERT, DANIEL, of New York, a medical student at Edinburgh University around 1768. [EUL]

ROBERTS, CHRISTOPHER, son of Christopher Roberts in Dominica, a student at King's College, Aberdeen, 1788 to 1789. [KCA]

ROBERTS, JAMES WATSON, of Antigua, graduated MD at Edinburgh University in 1786. [EMG]

ROBERTS, MERCER, son of Edward Roberts a saddler in Williamsburgh, Virginia, was apprenticed to Baillie Blinshall a saddler in Edinburgh for seven years on 15 October 1778. [ERA]

ROBERTS, WILLIAM, only son of Benjamin Roberts, a gentleman in Charleston, South Carolina, matriculated in 1770, and graduated MA and MD at Glasgow University in 1771. [RGG]

ROBERTSON, ALEXANDER, on the Wicomico River, Somerset County, Maryland, a letter to George Robertson in 1769. [NRS.NRAS.0247]

ROBERTSON, ALEXANDER, emigrated from Scotland to America in 1770, an Indian trader on the Ohio River, Pennsylvania, a Loyalist, in Shelburne, Nova Scotia, on 26 June 1786. [PAO.LC.77]

ROBERTSON, ALEXANDER, in Jamaica, a deed, 12 July 1779. [NRS.RD3.243.485]

ROBERTSON, ANDREW, emigrated from Scotland to America in 1756, settled in Charleston, South Carolina, moved to Savannah, Georgia, in 1773, a planter, a Loyalist who moved to England in 1783. [TNA.AO12.51.111, etc]

ROBERTSON, ARTHUR GRANT, of Antigua, graduated MD at Edinburgh University in 1783. [EMG]

ROBERTSON, CHARLES, via Greenock to St John, New Brunswick, in 1803, settled in Sussex Vale. [PANB.mc1672]

ROBERTSON, GEORGE, late of Virginia, a contract of marriage with Jean McKenzie, 1784. [NRS.RD2.242/2.209]

ROBERTSON, JAMES, from Edinburgh, a Loyalist soldier, from Florida to London by 1784, hoping to go to Nova Scotia. [TNA.AO13.36.1430, etc]

ROBERTSON, JAMES, in Jamaica, a deed, 7 March 1788. [NRS.RD3.247.401]

ROBERTSON, JAMES, of Barbados, graduated MD at King's College, Aberdeen, on 15 October 1794. [KCA]

ROBERTSON, JAMES, son of James Robertson MD in Jamaica, a student at King's College, Aberdeen, 1810 to 1814, graduated MA, later a Member of the Royal College of surgeons in St Ann's, Jamaica. [KCA]

ROBERTSON, JAMES, a minister in St John's, Newfoundland, letters dated 1829. [NRS.NRAS.2314]

ROBERTSON, JOHN, of Ernock, a letter from Boston, New England, dated 1710 to the Duke of Hamilton re 4 of the Grand Sachems. [NRS.NRAS.0332/1291]

ROBERTSON, JOHN, of Canada, graduated MD from Edinburgh University in 1813. [EMG]

ROBERTSON, PATRICK, in America, a deed of factory in favour of Arthur Robertson, 3 January 1772. [NRS.RD4.211/1.53]

ROBERTSON, PATRICK, MA, of America, a student at King's College, Aberdeen, 1767 to 1771. [KCA]

ROBERTSON, PETER, in St Thomas, a deed of attorney with Duncan McDonald, 30 December 1798. [NRS.RD4.270.507]

ROBERTSON, WALTER, in Tobago, a deed of attorney in favour of Dr A. Robertson, 7 June 1771. [NRS.RD3.238/2.23]

ROBERTSON, WILLIAM, son of Alexander Robertson in Grenada deceased, a student at King's College, Aberdeen, from 1796 to 1799. [KCA]

ROBERTSON, WILLIAM, son of John Robertson in America, a student at King's College, Aberdeen, graduated MA in 1823. [KCA]

ROBINSON, ALEXANDER, third son of James Robinson in Bishop Mill, Moray, the Naval Officer of Kingston, Jamaica, died at Port Royal, Jamaica, on 19 September 1791. [GM.61.1062]

ROBINSON, JAMES, in Demerara, a deed of attorney with George Robinson, 20 April 1801. [NRS.RD2.282.669]

ROBISON, JAMES, a farmer at Still Water Village, New York State, a letter dated 1830. [NRS.GD16.35.68]

ROBISON, WILLIAM, servant to William Salmond a merchant in Antigua, was admitted as a burgess and freeman of Ayr on 5 February 1757. [ABR]

ROGERS, JOHN, of New York, graduated DD at Edinburgh University on 29 June 1768. [GEU]

ROGERS, JOHN R. B., of New York, graduated MD at Edinburgh University in 1785. [EMG]

ROGERS, NATHANIEL, of Boston, New England, graduated MA from Glasgow University in 1750. [RGG]

ROGERSON, SAMUEL, landed at St John's, Newfoundland, in November 1820, a letter to his brother William Rogerson in Hutton near Lockerbie, Dumfries-shire, dated 18 November 1820. [NRS.GD1.620.66]

ROMAYNE, NICOLAS, (1756-1817), of New York, graduated MD at Edinburgh University in 1780. [EMG]

ROSE, ALEXANDER, a merchant from Inverness, at Cromarty bound as a passenger aboard the Hope for Carolina in 1736, a petition before the High Court of the Admiralty of Scotland in 1736. [NRS.AC10.227]

ROSE, CHARLES, Depute Judge of the Admiralty in Antigua, graduated as a Doctor of Law from King's College, Aberdeen, on 1 February 1748. [KCA]

ROSE, Dr HUGH, born in Scotland, a physician and surgeon in St John's parish, Berkley County, South Carolina, for over 18 years, a Loyalist, via East Florida and New Providence to England in 1786, later in Stonehaven, Kincardineshire, by 1788. [TNA.AO12.3.156, etc]

ROSE, HUGH, son of John Rose in Jamaica, a student at King's College, Aberdeen, 1789. [KCA]

ROSE, HUGH, in Grenada, an indenture with Robert Riddell, 8 May 1792. [NRS.RD3.256.57]

ROSE, JAMES, in St Vincent, later in Dundee, testament 7 December 1822, Comm. Brechin. [NRS]

ROSE, WILLIAM BROMLEY, of Jamaica, graduated MD from Edinburgh University in 1824. [EMG]

ROSS, DANIEL, formerly in Charleston, South Carolina, later in Antigua, letters to his cousin Munro Ross of Pitcalny, dated between 1777 and 1780. [NRS.GD199.255/273]

ROSS, GEORGE, from Greenock to St John, New Brunswick, in 1803. [PANB.mc1672]

ROSS, HECTOR, a merchant in Colchester, Virginia, conveyances, 1771, 1774. [see TNA.AO13.134.392-406]

ROSS, HERCULES, in Jamaica, bonds, 24 May 1784. [NRS.RD3.243.755/765]

ROSS, JAMES, son of Benjamin Ross in Barbados a student at King's College, Aberdeen, 1805 to 1807. [KCA]

ROSS, JOHN, a settler on the north-west branch of the Cape Fear River, North Carolina, petitioned the Synod of Argyle for a Gaelic speaking minister, on 2 September 1748. [NRS.NRAS.1209.553]

ROSS, JOHN, a shipbuilder on Cape Fear, North Carolina, a Loyalist who moved to Kingston, Jamaica, in 1783. [TNA.AO12.36.327]

ROSS, JOHN, of Arnage, a factor in East Florida, papers from 1775 until 1790. [NRS.GD186.box 4, bundle 10]; a ledger from 1782 to 1795. [NRS.GD186.12.5]

ROSS, ROBERT, from Aberdeen, a merchant in Pensacola, West Florida, from 1764, then in Mississippi from 1772 as a merchant and planter. [TNA.AO.13.26.414]; a letter from Carolina on 2 October 1781. [NRS.GD44.43.261]

ROSS, THOMAS, from Drumvaich, emigrated from Scotland to America in 1773, settled at Johnson's Bush, Tryon County, New York, a Loyalist soldier, moved to New Johnstown. [PAO.LC.1104]

ROSS, WILLIAM, from Barbados aboard the ketch William and Susan, master Ralph Parker, bound for New England on 21 March 1679. [TNA]

ROSS, WILLIAM, a merchant from Fortrose, at Cromarty bound as a passenger aboard the Hope for Carolina in 1736, a petition before the High Court of the Admiralty of Scotland in 1736. [NRS.AC10.242]

ROULE, MATTHEW, from Greenock to St John, New Brunswick, in 1803. [PANB.mc1672]

ROXBURGH, ANTHONY, from Scotland to Virginia in 1767, settled in Nansemond County, Virginia, a Loyalist, settled in St Augustine, East Florida, by 1784. [TNA.AO12.106.31]

ROXBURGH, GEORGE, from Greenock to St John, New Brunswick, in 1803. [PANB.mc1672]

ROY, JAMES, in New York, a deed dated 25 June 1777. [NRS.RD2.222/2.362]

ROY, Mrs ELIZABETH, in New York, a deed in favour of Sir L. Dundas, dated 25 November 1777. [NRS.RD4.223/1.628]

RUAN, WILLIAM, a planter in St Jan, Danish West Indies, died 29 July 1835, probate St Jan, 1826-1836, fo.236-252. [RAK]

RUDDACH, JOHN, in Jamaica, a deed of factory dated 11 June 1787. [NRS.RD3.249.423]

RUSH, BENJAMIN, of Pennsylvania, graduated MD at Edinburgh University in 1768. [EMG][IUB][PU][CPP][PHS/lcp]

RUSSELL, CHARLES, (1739-1780), of Massachusetts, graduated BA from Harvard in 1757, and MD from Marischal College, Aberdeen, in 1765. [MCA] [SNQ.XII.95]

RUSSELL, DAVID, from Scotland to Virginia, as a partner of a merchant house in Glasgow, based in Blandford, returned to Glasgow in 1775. [TNA.AO12.109.260]

RUSSELL, FRANCIS, a merchant in Leith, trading with South Carlina and New Providence from 1752 until 1760. [NRS.CS96.1583]

RUSSELL, JAMES, of Barbados, graduated MD from Edinburgh University in 1822. [EMG]

RUSSELL, JAMES, a merchant in Augusta, Georgia, a letter dated 1823. [NRS.NRAS.1267]

RUSSELL, LOCKHART, in Antigua, a deed dated 22 October 1787. [NRS.RD3.247.403]

RUSSELL, SAMUEL, a merchant in Marblehead, Essex County, Massachusetts, a will dated 1722. [NRS.GD155.705]

RUSSELL, WILLIAM, in Charleston, South Carolina, a letter dated 1825, another dated Philadelphia, Pennsylvania, in 1832. [NRS.NRAS.1267]

RUSTON, THOMAS, of Pennsylvania, graduated MD at Edinburgh University in 1765. [EMG][LC]

RUTHERFORD, GEORGE, in Antigua, an inventory, 1797-1806. [NMM.C108.245]

RUTHERFORD, JOHN, of Edgerston, an advocate, letters from his tour of America and the Indian Nations, dated 1742. [NRS.GD110.911.6-7]

RUTHERFURD, JOHN, of Bowland, a merchant on Cape Fear, North Carolina, deeds dated 22 January 1752. [NRS.RD2.171/2.272; RD3.211/2.366]; a contract dated 26 October 1752. [NRS.RD4.178/2.364]; indentures dated 26 October 1752, [NRS.RD4.178/2.365; contract dated 1 November 1752, [NRS.RD4.178/2.363]; Receiver General and a Member of the Council of N.C. was suspended from duty by Governor Dobbs, a memorial on 15 March 1758. [JCTP.65.]

RUTHERFORD, W., who had lost several hundred pounds improving the Niagara Portage, petitioned for a land grant in New York on 13 February 1765. [RPCCol.vi.387]

RUTLEDGE, CHARLES, of South Carolina, a student in Edinburgh, from 1794 to 1796. [EUL][UNC]

RUTLEDGE, JOHN, in Charlestown, South Carolina, a missive letter, 15 March 1748. [NRS.RD2.171/1.312]

SADLER, JAMES EDWARD ASH, of St Kitts, graduated MD from Edinburgh University in 1823. [EMG]

SALMON, JOHN, of Jamaica, graduated MD from Edinburgh University in 1819. [EMG]

SALMOND. WILLIAM, in Antigua, was admitted as a burgess and guilds-brother of Ayr on 5 February 1757. [ABR]

SAMUELS, EDWARD, born 1813, son of Dr Samuels in Jamaica, educated at Edinburgh Academy from 1824 to 1828. [EAR]

SAMUELS, PAUL STEVENS, of Jamaica, graduated MD at Edinburgh University in 1798. [EMG]

SANDBERG, PETER, of St Cruz, (St Croix), graduated MD from Edinburgh University in 1813. [EMG]

SANDERS, GEORGE, of Barbados, graduated MD from Edinburgh University in 1810. [EMG]

SANTOS, DOMINIC FELISA, of Brazil, graduated MD at Edinburgh University in 1795. [EMG]

SCARLETT, ROBERT, of Jamaica, graduated MD at Edinburgh University in 1795. [EMG]

SCOTLAND, JAMES, a house carpenter in St Augustine, East Florida, from 1775, a Loyalist, later in London. [TNA.AO12.3.297]

SCOTLAND, JOHN, in Antigua, a deed of attorney dated 24 April 1773. [NRS.RD3.232.432]

SCOTT, ALEXANDER, in Antigua, a bond dated 2 January 1779. [NRS.RD4.226.1004]

SCOTT, CHRISTOPHER, from Greenock, a merchant, late of St Andrews, Charlotte County, New Brunswick, now in London, probate 29 July 1833. [PANB]

SCOTT, HUGH, of Gala, a letter dated 1791 at Niagara. [NRS.GD224.box 31, no. 19/2/6]

SCOTT, JAMES, from England aboard the South Sea Company's snow St Philip bound for America, a letter from Panama in 1735. [NRS.GD157.2810.1]

SCOTT, JAMES, of Virginia, a medical student at Edinburgh University in 1799-1800. [EUL]

SCOTT, JOHN, a merchant in Jamaica and New York, letters to his father Sir John Scott of Ancrum, in 1700 and 1701, one from Port Royal, Jamaica, another from New York, and one from Duckesburg, Staten Island, N.Y. [NRS.GD259.box 4, bundle 2]

SCOTT, JOHN, was proposed for the Council of Jamaica on 20 October 1753. [JCTP.61/2]

SCOTT, JOHN, son of James Scott in Westwood, Virginia, a student from 1766 to 1768, graduated MA at King's College, Aberdeen, on 29 March 1768. [KCA]

SCOTT, JOHN, in Demerara, a deed of factory with Mrs Scott, 20 February 1802. [NRS.RD3.295.657]

SCOTT, THOMAS, a merchant late of Blandford, Virginia, settled in Glasgow by 1786, a deposition. [TNA.AO13.28.415]

SCOTT, THOMAS, Customs Controller of Quebec, a letter of attorney. 1774. [NLS. Stewart pp.3929]

SCOTT, THOMAS, with his wife Elizabeth and their children settled in Canada, he was brother of Sir Walter Scott, letters from 1815 until 1820. [NRS.NRAS.0231]

SCOTT, WILLIAM J., in Savannah, Georgia, a probative will, 6 October 1823. [NRS.RD433.539]

SCREVEN, RICHARD BEDON, of South Carolina, a medical student at Edinburgh University 1797-1798, graduated MD at Edinburgh University in 1799. [EUL][EMG]

SCROGGIE, JOHN, in Jamaica, a deed, 1 June 1767. [NRS.RD4.220.1144]

SEABURY, SAMUEL, born in 1729, of Connecticut, a physician educated at Edinburgh University 1752, died 1796. [Bio. Notices of Grads. of Yale College]

SEAMAN, GEORGE, in Charleston, South Carolina, a letter dated 1756. [NRS.GD199.227]

SEDGEWICK, SAMUEL, of Antigua, graduated MD from Edinburgh University in 1819. [EMG]

SELBY, WILLIAM D., of America, graduated MD from Edinburgh University in 1810. [EMG]

SELDEN, WILLIAM B., born in 1773, of Virginia, a medical student at Edinburgh University 1797-1798, born 1849. [EUL]

SELKIRK, JOHN, son of Robert Selkirk late a merchant in Boston, was apprenticed to William Jameson a mason in Edinburgh for six years on 20 November 1788. [ERA]

SEMPLE, JOHN, a merchant in Portobacco, Maryland, partner of James Lawson, a merchant in Glasgow, around 1765. [NRS.CS96.1176]

SEMPLE, WILLIAM, formerly in Bengal, applied for a grant of 15,000 acres in Nova Scotia, in 1771. [JCTP.78.105]

SETON, JOHN, in Jamaica, a deed, 18 August 1777. [NRS.RD2.9]

SEWALL, JOSEPH, born 26 August 1688 in Boston, New England, Pastor of the Old South Church in Boston from 1713 to 1769, graduated DD from Glasgow University in 1731, died in Boston on 27 June 1769. [RGG]

SEYBERT, ADAM, (1733-1825), of Pennsylvania, a medical student at Edinburgh University in 1794-1795. [EUL]

SHAAF, JOHN THOMAS, of Maryland, a medical student at Edinburgh University, 1788 to 1790, died 1817. [EUL]

SHAND, JOHN, son of John Shand in Jamaica, a student at King's College, Aberdeen, 1817 to 1819. [KCA]

SHARP, GILES, son of Henry Sharp on St Kitts, was apprenticed to Charles Congalton an apothecary in Edinburgh on 25 July 1764. [ERA]

SHAW, ALEXANDER, son of the late Reverend John Shaw in Greenock, died in Jamaica on 10 August 1804. [GM.74.1071]

SHAW, DAVID, of Jamaica, graduated MD from Edinburgh University in 1817. [EMG]

SHAW, DOUGHIE [DOWIE?], a settler on the north-west branch of the Cape Fear River, North Carolina, petitioned the Synod of Argyle for a Gaelic speaking minister, on 2 September 1748. [NRS.NRAS.1209.553]

SHAW, DUNCAN, a settler on the north-west branch of the Cape Fear River, North Carolina, petitioned the Synod of Argyle for a Gaelic speaking minister, on 2 September 1748. [NRS.NRAS.1209.553]

SHAW, JOHN, a settler on the north-west branch of the Cape Fear River, North Carolina, petitioned the Synod of Argyle for a Gaelic speaking minister, on 2 September 1748. [NRS.NRAS.1209.553]

SHAW, JOHN SMITH, of Virginia, graduated MD from Edinburgh University in 1777, died 1811. [EMG]

SHAW, NEILL, [1], a settler on the north-west branch of the Cape Fear River, North Carolina, petitioned the Synod of Argyle for a Gaelic speaking minister, on 2 September 1748. [NRS.NRAS.1209.553]

SHAW, NEILL, [2], a settler on the north-west branch of the Cape Fear River, North Carolina, petitioned the Synod of Argyle for a Gaelic speaking minister, on 2 September 1748. [NRS.NRAS.1209.553]

SHAW, NEILL, with three others, emigrated from Campbeltown, Argyll, aboard the Edinburgh of Campbeltown, master John McMichael, in July 1771 bound for Prince Edward Island. [NRS.SC54.2.106]

SHAW, WILLIAM, late of Quebec, was admitted as a burgess and guilds-brother of Ayr on 7 February 1784. [ABR]

SHAW, WILLIAM, born 1831, died in Carriecou near Grenada on 9 October 1864, son of Alexander Shaw, in Eelegie, Aberdeenshire, born 1790, died 7 July 1859. [Crathie gravestone]

SHEDDEN, WILLIAM, a letter from St George's to Governor William Browne dated 27 June 1782. [HMC.American ii.545]; a merchant in Bermuda and New York, letters between 1780 and 1794. [NRS.GD1.67.1]

SHEPHERD, WILLIAM, of Connecticut, a student of medicine at Edinburgh University from 1790 to 1791. [EUL]

SHERIFF, CHARLES, in Quebec, a letter to A. W. Cochrane re lumbering, dated 20 January 1827. [NRS.GD45. Section 3.452]

SHERIFF, JOHN, in St Thomas, a deed, 7 November 1783. [NRS.RD4.234.764]

SHERIFF, SAMUEL M., of Antigua, graduated MD from Edinburgh University in 1822. [EMG]

SCHEVIZ, ALEXANDER, a merchant late of Blandford, Prince George County, Virginia, settled in Glasgow, by 1786, a deposition. [TNA.AO13.28.415]

SHIACH, or CUTHBERT, Mrs MARGARET, from Banff, a shopkeeper in St John, New Brunswick, probate 15 June 1791, New Brunswick. [PANB]

SHIPPEN, WILLIAM, (1736-1808), of Pennsylvania, graduated MD at Edinburgh University in 1761. [EMG]

SHORE, JOHN, of Virginia, graduated MD at Edinburgh University in 1777. [EMG][SM.39.336]

SHORT, JOHN, in Virginia, a deed, 17 August 1787. [NRS.RD3.247.15]

SIBBALD, DAVID, in Jamaica, deeds, 21 July 1772, 25 March 1775, 29 March 1779, 28 March 1785. [NRS.RD2.232/1.794/795/796]

SIMONS, BENJAMIN BONNEAU, (1776-1844), of South Carolina, a medical student at Edinburgh University 1799-1800, graduated MD from Glasgow University in 1800. [EUL][RGG]

SIMONS, THOMAS YOUNG, of America, graduated MD from Edinburgh University in 1819. [EMG]

SIMPSON, ALEXANDER, in Jamaica, a letter dated 15 February 1766. [NRS.GD345.1180.12]

SIMPSON, ANNA, wife of John Simpson in Savannah, Georgia, a judicial ratification of disposition of 500 acres in Christ Church, Georgia, to John Bowman of Savannah, in 1774. [NRS.GD77.167]

SIMPSON, Captain HOUSTOUN, master of the Cumberland of Leith, was shipwrecked on passage from Jamaica on 22 August 1806, died in Baltimore, Maryland, on 24 September 1806. [GM.76.1168]

SIMPSON, WILLIAM and GEORGE, in Jamaica, a deed of attorney, 26 January 1788. [NRS.RD4.244.318]

SIMS, JOHN, of Pennsylvania, graduated MD from Edinburgh University in 1774. [EMG]

SINCLAIR, ALEXANDER, settled in Charlotte County, New Brunswick, in 1804. [PANB.MC1672]

SINCLAIR, ARCHIBALD, in Jamaica, a deed, 11 March 1771. [NRS.RD4.211/1.200]; a deed, 10 May 1774. [NRS.RD4.215.54227.237]; a deed of attorney in favour of Loudon Craig, 11 November 1783. [NRS.RD2.236/1.651]

SINCLAIR, MARGARET, in Jamaica, a deed of factory in favour of Hugh Polson, 25 July 1778. [NRS.RD4.232.906]

SINCLAIR, ROBERT, in New York, a probative bill, 13 July 1771. [NRS.RD4.212/1.95]

SINCLAIR, ROBERT, in Jamaica, a deed of attorney with David Thomson, 1 June 1800. [NRS.RD4.289.454]

SINCLAIR, THOMAS, settled in Charlotte County, New Brunswick, in 1804. [PANB.MC1672]

SINCLAIR, WILLIAM, of Lochend, Orkney a letter to US Major General Arthur St Clair, seeking his help to settle in America, a letter dated 1793. [NRS.GD136.465]

SISE, JEAN, in New York, a deed of factory, 18 June 1786. [NRS.RD3.245.1065]

SKEETE, THOMAS, of Barbados, born 1757, graduated MD from Glasgow University in 1785, a physician in London, died on 29 May 1789. [RGG]

SKENE, A., petitioned the boundary commissioners of South and North Carolinas on 14 June 1737. [RPCCol.vi.245]

SKENE, Dr JAMES, a physician in South Carolina from 1767 until 1778, moved to Kingston, Jamaica, before 1788. [TNA.AO12.52.163]; a Loyalist who settled in Jamaica, a letter dated 8 April 1783. [HMC. American.iv.19]

SKENE, PHILIP, Lieutenant Governor of Ticonderoga and Crown Point, New York, a Loyalist in 1776, in London by 1784. [TNA.AO12.24.118]

SKINNER, JAMES, in Louisbourg, Acadia, a letter, 1753. [NRS.NRAS.0036]

SMART, ADAM, in Antigua, a letter dated 1758. [NRS.GD219.289.6]

SMIBERT, WILLIAM, (1732-1774), of Massachusetts, graduated MD at Edinburgh University in 1762. [EMG]

SMITH, ARCHIBALD, emigrated aboard the Edinburgh of Campbeltown, master John McMichael, from Campbeltown on 1 July 1771 bound for North Carolina. [NRS.SC54.2.166]

SMITH, AUGUSTINE, of Virginia, graduated MD at Edinburgh University in 1787. [EMG]

SMITH, HADDON, a minister in Virginia, graduated DD at Edinburgh University on 20 May 1785. [GEU]

SMITH, JAMES, (1741-1812), of New York, a medical student at Edinburgh University 1762-1763. [EUL]

SMITH, JOHN, of Georgia, graduated MD at Edinburgh University in 1787. [EMG]

SMITH, JOHN, commander of the snow Adventure, is to sail from the Clyde to Jamaica on the 10th Day of July next, and is to take in Goods and Passengers, for whom the Master has very good Accommodation. He will also take Servants, any Tradesmen, who incline to hire themselves, to whoever will give all reasonable encouragement. Any Persons who have a mind to hire themselves for Servants, may apply to Captain Hugh MacLauchlan or William MacGowan merchants in Glasgow, or to John Watterston to be found at the Laigh Coffee-house in Edinburgh.' Source – the Caledonian Mercury, 22 June 1749.

SMITH, MALCOLM, a settler on the north-west branch of the Cape Fear River, North Carolina, petitioned the Synod of Argyle for a Gaelic speaking minister, on 2 September 1748. [NRS.NRAS.1209.553]

SMITH, MARSHALL KEITH, son of William Smith in the Bahamas, a student at King's College, Aberdeen, around 1815. [KCA]

SMITH, NATHAN, (1762-1829), of New Hampshire, studied medicine in Glasgow and Edinburgh, 1796-1797. [DAB]

SMYLLIE, MATTHEW, a settler on the north-west branch of the Cape Fear River, North Carolina, petitioned the Synod of Argyle for a Gaelic speaking minister, on 2 September 1748. [NRS.NRAS.1209.553]

SMYTH, HENRY, landed in Charleston, South Carolina, in 1761, a letter. [NRS.NRAS.0387]

SNODGRASS, NEIL, from Scotland to Virginia before 1758, a merchant there and later in Pasquotank County, North Carolina, a Loyalist who moved to London by 1778. [TNA.AO12.103.8]

SOMERVILLE, ALEXANDER, son of Reverend Somerville in Stirling, late in Barbados, 24 December 1807. [NRS.GD51.6.1567.1/2]

SOMERVILLE, JAMES, a planter on Forest Estate, Westmorland, Cornwall, Jamaica, versus Marion Shiells in Westruther, a Process of Divorce dated June 1794. [NRS.CC8.6.927]

SPALDING, HINTON, of Jamaica, graduated MD from Edinburgh University in 1807. [EMG]

SPALDING, JAMES, a merchant and planter on St Simon's Island, Frederica, Georgia, a Loyalist, in St Augustine in 1783. [TNA.AO13.83.523]

SPALDING, JAMES, a merchant in East Florida, title deeds and papers re Bonnington Mills in East Lothian, from 1770 to 1795. [NRS.GD174.2069/2071/2076/2082/2084]

STALKER, DUNCAN, formerly in Tobago, lately in Killean, Argyll, testament, 19 October 1798, Comm. Argyll, [NRS.CC2.3.12/309]

SPARK, ALEXANDER, a minister in Quebec, graduated DD at King's College, Aberdeen, on 31 January 1804. [KCA]

SPEED, JAMES, of Kentucky, a medical student at Edinburgh University in 1796. [EUL]

SPENCE, EDWARD JOHN, of Jamaica, graduated MD from Edinburgh University in 1820. [EMG]

SPENCE, GEORGE, of Jamaica, graduated MD at Edinburgh University in 1790. [EMG]

SPENCE, PETER, a merchant in Virginia, was admitted as a burgess and guilds-brother of Ayr on 7 May 1753. [ABR]

SPENCE, WILLIAM, of Virginia, a medical student at Edinburgh University in 1778, graduated MD from Glasgow University in 1780. He married Isabella, daughter of the late James Tennant a merchant in Glasgow, on 5 June 1780. [EUL][RGG]

SPENCER, MARY ELIZABETH, wife of Alexander Thomson late of Georgia, died in Edinburgh on 30 April 1777. [SM.40.222]

SPOONER, WILLIAM, (1760-1836), of Massachusetts, graduated MD at Edinburgh University in 1785. [EMG]

SPOTSISWOODE, ROBERT, 6th son of William Spottiswoods of Glenfernate [1767-1830, died in America in 1855. [Kirkmichael gravestone, Perthshire]

SPRATT, GEORGE DANIEL, of Virginia, graduated MD from Edinburgh University in 1804. [EMG]

SPRATT, ROBERT BEVERLEY, of Virginia, graduated MD at Edinburgh University in 1793. [EMG]

SPROWLE, ANDREW, a merchant in Gosport, Norfolk, Virginia, for over 40 years, a Loyalist, died in 1776. [TNA.AO12.54.283, etc]

STAIR, the Earl of, titles to the lordship and barony of Makgill in Nova Scotia, 1626-1627. [NRS.NRAS.0062]

STALKER, DUNCAN, sometime of Tobago, lately in Killean, Argyll, an edict of executry dated 18 September 1798, [TNA.CC8.102.7]; testament, confirmed on 19 October 1798. [NRS.CC2.3.12]

STARK, BOLLING, of Virginia, a medical student at Edinburgh University 1797-1799, graduated MD at Edinburgh University in 1799. [EUL][EMG]

STEEL, JOHN, in Jamaica, a probative bill, 10 May 1783. [NRS.RD2.235/1.825]

STEEL, RORY, settled on Prince Edward Island in 1790. [NLS.RHASS.Adv.73.2.13]

STEEL, ROBERT, arrived in Newcastle from Virginia, intended to return to Virginia, a letter dated 27 June 1696. [NRS.GD3.5.805]

STENHOUSE, ALEXANDER, emigrated from Scotland to America in 1759, a physician and surgeon in Baltimore by 1764, a Loyalist, moved to England 1776, who returned to Edinburgh by 1788. [TNA.AO12.6.60][PAO.LC.1158/1177]

STENHOUSE, JANE, emigrated from Scotland to North Carolina around 1763, a schoolmistress and needle-worker in Cross Creek, Cumberland County, N.C., a Loyalist in 1776, settled in England. [TNA.AO13.137.578]

STENNETT, JOHN, of Jamaica, graduated MD at Edinburgh University in 1792. [EMG]

STEPHENSON, GEORGE, in Jamaica, a deed of factory with Dan McLeod, 26 June 1810. [NRS.RD3.336.235]

STEPHENSON, JOHN, of Canada, graduated MD from Edinburgh University in 1820. [EMG]

STEPTOE, GEORGE, of Virginia, graduated MD at Edinburgh University in 1767. [EMG]

STEUART, ADAM, a merchant of Rock Creek, Maryland, a Loyalist, in Ayr, Scotland, by 1783. [TNA.AO12.8.54]

STEUART, GEORGE, emigrated to Maryland in 1728, a Loyalist in 1776, settled in Argarty, Stirlingshire, by 1784. [TNA.AO12.6.227]

STEUART, JAMES, (1755-1845), of Maryland, graduated MD at Edinburgh University in 1779. [EMG]

STEVEN, ALEXANDER, son of Alexander Steven in Tobago deceased, a student at King's College, Aberdeen, 1790. [KCA]

STEVENS, EDWARD, of the West Indies, graduated MD at Edinburgh University in 1777. [EMG]

STEVENSON, GEORGE PITT, (1768-1819), of Maryland, graduated MD at Edinburgh University in 1789. [EMG]

STEVENSON, HAMILTON, in Jamaica, a deed of attorney in favour of Robert Corbett, 20 February 1781. [NRS.RD2.231.892]

STEVENSON, HUGH, in Antigua, was admitted as a burgess and guilds-brother of Ayr on 4 June 1783. [ABR]

STEVENSON, JOHN, in Jamaica, a deed, 5 April 1783. [NRS.RD2.234.1440]

STEVENSON, ROBERT, son of the late Allan Stevenson a storekeeper in St Kitts, was apprenticed to Thomas Smith a white iron smith in Edinburgh, for six years on 2 June 1796. [ERA]

STEWART, ADAM, in Jamaica, a probative will, 31 May 1783. [NRS.RD2.237.825]

STEWART, ADAM, late of New York, now of Ayr, was admitted as a burgess and guilds-brother of Ayr on 4 June 1783. [ABR]

STEWART, AGNES, in Jamaica, a deed in favour of Thomas Buchanan, 3 June 1777. [NRS.RD3.237/1.36]

STEWART, ALEXANDER, emigrated from Scotland to North Carolina in 1775, a Loyalist soldier, in London by 1784. [TNA.AO12.100.90]

STEWART, ALEXANDER, in Dominica, a bond, 30 April 1774. [NRS.RD4.215.486]

STEWART, ANN, in Maryland, a deed of attorney, 5 April 1788. [NRS.RD4.246.179]

STEWART, BALFOUR, in Thurso, Nova Scotia, a letter to William Watt in Kirkwall, Orkney, dated 1773. [NRAS.1031]

STEWART, CHARLES, son of James Stewart a spoon-maker in Glamis, was found guilty of housebreaking and theft and was banished to the American Plantations for life, at Perth in June 1773. [SM.35.332]

STEWART, CHARLES, in Quebec, a deed of attorney, 2 July 1790. [NRS.RD4.247.1052]

STEWART, CHARLES and DAVID, sons of Dr George Stewart in Annapolis, Maryland, failed in their claim to the lands and barony of Argaty in 1793. [NRS.GD275.84]

STEWART, CHARLES, born 1725, formerly the Receiver General of Customs in America, died in Edinburgh on 27 November 1797. [GM.68.443]

STEWART, DANIEL, a surgeon in Dominica, a post nuptial marriage contract with Jean Murray, second daughter of William Murray a merchant in Edinburgh, on 24 October 1777, [NRS.CS238.F3/4]; a deed with H. Ferguson, 30 January 1778. [NRS.RD4.223/1.624]

STEWART, DAVID, from Virginia, graduated MD from Edinburgh University in 1777. [SM.39.336]

STEWART, DUGALD, with one other, emigrated from Campbeltown, Argyll, aboard the Edinburgh of Campbeltown, master John McMichael, in July 1771 bound for Prince Edward Island. [NRS.SC54.2.106]

STEWART, DUNCAN, emigrated to America in 1764 as Collector of Customs in New London, a Loyalist, left America in 1777. [PAO.LC.1137]

STEWART, LEONARD, of Bermuda, graduated MD from Edinburgh University in 1819. [EMG]

STEWART, ROBERT, was appointed councillor of the Bahamas on 11 December 1753. [JCTP.61/2.26]

STEWART, Mrs ROBERT, with eight others, emigrated from Campbeltown, Argyll, aboard the Edinburgh of Campbeltown, master John McMichael, in July 1771 bound for Prince Edward Island. [NRS.SC54.2.106]

STEWART, ROBERT, a merchant in Norfolk, Virginia, before 1776, he was appointed Customs Controller of Norfolk in 1776, a Loyalist, later in Greenock. [TNA.AO12.54.418, etc]

STEWART, ROBERT, of Rhode Island, a medical student at Edinburgh University in 1765. [EUL]

STEWART, ROGER, a merchant in Norfolk, Virginia, before 1776, a Loyalist, later in Greenock. [TNA.AO12.54.418, etc]

STEWART, THOMAS, a blacksmith in Portsmouth, Virginia, a Loyalist who settled in Port Roseway, Nova Scotia, in 1783. [TNA.AO13.83.604]

STEWART, WILLIAM, formerly a soldier of the 14th Regiment, and his daughter Agnes Stewart, in the Hilltown of Dundee, were found guilty of resetting stolen goods, were banished to the American Plantations for life, in Perth in June 1773. [SM.35.332]

STEWART, WILLIAM, in Jamaica, a deed of factory, 30 May 1776. [NRS.RD2.220.656]

STEWART, WILLIAM, only son of Samuel Stewart a merchant in the island of New Providence, matriculated at Glasgow at Glasgow University in 1761, graduated MA there in 1764. [RGG]

STILES, EZRA, of Newport, Rhode Island, graduated DD at Edinburgh University on 28 March 1765. [GEU]

STIRLING, ARCHIBALD, in Jamaica, a deed of factory, 4 November 1793. [NRS.RD3.263.51]

STIRLING, CHARLES, in Jamaica, a will, 7 November 1768. [NRS.RD2.214/2.75]

STIRLING, EDWARD, of Jamaica, a student at King's College, Aberdeen, around 1818. [KCA]

STIRLING, ROBERT, a merchant in Jamaica, was admitted as a burgess and guilds-brother of Ayr on 4 April 1751, [ABR]; in Kingston, Jamaica, a letter, 30 September 1753. [GCA.T-SK11.2.81]

STIVEN, WILLIAM, a merchant in Aberdeen, settled at Gunaboa, Jamaica, in 1715, formerly an apprentice to William Martin a merchant in Aberdeen, 1734. [ACA.APB.3]

STOBO, Reverend ARCHIBALD, in Charleston, South Carolina, letters, 1705-1708. [NRS.CH1.2.24.2.3; CH1.2.27.3.226]; husband of Elizabeth Park, a deed, 1707. [NRS.RD2.94.513]; a letter requesting a young Presbyterian minister for James Island, S.C., dated 1712. [NRS.CH1/2.32.fos.531-540]; John Squire left James Island by 1725. [NRS.CH1/2.51.fo.99]

STOBO, JOHN, of Tortula, graduated MD at Marischal College, Aberdeen, on 3 May 1816. [MCA]

STOCK, THOMAS, of America, graduated MD from Edinburgh University in 1802. [EMG]

STRACHAN, Sir ALEXANDER, of Thorntoun, Kincardineshire, a sasine, 14 July 1625, Nova Scotia. [NRS.RS1.17.342]

STRACHAN, JOHN B., of Virginia, graduated MD from Edinburgh University in 1809. [EMG]

STRACHAN, JOHN, Bishop of Toronto, a letter, 16 October 1850. [NLS.ms930/130]

STRACHAN, JOHN, a minister in Cornwall, Canada, graduated DD at King's College, Aberdeen, on 22 November 1811. [KCA]

STRAGHAN, HARBOURNE GIBBES, of Barbados, graduated MD from Edinburgh University in 1821. [EMG]

STRACHAN, PETER, a physician in Virginia for over 30 years before 1776, a Loyalist who moved to London by 1784. [TNA.AO13.83.640]

STRACHAN, Dr, from Banff, a letter re his journey from Nova Scotia via Boston, New York to London in 1823. [NRS.GD45.318]

STRAKER, CHARLES D., of Barbados, graduated MD from Edinburgh University in 1822. [EMG]

STRAKER, THOMAS, son of John Straker a gentleman in Barbados, a student at King's College, Aberdeen, in 1800. [KCA]

STRINGHAM, JAMES SACKETT, (1755-1817), of New York, America, graduated MD at Edinburgh University in 1799. [EMG]

STRUTHER, A., in Pensacola, a letter re the death of George Aikman in Florida, dated 1781. [NRS.NRAS.0174]

STUART, ANDREW, in Quebec, a letter re the boundaries between Lower Canada, New Brunswick, and the USA, dated May 1828. [NRS.RD45.323]

STUART, DAVID, born in 1753, of Virginia, graduated MD at Edinburgh University in 1777. [EMG]

STUART, DAVID, emigrated from Scotland to America in 1757, settled at Fort George, Charlotte County, New York, a Loyalist, moved to Canada in 1778, settled at Sorel by 1783. [PAO.LC.1022]

STUART, GILBERT, a letter from George Washington arranging a sitting with the artist, dated 1796. [NRS.RH1/2.561]

STUART, WILLIAM, Lieutenant Governor of Dominica, a letter dated 24 August 1773. [JCTP.80.148]

SURGEON, JOHN, a gentleman in Jamaica, was admitted as a burgess and guilds-brother of Ayr on 4 April 1751. [ABR]

SUTHERLAND, ALEXANDER, on Nantasket Road six miles from Boston, Massachusetts, reporting armed American schooners off the New England coast, a letter dated 10 June 1776. [NRS.GD153.box1]

SUTHERLAND, DONALD, in Jamaica, a deed of attorney in favour of William Sutherland, 2 September 1780. [NRS.RD2.228/2.652]

SUTHERLAND, D., in Quebec, a letter to Sir Walter Scott, 1822. [NLS.ms867/180]

SUTHERLAND, JAMES CUBBISTON, only son of Arthur Sutherland in Jamaica, was apprenticed as a writer to (1) A. L. Ramage, (2) John Blair; was admitted to the Society of Writers to the Signet in Edinburgh on 3 July 1820. [HWS].40]

SUTHERLAND, PATRICK, at Lunenburg, Nova Scotia, in 1755. [JCTP.64]

SWABY, GEORGE, of Jamaica, graduated MD from Edinburgh University in 1822. [EMG]

SWANSTON, Dr WILLIAM, in St Kitts, a commission with John Grieve, 10 November 1801. [NRS.RD3.291.782]

SWETT, JOHN B., (1752-1796), of Massachusetts, a medical student at Edinburgh University in 1779. [EUL]

SWIFT, JONATHAN, in Virginia, a bond, 14 July 1793. [NRS.RD4.253.374]

SYME, JOHN, from Scotland to Virginia in 1764, a merchant in Norfolk, Virginia, before 1776, a Loyalist who moved to Bermuda. [TNA.AO13.83.682]

SYM, Mrs C., in Jamaica, a deed with William Gibb, 15 November 1808. [NRS.RD2.309.103]

SYMS, PHILLIP, (1768-1837), a physician in Philadelphia, graduated MD at Edinburgh University in 1792. [EMG]

TAILOUR, GEORGE, 'who had practiced Medicine fifteen years in St Christopher's with great approbation and success', graduated M.D. from Glasgow University in 1768. [RGG]

TAILOUR, JOHN, of St Kitts, graduated MD at Edinburgh University in 1776. [EMG][SM.38.512]

TALIAFERRO, JOHN, of Virginia, a medical student at Edinburgh University in 1796-1797, graduated MD from Edinburgh University in 1798. [EUL][EMG]

TALIAFERRO, WILLIAM, of Virginia, a medical student at Edinburgh University in 1796-1797. [EUL]

TANKARD, JOHN, of Virginia, a medical student at Edinburgh University in 1785-1786. [EUL]

TAPSCOT, JAMES, of Pennsylvania, graduated MD from Edinburgh University in 1765. [EMG]

TARPLEY, THOMAS, GRIFFIN, born 1748, from Virginia, a medical student at Edinburgh University, 1756-1757. [EUL]

TAWSE. PETER, born 1798, son of John Tawse and his wife Isabella Dunbar in Milton of Edinglassie, died in Jamaica in May 1828. [Strathdon gravestone, Aberdeenshire]

TAYLOR, JAMES, son of Robert Taylor a mason in Aberdeen, apprentice to Robert Alison a mason in Edinburgh, absconded to Virginia in 1667. [ERA]

TAYLOR, JAMES, of Virginia, a medical student at Edinburgh University, 1756-1757. [EUL]

TAYLOR, JOHN HANBURY, of Jamaica, graduated MD at Edinburgh University in 1751. [EMG]

TAYLOR, JOHN, born 1755 in Marykirk, Kincardineshire, a factor and merchant in Glasgow, Virginia, New York, and by 1782 in Jamaica as a slave trader, moved to London in 1798, died at Kirtonhill near Montrose, Angus, in 1816.

TAYLOR, JOHN, of Virginia, graduated MD from Edinburgh University in 1806. [EMG]

TAYLOR, SIMON, born 1740, son of John Taylor and his wife ..... McCall, a planter, entrepreneur and attorney in Jamaica, an assemblyman there, died in Port Royal, Jamaica, on 14 April 1813. [GM.83.660]

TAZWELL, JOHN, of Virginia, a medical student at Edinburgh University 1795-1796. [EUL]

TAZWELL, WILLIAM, of Virginia, a medical student at Edinburgh University 1796. [EUL]

TEASDALE, WILLIAM, son of William Teasdale a merchant in Jamaica deceased, a student at King's College, Aberdeen, in 1820. [KCA]

TELFAIR, ALEXANDER, emigrated from Scotland to America in 1759, a merchant in Halifax, North Carolina, a Loyalist, died in 1777. [TNA.AO12.34.351]

TELFAIR, WILLIAM, a Loyalist who settled in Jamaica, a letter dated 8 April 1783. [HMC. American.iv.19]

TELFER, ALEXANDER, in Virginia, a deed, 30 January 1779. [NRS.RD2.225.1299]

TENNANT, JOHN, in Jamaica, a deed of attorney in favour of Thomas Baillie, 10 June 1778. [NRS.RD4.773/1.563]

TENNANT, JOHN VAN B., born in New Jersey, settled in New York, a medical student at Edinburgh University in 1763, died 1770. [EUL]

TENNANT, JOHN, of Virginia, a medical student at Edinburgh University 1793-1794. [EUL]

THATCHER, PETER, MA, of Boston, New England, graduated DD at Edinburgh University on 26 July 1791. [GEU]

THIBON, JAMES, of Antigua, a student at Marischal College, Aberdeen, in 1757, then at King's College, Aberdeen, [KCA]

THIERENS, MATTHIAS, from Essequibo, graduated MD from Glasgow University in 1816. [RGG]

THOM, ALEXANDER, son of James Thom a merchant in Nova Scotia, a student at King's College, Aberdeen from 1818 to 1822, later a merchant in Aberdeen. [KCA]

THOMAS, EDWARD, of South Carolina, a medical student at Edinburgh University in 1796-1797. [EUL]

THOMAS, NATHAN, of Delaware, a medical student at Edinburgh University in 1785. [EUL]

THOMAS, REYNOLDS C., of Barbados, graduated MD from Edinburgh University in 1818. [EMG]

THOMAS, SAMUEL, from America, graduated MD from Glasgow University in 1801. [RGG]

THOMSON, ALEXANDER, in Jamaica, a deed of attorney, [NRS.RD2.221/1.170]; was admitted as a burgess and guilds-brother of Ayr on 4 April 1751. [ABR]

THOMPSON, ALEXANDER, Customs Collector at Savannah, Georgia, in 1772, a Loyalist, settled in Edinburgh by 1788. [TNA.AO12.4.251]

THOMSON, ALEXANDER, in Halifax, [Nova Scotia?], a deed, 3 August 1779. [NRS.RD4.229.1111]

THOMPSON, ARCHIBALD, emigrated to America in 1773, a farmer in Tryon County, New York, a Loyalist in 1776, moved to Niagara by 1783. [TNA.AO12.28.69]

THOMPSON, GEORGE, emigrated from Scotland to Charleston, South Carolina, in 1772, a merchant there, a Loyalist, moved from Charleston via Jamaica to England in 1777. [PAO.LC.1164]

THOMSON, JOHN, in Charleston, South Carolina, a deed, 2 September 1777. [NRS.RD3.236.818]; a deed of factory in favour of William Lumsdaine, 26 July 1784. [NRS.RD3.245.908]

THOMPSON, JOHN, a merchant in Halifax, North Carolina before 1776, a Loyalist who moved via Charleston and St Augustine to London, settled in Dumfries, Scotland, by 1787. [TNA.AO12.102.125, etc]

THOMSON, WILLIAM, in St Kitts, a deed of attorney, 25 September 1764, [NRS.RD4.197/1.559]; a deed, 3 November 1784. [NRS.RD2.239/1.201]

THOMSON, WILLIAM, of Virginia, a medical student at Edinburgh University 1797-1798. [EUL]

THORBURN, JOHN, born 1756 in Penicuik, Midlothian, emigrated to America in 1775, a joiner and house-carpenter in Morris Town, New Jersey, a Loyalist, returned to Penicuik in 1779. [TNA.AO12.17.119]

THORNDYKE, OLIVER, of Boston, Massachusetts, "studied medicine for 3 years in Edinburgh", graduated MD at King's College, Aberdeen, on 7 August 1820. [KCA]

THORNTON, THOMAS, a merchant in Glasgow, a contract with Garret Garrett, master of the brigantine Hanover to convey a cargo of trade goods, under Alexander Horseburgh his factor, to the Coast of Guinea, dated at Greenock on 13 November 1719.

THORNTON, WILLIAM, master of the Fame of Dundee at Madeira bound for Charleston, South Carolina, in 1775. [MRA]

THURSTON, JOHN ROBINSON, of St Kitts, graduated MD at King's College, Aberdeen, on 22 February 1800. [KCA]

TIDYMAN, PHILIP, of South Carolina, a medical student at Edinburgh University 1797-1800. [EUL]

TITLEY, JOHN M., of St Kitts, graduated MD from Edinburgh University in 1810. [EMG]

TOD, ALAN, in Philadelphia, a deed of attorney in favour of Alan Hepburn, 9 September 1755. [NRS.RD4.218.858]; a deed, 8 December 1790. [NRS.RD3.251.497]

TODD, GEORGE, a surgeon in Caroline County, Virginia, son of Charles Todd in Westshore, Holm, Orkney, papers 1763. [NRS.NRAS.1246]

TODD, JAMES, in Jamaica, a deed of attorney, 25 July 1787. [NRS.RD4.243.131]

TODD, JOHN, emigrated from Scotland to America in 1771, a planter in St George's parish, Georgia, a Loyalist, via St Augustine to Halifax, or St John, by 2 December 1785. [PAO.LC.1]

TOLMIE, DAVID, master of the Mary of Inverness, and David Robertson the mate, a petition to the High Court of the Admiralty of Scotland, concerning a voyage from Inverness to Virginia for tobacco, in 1729. [NRS.AC10.151]

TOLMIE, MURDOCH, in Nova Scotia, son of John Tolmie in Dunvegan, Skye, a letter dated 1809. [NRAS.2237]

TOWER, JOHN, son of James Tower MD in St Thomas Island, a student at King's College, Aberdeen, 1804. [KCA]

TOWTON, GEORGE WILLIAM, of Jamaica, graduated MD from Edinburgh University in 1815. [EMG]

TOWTON, HENRY V., of Jamaica, graduated MD from Edinburgh University in 1817. [EMG]

TRAIL, THOMAS, born 1720, late of Dominica, died in July 1763. [St Andrews Cathedral gravestone]

TRAVERS, DEVEREUX, from Maryland to Edinburgh in 1793, to study medicine at Edinburgh University, residing in College Street, Edinburgh, in 1794. [ECA.SL115.1.1]

TRENCH, WILLIAM, son of William Trench a merchant in Jamaica, a student at King's College, Aberdeen, from 1824 to 1825. [KCA]

TRESTLER, JOHN BAPTIST CURTIUS, of Canada, graduated MD from Edinburgh University in 1821. [EMG]

TROTTER, ALEXANDER, in Halifax, Nova Scotia, a letter, 1774. [NRS.NRAS2709, bundle 31]

TROUP, JOHN IRVINE, of Maryland, to Edinburgh in 1792, residing in Nicolson Square, Edinburgh, graduated MD at Edinburgh University in 1793. [EMG] [ECA.SL115.1.1]

TRUMBULL, JONATHAN, the Governor of Connecticut, graduated LL.D. at Edinburgh University on 7 February 1785. [GEU]

TUCKER, EDWARD, of Jamaica, graduated MD from Edinburgh University in 1821. [EMG]

TUCKER, SAMUEL, of Jamaica, graduated MD from Edinburgh University in 1822. [EMG]

TUCKER, THOMAS, of Bermuda, graduated MD at Edinburgh University in 1770. [EMG][WMC]

TUCKER, THOMAS BIRCH, of Bermuda, graduated MD at Edinburgh University in 1801. [EMG]

TUITE, RICHARD, of St Cruz, (St Croix), graduated MD from Edinburgh University in 1819. [EMG]

TURNBULL, Dr ANDREW, born 1719 in Annan, Dumfries-shire, a physician, died in Charleston, South Carolina, on 16 March 1792. [GM.62.673]; Governor Patrick Tonyn of East Florida, claimed that Dr Turnbull was aiding the rebels, a letter dated St Augustine on 27 May 1780. [HMC. American. ii.127]

TURNBULL, THOMAS, of Jamaica, graduated MD from Edinburgh University in 1822. [EMG]

TURNER, EDWARD, of Jamaica, graduated MD from Edinburgh University in 1819. [EMG]

TURNER, WILLIAM, of Jamaica, graduated MD from Edinburgh University in 1820. [EMG]

TURPIN, PHILIP, of Virginia, graduated MD at Edinburgh University in 1774. [EMG]

TWEEDIE, ROBERT, in Antigua, a deed with William Cunningham, 27 June 1808. [NRS.RD2.304.769]

TYLER, JOHN, (1764-1841), a medical student in London and Edinburgh. [Toner pp, Library of Congress]

URQUHART, ALEXANDER, from Barbados aboard the sloop Hopewell bound for Antigua on 8 November 1679. [TNA]

URQUHART, ROBERT, born in Cadboll, Easter Ross, died in Charleston, South Carolina, on 11 August 1800. [GM.70.1107]

VERNON, JAMES, of Jamaica, graduated MD at Edinburgh University in 1796. [EMG]

VETCH, SAMUEL, in Boston, a letter introducing Colonel Schuyler and the Indian ambassadors, 1710. [NRS.NRAS.0332/1282/1327]

VIRGO, JAMES, of America, a medical student at Edinburgh University in 1765. [EUL]

VOZE, JAMES, of New York, graduated MD from Edinburgh University in 1809. [EMG]

WALKER, ALEXANDER, a merchant in Virginia, a deed, 22 November 1751. [NRS.RD2.170.304]

WALKER, DAVID, of Virginia, to Edinburgh in 1793, residing in Potter Row, Edinburgh, 1794, a medical student at Edinburgh University 1794-1795, graduated MD at Edinburgh University in 1796. [EUL][EMG] [ECA.SL115.1.1]

WALKER, FRANCIS, born in Kincardineshire, was educated at King's College, Aberdeen, a schoolmaster in Portobacco, Maryland, a Loyalist, sailed for Glasgow in 1775. [TNA.AO13.13.40]

WALKER, JOHN, emigrated from Scotland to South Carolina, in 1760, a merchant in Charleston, S.C., moved to England in 1775. [TNA.AO13.132.262][NRS.GD1.128.43]

WALKER, JOHN, of Jamaica, a student at King's College, Aberdeen, around 1803. [KCA]

WALKER, ROBERT, of Virginia, graduated MD at Edinburgh University in 1787, died 1820. [EMG]

WALKER, WILLIAM, born in Scotland, an indentured servant who absconded from the brigantine William and Mary at Corbett's Wharf, Jamaica, in 1754. [Jamaica Courant, v.295]

WALKER, WILLIAM, born 1801, son of David Walker a farmer in Siviedly, Keig, died in Grenada on 2 September 1838. [Kildrummy gravestone, Aberdeenshire]

WALKINSHAW, JOHN, a merchant in Glasgow, deputised for a group of Glasgow merchants, on a trading voyage aboard the Robert of Londonderry to Virginia, a letter dated 14 March 1691. [NRS.GD3.5.805]

WALL, GEORGE, in Montreal, a deed, 18 February 1804. [NRS.RD.336.34]

WALLACE, ARCHIBALD, from St Andrews, Fife, a writer who died in Quebec on 21 June 1832. [FH]

WALLACE, HUGH, in Jamaica, a deed, 28 March 1772. [NRS.RD2.211.805]

WALLACE, JAMES, in Virginia, 26 April 1704. [JCTP]

WALLACE, JAMES WESTWOOD, of Virginia, a medical student at Edinburgh University in 1791-1792. [EUL]

WALLACE, JOHN, a merchant in Nansemond County, Virginia, before 1776, a Loyalist who moved to Halifax, Nova Scotia, by 1786. [TNA.AO12.55.706, etc]

WALLACE, MICHAEL, a merchant in Nansemond County, Virginia, before 1776, a Loyalist who moved to Halifax, Nova Scotia, by 1786. [TNA.AO12.55.706, etc][PAO.LC.602]

WALLACE, WILLIAM, in Carolina, was despatched golf balls there by Andrew Wallace in Edinburgh, 1739-1741. [NRS.GD377.401.]

WALLEN, JOHN, MA, son of Matthew Wallen in Jamaica, a student at King's College, Aberdeen, 1773 to 1777. [KCA]

WALROND, MAINE, of the West Indies, graduated MD at Edinburgh University in 1800. [EMG]

WALTER, WILLIAM, graduated BA from Harvard in 1756, and DD from King's College, Aberdeen, in 1784. [SNQ.XII.9]

WALTON, GEORGE, of Barbados, a student at King's College, Aberdeen, in 1783. [KCA]

WALWIN, JOHN, of St Kitts, graduated MD at Edinburgh University in 1769. [EMG]

WARDROPE, WILLIAM, in Virginia, a deed of factory in favour of B. Whyte, 8 September 1778. [NRS.RD4.225/1.201]

WARWICK, ALEXANDER, a merchant in Virginia, moved to London by 1778. [TNA.AO13.2.661]

WARWICK, ANTHONY, emigrated to Virginia around 1760, a merchant in Nansemond County, partner in the firm Cuming, Warwick and Company in Glasgow. a Loyalist who moved to London. [TNA.AO12.56.100, etc]

WATERHOUSE, BENJAMIN, (1754-1846), of Rhode Island, a medical student at Edinburgh University in 1775-1776. [EUL]

WATKINS, JOHN, of Kentucky, to Edinburgh in 1792, residing in Cooper's Entry, Canongate, in 1794, a medical student at Edinburgh University in 1790. [EUL] [ECA.SL115.1.1]

WATSON, ALEXANDER, son of David Watson MD in Jamaica, a student at King's College, Aberdeen, 1791 to 1793. [KCA]

WATSON, ANDREW, born 1776, son of Alexander Watson, a mason in Fortrose, and his wife Isabella Fowler, died in Jamaica in April 1805. [Plaque, Rosemarkie Church, Easter Ross]

WATSON, COLIN, born 1771, son of Alexander Watson, a mason in Fortrose, and his wife Isabella Fowler, died in Jamaica in June 1793. [Plaque, Rosemarkie Church, Easter Ross]

WATSON, JAMES, a merchant in Kingston, Jamaica, a bond, 14 September 1749. [NRS.RD2.170.264]

WATSON, JOHN, born 1770, son of Alexander Watson, a mason in Fortrose, and his wife Isabella Fowler, late in Jamaica, died in Fortrose, Easter Ross, on 5 December 1810. [Plaque, Rosemarkie Church]

WATSON, JOHN, of Virginia, a medical student at Edinburgh University, 1797-1799, graduated MD at Edinburgh University in 1799. [EUL][EMG]

WATSON, SAMUEL, and his family, emigrated aboard the Edinburgh of Campbeltown, master John McMichael, from Campbeltown on 1 July 1771 bound for North Carolina. [NRS.SC54.2.166]

WATSON, WILLIAM, in Boston, Massachusetts, a letter dated 1771. [NRS.NRAS.0888.781]

WATT, ALEXANDER, son of Alexander Watt in Jamaica, a student at King's College, Aberdeen, in 1796. [KCA]

WATT, EDWARD LINDSAY, of Jamaica, graduated MD from Edinburgh University in 1818. [EMG]

WATT, JOHN, of Jamaica, graduated MD from Edinburgh University in 1809. [EMG]

WATT, JOHN, of America, graduated MD from Edinburgh University in 1809. [EMG]

WATT, ROBERT, son of Alexander Watt in Jamaica, a student at King's College, Aberdeen, from 1796 to 1800, graduated MA, and in 1803 MD at Edinburgh University. [KCA]

WEDDERBURN, ALEXANDER, possibly bought land in East Florida in 1775. [NRS.GD164.1713]

WEDDERBURN, JAMES, in South Carolina, a letter recommending troops to defend the frontier against the French, dated 1740. [NRS.GD150.3483.11]

WEDDERBURN, JAMES, in Jamaica, a probative contract with Isabel Blackburn, 7 March 1764. [NRS.RD2.286.468]

WEDDERBURN, JOHN, a surgeon in Westmoreland, Jamaica, 'copy attorney', 16 March 1750. [NRS.RD2.170.68]

WEEKES, NATHANIEL, of Barbados, graduated MD at Edinburgh University in 1799. [EMG]

WEEKS, THOMAS PYM, son of Thomas Weeks MD in Nevis, a student at King's College, Aberdeen, from 1805 to 1808. [KCA]

WEEMS, JOHN, of Maryland, graduated MD at Edinburgh University in 1792. [EMG]

WEIR, E. M., in Jamaica, a commission with Matthew Sandilands, 9 May 1808. [NRS.RD4.283.895also on 21 September 1810. [NRS.RD4.290.806]

WELCH, WILLIAM, of Barbados, graduated MD at Edinburgh University in 1799. [EMG]

WELLS, WILLIAM CHARLES, born 1757, graduated MD from Edinburgh University in 1780. [EUL]

WELLWOOD, ARCHIBALD, in Baltimore, Maryland, letters from his brother Sir Henry Moncreiff Wellwood from 1773 until 1799. [NRS.NRAS.0333]

WELSH, JOHN, of Canada, graduated MD from Edinburgh University in 1818. [EMG]

WELSH, WILLIAM, son of Edward Welsh in Barbados, a student at King's College, Aberdeen, 1793 to 1795, graduated MD at Edinburgh University in 1799. [KCA]

WEMYSS, ALEXANDER, in New York, a will, 5 August 1782. [NRS.RD3.154.772]

WEMYSS, Sir JOHN, of Wemyss, a sasine, 3 November 1626, Nova Scotia, [NRS.RS1.20.170]

WENTWORTH, JOHN, graduated BA from Harvard in 1755, and LL.D. from Marischal College, Aberdeen, in 1764. [SNQ.XII.95]

WEST, GREGORY, a pharmacologist in America, graduated MD at King's College, Aberdeen, on 22 August 1786. [KCA]

WHARTON, JOHN, of Virginia, graduated MD from Edinburgh University in 1806. [EMG]

WHEELOCK, ELEAZOR, of Dartmouth, New Hampshire, graduated DD at Edinburgh University in June 1767. [GEU]

WHITE, ANDREW, of Jamaica, graduated MD from Edinburgh University in 1811. [EMG]

WHITE, JOHN, son of David White a gentleman in Jamaica, a student at King's College, Aberdeen, from 1806 to 1810, graduated MA. [KCA]

WHITE, SIMS, of South Carolina, a medical student at Edinburgh University 1796-1798, graduated MD at Edinburgh University in 1798. [EUL][EMG]

WHITEHEAD, ALEXANDER, of Virginia, a medical student at Edinburgh University 1796-1798. [EUL]

WHYTE, JOHN GORDON, in Jamaica, a deed of factory, 3 June 1790. [NRS.RD2.249.1059]

WIGHTMAN, CHARLES, in Tobago, a deed of factory with James Walker, 3 May 1800. [NRS.RD3.287.534]

WIGGLESWORTH, EDWARD, Harvard College, New England, graduated DD at Edinburgh University on 2 June 1730. [GEU]

WILKIE, JOHN, settled in Gloucester County, Virginia, as a merchant in 1772, a Loyalist in 1776, moved to Shelburne, Nova Scotia, by 1786. [TNA.AO12.102.203]

WILKIE, PATRICK, was assigned land on St Vincent on 28 January 1777. [JCTP]

WILL, THOMAS, born 1793, son of Robert Will [1749-1839] a farmer in Woodside, Echt, and his wife Agnes Thow, [1765-1845], died in Montreal Quebec, on 12 October 1819. [Strachan gravestone, Kincardineshire]

WILLIAMS, FREDERICK, a Loyalist late of Petersburg, Virginia, settled in Irvine, Ayrshire, by 1786, a deposition. [TNA.AO13.28.415]

WILLIAMS, JAMES, son of Dr Williams in Jamaica deceased, a student at King's College, Aberdeen, 1791. [KCA]

WILLIAMS, SAMUEL, Professor of Mathematics at Cambridge, New England, graduated LL.D. at Edinburgh University on 7 February 1785. [GEU]

WILLIAMS, WILLIAM, searcher of Customs at Montreal, a letter of attorney, 1778. [NLS.Stewart pp.3969]

WILLIAMSON, ARCHIBALD, probably from Argyll, a shipwright in St John, New Brunswick, probate 22 September 1827. St John. [PANB]

WILLIAMSON, HUGH, (1736-1819), a medical student at Edinburgh University 1764-1765. [EMG]

WILLIAMSON, JOHN, of Meiklour, born 1801, late of New York, died in Blairgowrie on 9 August 1871. [Lethendy gravestone, Perthshire]

WILLMAN, JAMES or JACOB, of South Carolina, graduated MD at Edinburgh University in 1795. [EMG]

WILLOUGHBY, EDWARD, of Barbados, graduated MD from Glasgow University in 1818. [RGG]

WILSON, ANDREW, emigrated from Campbeltown, Argyll, aboard the Edinburgh of Campbeltown, master John McMichael, in July 1771 bound for Prince Edward Island. [NRS.SC54.2.106]

WILSON, BARBARA, a vagrant, was found guilty of theft at the St John's fair at Banff, was sentenced to be banished to the American Plantations, with seven years' service there, at Aberdeen in June 1773. [SM.35.333]

WILSON, CUMBERLAND, from Scotland to Virginia in 1760, from 1764 he was a partner of Colin Dunlop and Company in Glasgow, from 1768 to 1776 he was a merchant in Maryland. [TNA.AO12.109.306]

WILSON, HENRY BROUNCKER, of St Kitts, graduated MD at Edinburgh University in 1784. [EMG]

WILSON, JOHN, of St Martin's, graduated MD at Edinburgh University in 1795. [EMG]

WILSON, JOSEPH NICHOLAS, of South Carolina, graduated MD at Edinburgh University in 1788. [EMG]

WILSON, JOSEPH, of Barbados, graduated MD from Edinburgh University in 1816. [EMG]

WILSON, LILIAS, daughter of Alexander Wilson, a merchant in Inverness, married Alexander Robertson, a surgeon in Jamaica, on 25 October 1802. [GM.72.1224]

WILSON, PHILIP, in the West Indies, a deed, 1 August 1778. [NRS.RD2.234.797]

WILSON, ROBERT, jr., of South Carolina, to Scotland 1791, graduated MD at Edinburgh University in 1794. [EMG] [ECA.SL115.1.1]

WILSON, SAMUEL, (1763-1827), of South Carolina, a medical student at Edinburgh University 1784-1786, graduated MD from Glasgow University in 1786. [EUL][RGG]

WILSON, SAMUEL, of Virginia, a medical student at Edinburgh University in 1790-1792, graduated MD at Edinburgh University in 1792. [EUL][EMG]

WILSON, SAMUEL, of America, graduated MD from Glasgow University in 1786. [RGG]

WILSON, THOMAS, from Fife, a mason on Prince Edward Island, a letter, 1818. [NLS.Acc.6981]

WILSON, WILLIAM, a merchant in Boston, New England, was admitted as a burgess and guilds-brother of Ayr on 15 July 1717. [ABR]

WILSON, WILLIAM, emigrated from Scotland to South Carolina in 1769, a merchant and trader in Charleston, S.C., died there in 1779, his brother Gilbert Wilson died there 20 October 1784. [TNA.AO12.48.363, etc]

WINDSHIP, CHARLES, of Boston, America, a medical student at Edinburgh University in 1796, graduated MD from Glasgow University in 1797. [EUL][RGG]

WINT, THOMAS K., of Jamaica, graduated MD from Edinburgh University in 1807. [EMG]

WINTHROP, JOHN, Professor of Mathematics in Cambridge, Massachusetts, graduated LL.D. at Edinburgh University on 4 July 1771. [GEU]

WISHART, ELIZABETH, in New York a deed of factory in favour of Sir L. Dundas, 5 June 1778. [NRS.RD2.223.173]

WISTAR, CASPAR, (1761-1818), of Pennsylvania, graduated MD at Edinburgh University in 1786. [EMG][PHS/Vaux pp]

WOOD, JOHN, in St Kitts, a deed of attorney, in favour of William Chalmers, 18 November 1775. [NRS.RD4.227.789]

WOOD, JOHN, a merchant in Savannah, Georgia, a Loyalist soldier, moved to Providence while his wife and children settled in Scotland. [TNA.AO12.109.308, etc]

WOOD, JOHN, of St Thomas Island, graduated MD from Glasgow University in 1817. [RGD]

WOODCOCK, SAMUEL, of St Kitts, graduated MD from Edinburgh University in 1809. [EMG]

WOODSIDE, JAMES, with one other, emigrated from Campbeltown, Argyll, aboard the Edinburgh of Campbeltown, master John McMichael, in July 1771 bound for Prince Edward Island. [NRS.SC54.2.106]

WORDROP, WILLIAM, a merchant, late in Virginia, a sasine, 26 January 1779. [NRS.RS27.243.29]

WRAG, JOHN, of America, graduated MD from Edinburgh University in 1806. [EMG]

WRIGHT, ROBERT B., of Jamaica, graduated MD from Edinburgh University in 1808. [EMG]

WYKE, ANTONY, son of Antony Wyke in Antigua, a student at King's College, Aberdeen, 1782. [KCA]

YOUNG, ALEXANDER and JAMES YOUNG, vagrants, were found guilty of theft at the St John's fair at Banff, was sentenced to be banished to the American Plantations, with seven years' service there, in June 1773. [SM.35.333]

YOUNG, FRANCIS, of Honduras, graduated MD from Edinburgh University in 1820. [EMG]

YOUNG, JAMES BOX, of Georgia, graduated MD at Edinburgh University in 1789. [EMG]

YOUNG, JOHN, in Tobago, a bond of relief, 4 September 1771. [NRS.RD2.224/2.646]

YOUNG, JOHN 'AGRICOLA', in Halifax, Nova Scotia, letters, 1819-1823. [NLS.ms790, ms792]

YOUNG, N. L., of Barbados, graduated MD from Edinburgh University in 1817. [EMG]

YOUNG, ROBERT BOYD, of Tobago, graduated MD at King's College, Aberdeen, on 18 May 1811. [KCA]

YOUNG, THOMAS, of Barbados, a student at King's College, Aberdeen, 1803 to 1805. [KCA]

YOUNG, WILLIAM, in Grenada, a bond, 8 August 1774. [NRS.RD3.239/1.161]

YUILL, JAMES, in Williamsburg, Virginia, a letter dated 1799. [NRS.GD47.742]

www.ingramcontent.com/pod-product-compliance
Lightning Source LLC
Chambersburg PA
CBHW070330230426
43663CB00011B/2270